Match of My Life

ENGLAND WORLD CUP

£1 from the purchase of this book will be donated
to the Bobby Moore Fund for Cancer Research UK
to help tackle bowel cancer
Registered Charity 1089464

Know The Score Books Sports Publications

MATCH OF MY LIFE

ENGLAND WORLD CUP
Louis Massarella &Leo Moynihan   ISBN 1-905449-52-6

EUROPEAN CUP FINALS
Ben Lyttleton   ISBN 1-905449-57-7

FULHAM
Michael Heatley   ISBN 1-905449-51-8

LIVERPOOL
Leo Moynihan   ISBN 1-905449-50-X

WOLVES
Simon Lowe   ISBN 1-905449-56-9

CULT HEROES

CHELSEA   Leo Moynihan   ISBN 1-905449-00-3

AUTOBIOGRAPHY

TACKLES LIKE A FERRET (England cover)
Paul Parker with Pat Symes   ISBN 1-905449-47-X

TACKLES LIKE A FERRET (Manchester United cover)
Paul Parker with Pat Symes   ISBN 1-905449-46-1

FOOTBALL FICTION

BURKSEY: The Autobiography of a Football God
Peter Morfoot   ISBN 1-905449-49-6

Forthcoming Sports Publications in 2006

MATCH OF MY LIFE

ASHES	Sam Pilger &Rob Wightman	ISBN 1-905449-63-1
FA CUP FINALS 1953-1969	David Saffer	ISBN 1-905449-53-4
LEEDS UNITED	David Saffer	ISBN 1-905449-54-2
MANCHESTER UNITED	Sam Pilger	ISBN 1-905449-59-3
SHEFFIELD UNITED	Nick Johnson	ISBN 1-905449-62-3
STOKE CITY	Simon Lowe	ISBN 1-905449-55-0
SUNDERLAND	Rob Mason	ISBN 1-905449-60-7
SPURS	Matt Allen &Louis Massarella	ISBN 1-905449-58-5
WEST HAM	Simon Lowe	ISBN 1-905449-61-5

CULT HEROES

NEWCASTLE	Dylan Younger	ISBN 1-905449-03-8
SOUTHAMPTON	Jeremy Wilson	ISBN 1-905449-01-1
WEST BROM	Simon Wright	ISBN 1-905449-02-X

GENERAL

HARRY HARRIS WORLD CUP DIARY
Harry Harris with Pelé   ISBN 1-905449-90-9

HOLD THE BACK PAGE
Harry Harris   ISBN 1-905449-91-7

Match of My Life

ENGLAND WORLD CUP

Editors: Louis Massarella & Leo Moynihan
Series Editor: Simon Lowe

www.knowthescorebooks.com

First published in the United Kingdom
by Know The Score Books Limited, 2006

The right of Louis Massarella & Leo Moynihan to be identified as the authors of this work has been asserted by them in accordance with sections 77 and 78 of the Copyright, Designs and Patents Act, 1988.

Know The Score Books Limited
118 Alcester Road
Studley
Warwickshire
B80 7NT
United Kingdom

www.knowthescorebooks.com

A CIP catalogue record is available for this book from
the British Library
ISBN 1-905449-52-6

Jacket and book design by Lisa David

Typeset by James Bridgman

Printed and bound in Great Britain
By Cromwell Press, Trowbridge, Wiltshire

Editor's Acknowledgements

Louis would like to thank all the participants. Janet Parr at Preston North End, Judith Horey, JP Shaw, Jonathan Sim at Sky Sports, Matt Hayes at Champions. But most of all I would like to thank my mum for lending me her car and the TV - my best friend during a lonely time.

Leo would also like to thank the players themselves for all their help and enthusiasm. Brian Glanville, John Moynihan, Candy Moynihan, Ian Callaghan, Oliver Holt, Andy Bate at the BBC, Roger Martin, Laraine Smith, Steve Taylor.

Louis Massarella & Leo Moynihan
April 2006

Photographs in this book are reproduced by kind permission of: EMPICS & Ivor Broadis

Front cover:
Left David Beckham celebrates his redemption after scoring the winning goal against Argentina from a penalty kick in Sapporo in 2002
Right Inspirational captain Bobby Moore joyfully lifts the Jules Rimet trophy high into the Wembley sky in 1966

Rear cover:
Top Left The Programme for the triumphant 1966 World Cup in England
Top Middle The line-up for the 1986 quarter-final against Argentina, blissfully unaware of the controversial fate that would befall them
Top Right Tony Adams marshals England's defence during the epic 1998 second round match against Argentina
Bottom Terry Butcher consoles Paul Gascoigne following agonising defeat to the West Germans in the semi-final of Italia 90

Contents

Foreword

STEPHANIE MOORE MBE   Founder, Bobby Moore Fund

Football was Bobby's life. He loved every minute of his involvement with England and took great pride in being captain on that glorious day in 1966 when he lifted the Jules Rimet trophy high into the Wembley sky – a moment relived in detail by Roger Hunt in this book.

I founded the Bobby Moore Fund, in partnership with Cancer Research UK, in 1993 after Bobby's tragic death from bowel cancer at the early age of 51. Since then we have raised several million pounds for the vital research into this terrible disease. The Fund not only raises money for much needed research, but also raises the profile of bowel cancer and informs people about the high risk symptoms of the disease.

Bowel cancer is the second highest cause of cancer death after lung cancer – 45 people die every day in the UK from this form of the disease. However, bowel cancer is a highly curable form of cancer if caught at an early stage. Unfortunately, the symptoms of bowel cancer often go unrecognised and the cancer progresses to an advanced stage if untreated. It is then often untreatable, so it is vital that awareness is raised in order to save as many lives as possible.

In order to ensure the very best quality research, we have established a series of Bobby Moore Research Fellowships. These are awarded on a competitive basis to ensure that only the very best scientists are chosen. A committee of senior Cancer Research UK scientists award the grants.

In the past year, the Bobby Moore Fund has appointed its 15th bowel cancer Research Fellow and opened the Bobby Moore Laboratory at St Mark's Hospital, Northwick Park, Middlesex, which cost £425,000, a sum which was raised entirely by Bobby Moore Fund supporters. St Mark's is recognised as the leading centre of excellence, both clinically and scientifically, in all of Europe, so I am very proud that Bobby's name should be linked with such a fine institution.

2006 is a very important year for the Bobby Moore Fund as it marks the 40th anniversary of Bobby leading the England team to World Cup victory at Wembley Stadium in 1966. We have many exciting activities planned for the year and hope to raise £3 million for our research.

I am delighted that a donation of £1 is being made to the Bobby Moore Fund from the sale of each copy of this book. I hope that you enjoy reading with the knowledge that you have contributed to our aim of tackling bowel cancer.

Best wishes

Stephanie Moore

Stephanie Moore MBE

For more information about bowel cancer, please visit the charity's patient website at www.cancerhelp.org.uk.

To receive more information about our events and supporting the Bobby Moore Fund, please visit our website at www.bobbymoorefund.org or call us on 020 7009 8881.

Registered Charity No. 1089464

Dedication

SIR TOM FINNEY
RIGHT-WINGER

BRAZIL 1950

BORN   5th April 1922, Preston
CLUB   Preston North End
INTERNATIONAL DEBUT   September 1946 v Northern Ireland
ENGLAND CAREER   76 caps, 30 goals
INTERNATIONAL FAREWELL   October 1958 v Soviet Union

The classic selection dilemma of post-war English football was: Finney or Matthews? Both men laid rightful claim to footballing genius, but Tom Finney, the Preston Plumber, so called because of his plumber's training, assisted the England selectors' dilemma by proving to be more than adept on either wing. Despite being mostly a creative player, Finney set a new English goalscoring record of 30, which stood until the arrival of Jimmy Greaves in the 1960s. Tom Finney was knighted for his services to football in 1998.

ENGLAND 0 v USA 1

World Cup Finals – Pool II
Thursday 29 June 1950

Estádio Independencia, Belo Horizonte, Brazil
Attendance 10,151

'No-hopers' shock 'Kings of Football' to leave England's inaugral World Cup hopes in tatters

Teams

Walter Winterbottom	**Managers**	Walter John Giesler
Bert Williams	1	Frank Borghi
Alf Ramsey	2	Harry Keough
John Aston	3	John Maca
Billy Wright	4	Edward McIlvenny
Laurie Hughes	5	Charles Colombo
Jimmy Dickinson	6	Walter Bahr
Tom Finney	7	Frank Wallace
Wilf Mannion	8	Gino Pariani
Roy Bentley	9	Joe Gaetjens
Stan Mortensen	10	John Souza
Jimmy Mullen	11	Edward Souza
	Scorers	Gaetjens 38

Referee: Generoso Dattilo (Italy)

IT WAS A catastrophe. The United States of America 1, England 0. It was a major shock at the time, certainly the biggest shock in the entirety of the four World Cups to date. But I'm sure none of us unlucky enough to be playing that day would have predicted that 56 years on, the World Cup still wouldn't really have produced an upset of such titanic proportions.

It was a big shock when Cameroon beat the holders Argentina in the opening game of the 1990 World Cup finals in Italy, but the so-called minor footballing nations and 'Third World' countries had come on leaps and bounds by then – even more so by 2002, when again the reigning champions were beaten 1-0 in the opening game by an African nation. But the Senegal team that beat France had a European coach and several players who would soon be plying their trade for top European clubs, many of them in our own English Premiership.

Without being disrespectful, most of the USA players that day would have struggled to get a game for an English Third Division side. Although they had been semi-finalists in 1930, the World Cup was not yet a major international tournament and the majority of Europe's best sides, including the four home nations, declined the invitation to take part. The USA team was made up of part-time players from a country where football was regarded as a minority sport. It still is, I suppose, even though the USA are now an extremely accomplished international side – ranked above England, in fact, as I write. In 1950, the England team, on the other hand, were considered to be *the* major world force. When we arrived in Brazil for our first ever World Cup, the local newspapers even ran headlines calling us 'The Kings of Football'. This game was supposed to be a walkover.

I was lucky enough to go to three World Cup finals. I say lucky because, although we didn't exactly set the world alight during those tournaments, most players don't even get the opportunity to play in one, let alone three, so I regard myself as being very fortunate. I've always looked at it that way, although obviously I would have liked to have fared better.

I admit my World Cup record doesn't exactly make impressive reading – played seven, won two, drawn two, lost three and we only progressed past the first group stage once – especially since we were well-fancied at all three tournaments (when are England not well-fancied?!). You can look for all the excuses in the world, but to this day I can't properly explain why we did so poorly.

But like I said, I prefer to dwell on the positives. Making my England debut against Northern Ireland in 1946 remains my proudest moment in football. Playing for your country is the ultimate honour and I felt similar pride every time I pulled on an England shirt. I suppose I would say this now, given my World Cup record, but because I loved playing for England so much I always felt it was about more than just results. We weren't just footballers, we were ambassadors for our country. With my debut coming shortly after the Second World War, I felt a great affinity with the soldier on the battlefield. I myself had fought in Africa during the conflict. Stanley Mortensen, the great Blackpool centre-forward and my England team-mate in 1950, was lucky to be playing football at all, having overcome serious head and back injuries, suffered during a wartime crash in a Wellington bomber.

As in the war, we weren't only representing ourselves and our families, but the entire nation – the nation that had introduced football to the world. And to be able to do it on the biggest stage of all, rubbing shoulders with the best players in the world, made it an even greater privilege. I was lucky enough to travel the world, playing in countries I could have only dreamed of visiting otherwise, experiencing different cultures, all this whilst playing the game I loved. Me, a one-time plumber's apprentice from Preston! How can I complain?

Of course, qualification for the World Cup was very different in 1950. The competition's organising committee decided that a total of 16 teams would compete in the finals. In the end, only 13 took part, due in part to the stubbornness of the Auld Enemy, Scotland. The winners and the runners-up of the 1949-50 Home Championships would be invited to the finals – rather generously, if you think about it, as no British team had competed in any of the three previous World Cups. You could say this was rather harsh on Wales and Northern Ireland. In the Home Championships, each team played each other just once, and in 1950, ourselves and Scotland both had two home games, to Wales' and Northern Ireland's one. It wasn't the fairest way of deciding who should go, perhaps, but it was certainly the most practical.

As expected, it came down to our match against Scotland at Hampden Park, in front of 134,000 raucous Scots! In theory, we had both already booked our places in the finals. But following FIFA's announcement that two teams from the British Isles would be invited to compete in the 1950 Finals, the Scottish Football Association – soon followed by Wales and Northern Ireland – declared that they would only take part as British Champions. Pride had obviously got the better of them, but it was a crazy decision nonetheless.

So we went into the game at Hampden in the strange knowledge that we were already assured of a place in the finals. The Scots, however, needed at least a draw to join us. But England and Scotland were never going to play out a tame draw; instead the scenario added extra spice to the game. Despite the partisan crowd, we were slight favourites and in truth our 1-0 win was pretty comfortable, even if it did come courtesy of a scrappy goal, scored by Chelsea's Roy Bentley.

The Scottish public didn't particularly agree with the SFA's stance and they made their feelings known at the final whistle, but it was the Scotland players I felt extremely sorry for. I never liked losing to them, but there were many Scottish players at Preston during my time, such as Tommy Docherty and Bill Shankly, so I felt a certain fondness for them. I remember our captain Billy Wright urging his opposite number in the Scotland team, George Young, to get the SFA to reverse their decision, but the SFA refused to back down. Could you imagine anybody turning down a place in the World Cup finals these days?!

That game against Scotland was the last time Stoke City's Neil Franklin ever played for England. Put quite simply, Neil was the best defender I ever played with or against and many others, Stanley Matthews included, said the same. Neil and I were also great pals – he was probably my best mate in the England squad. We were the same age, made our international debuts together and he went on to play 25 consecutive internationals. That was a record at the time, which was only broken by Billy Wright's phenomenal run of games which eventually led to him becoming the first ever international centurion.

At times, Franklin was faultless. But he was also a man with principles and often voiced his frustrations at how little English football's top players were paid, despite the amount of money pouring into the game. It wasn't the vast sums that enriches the Premiership clubs from TV money today, but it was a significant amount in terms of 1950 when the maximum wage was just £12 per week.

As we were lining up to sing the national anthems before the Scotland game, Neil, who was standing alongside me, said: "See that lot, Tom," nodding towards the band. "They're probably on more money than us." I laughed, but he didn't seem to be joking. Little did I know what was to happen next.

Just a few days later came the news that Neil and his Stoke team-mate George Mountford – soon to be followed by other English players, including, famously, Manchester United winger Charlie Mitten – had left Britain to play club football in Columbia. I was shocked – along with the rest of the footballing world. Neil had declined the chance to play in England's upcoming World Cup warm-up matches against Portugal and Belgium, but had told the FA it was because he wanted to look after his pregnant wife. Then came the news.

The FA were understandably furious and banned him indefinitely, while the press had a field day. From an England point of view, it was a major blow, coming just weeks before we were due to leave for the finals in Brazil. On a personal level, I was astonished. As it turned out, the riches Neil was promised in Columbia never materialised and he returned after a year or so, never to play in the First Division again. I believe he regretted the decision to go to his dying day.

In 76 games for England, in an international career spanning 12 years, there were three real low points and funnily enough, two of them came in World Cup warm-up matches. In May 1954, we were thrashed 7-1 by Hungary's 'Magical Magyars' in Budapest, with Ferenc Puskás to the fore. I'd been spared the embarrassment six months earlier, when injury ruled me out of our 6-3 humiliation to the same opposition at Wembley. For the return game, we knew what to expect, but still had no answer to their devastating passing and movement. It was depressing, but in hindsight it was no disgrace to be well-beaten by one of finest international sides of all time.

Four years later in Belgrade, I suffered more bitter disappointment, losing 5-0 to Yugoslavia. They were less skilful than the Hungarians, but they were well-organised and extremely physical. I was singled out for special treatment that day and was kicked black and blue, but there is no doubt they were the better side.

But our preparations for 1950 couldn't have been more different (little did I know what was in store for us in Brazil). In fact, in the first of our two warm-up games I produced one of my finest performances in an England shirt. The opposition were Portugal, who we'd humiliated 10-0 only three years earlier. Lisbon's Stadium of Light was again the venue, but by now Portugal were much improved. In a 6-3 win, I scored four goals, taking all the plaudits – and the headlines. Four days later we beat Belgium 4-1 in Brussels – a game in which Wolves winger Jimmy Mullen became England's first ever substitute, replacing Jackie Milburn. Everything had gone like clockwork and we approached the tournament with great confidence and an excellent spirit in the camp.

On paper, our 21-man squad looked impressive, particularly in attack, where, alongside yours truly, we could call upon the considerable firepower of Stanley Matthews, Stanley Mortensen, Jackie Milburn and Wilf Mannion.

Some people said afterwards that our squad was too old and inexperienced, but the war had robbed many players of their best years, so you'd be hard pushed to find players with plenty of experience who were also relatively young. At 28 and with 25 caps, I was probably one of only two who fell into that bracket, our captain Billy Wright being the other. Nevertheless, it was still a strong, well-balanced squad. In fact, Neil Franklin aside, the FA committee picked the strongest squad available. Neil's replacement was Laurie Hughes of Liverpool, who did as well as could be expected under the circumstances. His international career began and ended at those

World Cup finals, but Laurie certainly couldn't have been held accountable for our exit. It took England years to fill the void left by Neil Franklin, with Billy Wright eventually moving back into the centre of defence, before a certain Bobby Moore arrived on the international scene. No, he wasn't a bad player!

I'd be lying if I said the World Cup finals in 1950 were anywhere near the big deal they are today. After five teams dropped out [Argentina, Czechoslovakia and France, Scotland and Turkey], only 13 competed – compared to 32 these days – and you certainly didn't have every game beamed live to a television audience of billions. Don't get me wrong, there was a bigger sense of excitement and anticipation than usual in being part of the national squad as we left to a warm send-off in London, but none of us knew quite to expect.

After just three World Cup tournaments, World War Two had intervened. I was only 16 when Italy had won the last World Cup in 1938 and because England didn't compete, it barely warranted a mention in the press over here. Being an avid football fan, I knew a bit about it – previous winners, where it had been held, that sort of thing – but I suppose because England hadn't been involved I thought it couldn't have been that important. When we did finally compete, it meant as much to the other competing countries as it did to us.

If the flight to Brazil was anything to go by, we were in for a tough time. We were due to fly in to Rio de Janiero, but there was a mechanical problem with the aeroplane and we were forced to make an emergency landing in Recife – some way up the Brazilian coast – while repairs were carried out. We were there for several hours and when we did finally board the plane again, it's fair to say there was a bit of apprehension in the squad.

Commercial air travel was still a fairly new thing back then, remember. Three years later when we went to America on a summer tour (we got our revenge, beating the USA 6-3. Yes, three years too late, I know!) most of the lads still hadn't flown much – certainly not such a long way. I was well used to it by then and flying never really worried me anyway, but I couldn't say the same of some of the others.

Despite the blip, we were given a warm welcome in Rio, some would say too warm. The hotel was first class and we were well looked after by the staff. There was also plenty of opportunity for sightseeing. We were given £2 a day pocket money; not a lot – even in those days – but enough to get by. Relaxing between training and games however, was almost impossible.

Our hotel was situated right on the famous Copacabana Beach where there was a carnival atmosphere 24 hours a day. Singing, dancing, firecrackers, drum beats, you name it… it was one non-stop party. It was amazing – nothing like what I was used to back home in Preston – and the Brazilian doctor had to give us sleeping pills in an attempt to make sure we got enough rest. Personally, I didn't mind the noise. It was a different way of life and you just had to get on with it.

When it came to the business of winning football matches, though, it soon became apparent that everybody was out to get us. Along with the hosts, we were favourites to win the whole tournament, and because this was England's first World Cup, 'The Kings of Football' were seen as the prize scalp. I must say it was a bit strange to turn up in a country on the other side of the world to find that you're the star attractions.

One thing you had to say about the Brazilians was that they were mad about their football. We had heard things about their fanatical fans and how skilful their players were, without ever witnessing it first hand. That was the incredible thing about the World Cup in those days, we knew literally nothing about our opponents from other continents. With no Satellite TV and no blanket coverage from around the globe, we had no way of knowing anything at all. It was only when we saw close up what they were capable of that we realised just what we'd been missing.

A few days after we arrived, a small boy, dressed in just a pair of shorts and no shoes, approached a few of us outside our hotel. He put an orange on the instep of his right foot, flicked it into the air and caught it on his left instep. He did this about 20 times until we finally gave him a few coins for his troubles. We were gobsmacked. He must only have been about six years old and I don't think any of us could have performed that trick with a full size football, let alone an orange! But this was only a taste of things to come.

The following day we went the opening game of the tournament, Brazil versus Mexico, at the famous Maracana. It was like nothing I'd ever seen before. Nearly 200,000 fans were packed into the stadium and the noise was so loud it made the hairs on the back of your neck stand up. But that was nothing compared to the shock we got when the game got under way…

The Brazilian players were on another planet. The speed and skill with which they played made English football look laboured and awkward by comparison. Everything about them was different, from their physique to their boots and I was mesmerised by how easy they made it all look. Brazil won the game 4-0, but in the competition's other major shock, they would later lose in the final to Uruguay. Many people have said that Brazil side in 1950 was even better than the team that won the World Cup in 1970, so Uruguay must have been some side!

Were we surprised at how good Brazil were? Yes, to be honest. Just as we had arrived in Brazil with a big reputation, we only knew about them by reputation. Before 1950, English football was unashamedly insular. We didn't take much interest in foreign football and probably thought there was nothing we could learn from it. This was certainly a wake-up call.

Nevertheless, our opening game against Chile could not have gone much better. It was hot and humid for our first five days in Rio – indeed, many of us needed oxygen to get though training – but it absolutely chucked it down just before kick-off, making us feel right at home. This time there were only 30,000 in the Maracana, but having trained well, we were confident of victory, despite the unusually sparse crowd. Chile had just one familiar name in their line-up, Newcastle United striker, George Robledo.

I'd be lying if I said we had it all our own way. Chile started brightly and were comfortable on the ball, as you'd expect from a South American side, but we soon settled down and Morty headed in from Jimmy Mullen's cross just before half-time. Chile weren't about to lie down, though, and hit the post almost immediately.

In the second half, they again started strongly, but we weathered the storm and on 70 minutes, Morty fed me down the right and I crossed for Wilf Mannion to head in. It was fine goal and we never looked like losing after that, even though there were chances at both ends.

We didn't play our best by any means and we knew we would have to play much better if we were to have any chance of actually winning the tournament, but we'd done the most important thing and won the game. We were off the mark and could approach the next game with even more confidence.

Were we complacent? Did we take the USA lightly? I don't think so, no. Just two weeks earlier a strong England touring XI had only just scraped a 1-0 win against the USA World Cup team in New York on an FA tour of North America. More importantly, the USA had run Spain very close in their opening group game, leading 1-0 until a late surge saw the Spanish run out 3-1 winners. But like I said, most of their players were part-timers, some of ours were known the world over. Of course we expected to win.

The game was played 300 miles inland from Rio in a mining community called Belo Horizonte [pronounced 'Bel Orizonch'], but we weren't complaining; it was cooler and less humid in the mountains. The ground was fairly shabby and the changing facilities were so basic that we actually arrived for the game already changed into our kit. The pitch was also poor – bumpy, full of potholes and the grass was too long – but, to use an old football cliché, it was the same for both sides, so we couldn't use that as an excuse. Besides, we prepared for the game in relative comfort, as special guests of the Morro velho gold mine, an English-owned company who employed 2,000 British workers, so we had plenty of support among the 10,000 crowd. Unusually we played in blue shirts as the Americans also wore white, albeit with a diagonal sash. The ground was like a British non-league stadium of the time, with a red cinder track surrounding the pitch. Outside that stood a tall white wall around most of the ground. The feeling was very claustrophobic and the small crowd made plenty of noise within its confines.

Like Chile, the USA were quick out of the blocks and our keeper Bert Williams was forced into an early save from John Souza, the USA's goalscorer against Spain. But pretty soon we were on the attack and that's how it stayed for most of the first half. Morty, Wilf Mannion, Jimmy Mullen and I all missed decent chances before the Americans took the lead completely against the run of play.

Eight minutes before half-time, Roy Bentley lost possession and the Americans broke quickly up-field. McIlvenny, a Scottish-born defender who once played for Wrexham, fed Bahr 25 yards out and his speculative shot seemed to be heading straight for Bert Williams until Joe 'Larry' Gaetjens threw himself at the ball. The slightest deflection had Bert completely wrong-footed and we could only watch in horror as the ball sailed into the net.

Even then, I never thought we wouldn't win the game. In those seven minutes before half-time, Wilf Mannion and I both hit the post and we thought it was only a matter of time before we scored. That was the message at half-time: "Keep going, keep playing your football, the goal will come."

Again we poured forward in the second half. I lost count of the amount of chances we had; I was one of the guilty parties, blazing over the crossbar from close range. We hit the woodwork twice more, had several claims for a penalty waved away and the American keeper, Borghi, who was actually a professional baseball player, played out of his skin. Even as the clock ticked down, I always thought we would score. Only in the last minute when Jimmy Mullen's header was somehow scooped off the line by an American defender, did I think it wasn't going to be our day.

It was an awful feeling. I still cringe at the thought of it. As Gaetjens was hoisted onto his colleagues' shoulders and carried off the pitch at the final whistle to be immortalised in a famous photograph, we just stood with our hands on our hips looking at each other in total disbelief. Nobody said much in the dressing room afterwards. What can you say at a time like that?

The English press had a field day, of course. Don't get me wrong, it was nothing like the stick they would give you nowadays if a similar thing happened. Far fewer journalists travelled and nowhere near the number of column inches were dedicated to the national football team in those days, but it was the worst I can remember in my time.

Nobody was singled out for particular criticism, but the press lambasted the performance as a whole, one newspaper calling it "the worst ever by an England team," before naming and shaming the whole line-up. The fact that the result barely warranted a mention in the US press just goes to show how much of a minority sport football was in America. And the fact that the USA lost 5-2 to Chile only a few days later tells you how much of a one-off their victory over us was. Not that it was of any consolation to us.

The strange thing is, if we had beaten Spain in the Maracana three days later – and progressed to Round Two via a play-off against the same opposition – the defeat to the USA would have been forgiven, if not forgotten. It's a big if, I know, but not beyond the realms of possibility. After all, had we gone into the Spain game with two wins from two, we would have fully expected to beat them. Now the pressure was really on.

The FA selection committee responded, not unexpectedly, by making several changes to the team, especially in the forward line, with Stanley Matthews being flown in especially from the tour of North America and Jackie Milburn named at centre-forward.

It seemed to work a treat when Jackie rose to head home one of my crosses midway through the first half. Everybody except the referee thought it was a perfectly good goal (press photographs proved as much afterwards), but it was chalked off for offside. Despite the Spaniards' persistent fouling we dominated the first half, but again we faced a goalkeeper in inspired form and early in the second half we were hit with a sucker punch when Zarraonandia headed home after Laurie Hughes failed to clear a cross.

After that, Spain just sat back and played out time, with yet more blatant abuse of the rules going unpunished by the referee, to the increasingly loud jeers of the large home crowd, who wanted an England win. We did everything but score the goal our performance deserved and that was that. We were out of the World Cup, less than a fortnight after touching down in Brazil with high hopes.

For all the good it did, we held an inquest among ourselves in an attempt to work out what went wrong, but it kept coming back to the USA game. On returning home, again the media pilloried us over that performance – they just wouldn't let it go – and the FA were forced to offer an explanation. Sir Stanley Rous, Secretary to the FA, said the Americans had been "fitter, faster and better fighters" and even Walter Winterbottom said publicly that we'd played badly.

Although I was as embarrassed as everyone else by the result, I'm not sure I agree fully. I'm not saying we deserved to win, but it was just one of those days. If we hadn't created any chances I could understand the criticism more, but on another day we could have won comfortably.

If I was to be critical of our performance… perhaps we snatched at our chances a bit. I suppose as the game wore on we got more and more desperate, but we could have been playing all day and still wouldn't have scored.

I've said before that it took English football two years to get over that defeat and yes, I still maintain that belief to this day. Then, of course, in 1953 we suffered the humiliation of a 6-3 hammering at Wembley by Hungary and international football really began to mean something to everyone in this country. National pride was at stake and the notion that we were simply better than the rest of the world was knocked right into a cocked hat.

Playing right-back for us on both occasions was Alf Ramsey. We played together many times for England, but I never got to know him well – very few people did. He was a bit of a loner, even before he became a manager, and always seemed very serious. He obviously thought about the tactical side of the game from a very early age, though, and of course, 16 years after England's darkest hour, he led us to our finest; winning the 1966 World Cup on home soil. So he got to lay the ghost of 1950 to rest far earlier than the rest of us!

Of course, although I didn't know it at the time, my own World Cup adventures weren't over either. Far from it, in fact. Although I was 32, in 1954 I was arguably at my peak. Preston had been runners-up to Arsenal in the League only a year earlier, I captained North End in the FA Cup final, albeit in a losing cause, and my individual performances were recognised by my being named Footballer of the Year. For England, I won my 50th cap just before we departed for the finals in Switzerland – an odd choice to host the World Cup finals if you ask me – where we went one better than in 1950, reaching the quarter-finals before losing to Uruguay. My own form was patchy, however, so much so that I feared for my place before the Uruguay game – a match in which I scored – even though our problems were in defence rather than attack. To be honest, it was a bit of an anti-climax to what had, up until the FA Cup final, been a great season for me personally.

As I've said, despite not quite scaling the dizzy heights with England at international level, I feel lucky to have played in three World Cup finals. On a personal level, a bigger regret is that in 76 games, I never got to play against Brazil. You always want to pit your wits against the best and Brazil have proved consistently that they are worthy of that title, in terms of both results and entertainment.

In 1950, we would have played them in the second group stage. As it turned out, Spain, who went through instead of us, were beaten 6-1, but who's to say we would have suffered a similar fate? We eventually played them for the first time at Wembley in May 1956, but I was injured. Then the same fate befell me during the 1958 World Cup in Sweden. I'd scored a late equaliser from the penalty spot in our opening game against a 'physical' Russian side. That night during dinner my leg began to ache, but I thought it was just a knock and when I woke up the following morning – a day before the Brazil game – I was pretty confident I would be fit enough to take the field. But the knee was not ready for running or kicking – it turned out I had torn a muscle behind my knee – and I had to concede defeat.

Taking bad news on the chin is something I was always good at, but on this occasion, to coin a phrase, I was gutted. I knew this would probably be my last chance to play against Brazil and I felt like I'd been cheated out of it. The one consolation was that I got to watch Brazil at close quarters. We managed a well-earned 0-0 draw with them. Pelé and Garrincha were rested for that game as they were carrying injuries, but they swept aside all else before them. As a neutral, I was glad to see Brazil crowned World Champions. The skill with which they play is something I've always admired – and in Pelé they'd unearthed an absolute gem.

Years later, I met him in London at an event to celebrate a milestone for the FA – I forget how many years it was. He was the guest of honour and it was a great thrill to be introduced to the greatest player of all time. He'd heard of me too. "I remember my father once taking me to watch you play," he said. "Really?" I said, interested to know which game it was. "The World Cup in 1950," he replied. "You were playing for England in Belo Horizonte against…" I didn't even let him finish. "If it's all the same to you, I'd rather not talk about that particular game!" Pelé saw the funny side and we had a laugh about it. Looking back, I can just laugh about it now, but it certainly wasn't funny at the time!

IVOR BROADIS
INSIDE-FORWARD

SWITZERLAND 1954

BORN   18th December 1922, Isle of Dogs
CLUBS   Carlisle United, Sunderland, Manchester City, Newcastle United, Carlisle United, Queen of the South
INTERNATIONAL DEBUT   November 1951 v Austria
ENGLAND CAREER   14 caps, 8 goals
INTERNATIONAL FAREWELL   June 1954 v Uruguay

Ivor Broadis was a goalscoring inside-forward with an eye for goal. Aged almost 29, he fought off challenges from the likes of Wolves' Dennis Wilshaw, Manchester United's Tommy Taylor and West Bromich Albion's Johnny Nicholls to secure his place in the 1954 World Cup Finals team and scored twice in England's opening game against Belgium. He shouldered much of the blame for the quarter-final defeat to Uruguay along with goalkeeper Gil Merrick and never played for England again. Broadis is still involved in the game on a professional basis, although now he spends his time reporting on the progress of his former club Carlisle United.

ENGLAND 2 v URUGUAY 4

World Cup Quarter-final
Saturday 26 June 1954

St. Jakob Stadium, Basle
Attendance 50,000

A controversial goal sees underperforming England fall to the reigning World Champions to begin the curse of the quarter-final

Teams

	Managers	
Walter Winterbottom		Ivan Lopez
Gil Merrick	1	Roque Máspoli
Ron Staniforth	2	William Martinez
Roger Byrne	3	Jose Santamaria
Bill McGarry	4	Victor Andrade
Billy Wright	5	Obdulio Varela
Jimmy Dickinson	6	Luiz Cruz
Stanley Matthews	7	Julio César Abbadie
Ivor Broadis	8	Javier Ambrois
Nat Lofthouse	9	Omar Miguez
Dennis Wilshaw	10	Juan Schiaffino
Tom Finney	11	Carlos Borges

	Scorers	
Lofthouse 16, Finney 67		Borges 5, Varela 40, Schiaffino 50, Ambrois 79

Referee: Carl Erich Steiner (Austria)

Let me start off by saying that I absolutely loved playing for my country. Who wouldn't it? It was such a thrill. You can't help but enjoy it. People ask me to this day, "What's it like playing for England" and it is hard to explain. You pull on the England shirt and from that moment you love it. In fact just walking into a dressing room that is housing the country's best players is when you begin to get excited; the feeling is tremendous.

The World Cup in Switzerland was the highlight of my career. I was in my early thirties and although I would play for another four or five years at a good level, I was aware this was my chance to play against the best the world had to offer and I made sure that I was going to enjoy every minute and every kick. I did just that. I had played at Carlisle, even managed them on a shoestring and now here I was with the best of the best. I was adamant that I would do myself justice.

My England career had started three years prior to the World Cup. I had been playing well for Manchester City, but still, to be called into the team was a shock. We didn't have a phone and all I knew was that it had been announced that Stan Mortensen had been selected to play in the fixture. I played that Saturday and went back up to Carlisle to my in-laws' place. Stan got injured that day, but how was I to know? The first I knew that I had been selected to replace him was on the Sunday morning when a policeman came to my door and informed me that I was to travel down to London immediately and report to the England team for the match. It was very exciting I can tell you and I can't recall much about that long journey down to the capital. The game was against a good Austria side, who held us to a 2-2 draw at Wembley.

At this point I should tell you a bit about my background and how I even came to be selected for England. I was born Ivan Broadis, but when I signed my first registration form at Tottenham Hotspur they misread my handwriting and read it as Ivor. I've been Ivor ever since. Even my family call me Ivor.

Anyway, I was born on the Isle of Dogs and went to a rugby playing school called Coopers Company School in Bow. A lot of schools were founded by traders such as Ash Haberdashers. Coopers Companies were barrel makers and was founded in 1536. They played Rugby though. I, however, having got a scholarship came from a footballing family and was never going to switch codes. My father was an amateur at Millwall. My eldest brother played for Hampstead and Golders Green as an amateur as well and was a decent centre-half. I watched him a lot and got the bug.

Tottenham came along for me. They were a top team full of internationals, so it was wonderful. I was a teenager playing for Finchley and they asked if I would sign as an amateur, which I did.

Most of the London teams had nursery teams in the Kent League. Arsenal had Margate; Tottenham's was Northfleet, which became Gravesend and Northfleet. I played the first two games of the 1939/40 season for Northfleet aged 17. Then War broke out.

I worked for a firm called Grand Union Canal Company before being called up. What happened then was you were tied to a club. For the duration of the war, the team you were signed to, you remained signed to them. There were no transfers as such. So, about 12 months in I was back at Finchley, but then Millwall came in for me.

They signed another fella called Sid Tickridge. He was a schoolboy international and had been at Tottenham. Millwall were fined £1 for signing us both as it was against regulations. It's laughable now, £1. We had to eventually go back to Spurs.

We had good times at Millwall though. We played Watford during the war and we went out to play and suddenly the sirens are going off. It was the first daylight bombing raid on London. The referee took us off and when it was all clear we went back on. The crowd had stayed, mind.

There was a fella at Millwall called Jimmy Jinks. He was in the RAF. He was very smart, you know, took great pride in himself. An ordinary RAF uniform wasn't good enough for Jimmy. He had to have a better one made. He looked great with a pencil-thin moustache and, when we were brought off, the senior players got hold of him and shaved half of his moustache off. I was only a kid, but I thought it was brilliant. He struggled a bit, but accepted it.

I played for Spurs in the wartime London league. I loved it. I played against the likes of Cliff Bastin, the Compton brothers, Eddie Hapgood. The biggest influence came from Tottenham in the shape of Willy Hall. He played for England and even got five goals in one international. I played inside-right and he played behind me at wing-half. He was very, very good and was a lovely bloke, kept me right and really influenced me.

I soon got posted to Canada, but came back to guest for Bradford and, strangely enough, having no inkling of the shape my career would take, the other inside-forward there was Len Shackleton. We would later play together for Sunderland.

I also played twice for Manchester United during the war. I still have a letter from Matt Busby asking me to contact him once the war was finished. When I think about it, I was still playing in 1958 when the Munich disaster happened. Life is strange; I could have been on that plane, who knows.

I was then posted to Crosby-on-Eden, which is in Cumbria. The war had finished and a gentleman came along and asked if I would guest for Carlisle. I played a few games and then they said – when I came out of the air force – would I be going back to Tottenham? I wasn't sure. I had really grown to love this part of the country and the thought of going back to London and the rat-race worried me. I had met a girl as well, of course, but really loved the pace of life here.

Another factor in my decision to stay north was how tight they could be at Spurs. As an amateur I was paid expenses and that was it. They were very strict about it. I played a home game and got my expenses and the secretary who was a dour Scot said "Ivor, we paid you too much last week. We paid you a half crown extra. I have taken it off this week's money. Ok?" Half a bloody crown. That didn't weigh heavily, but I thought if they were that tight I shouldn't bother going back.

I was only 23, but Carlisle offered me the player-manager's job. I may have been inexperienced, but I took the job and I was demobbed in August 1946. I was due to go on a draft to India. I had guested on the Saturday and damaged ribs, reported sick and missed the draft. Meanwhile the local MP was doing his bit saying I had a new job to go to. The war was over, so I was soon free to became player-manager.

Looking back I learnt a lot about the game, but at 23 and with a board of directors of about twelve, average age maybe 65 and with the club not having two ha'pennies to rub together, it was going to be hard. The Chairman funnily enough was Bill Shankly's uncle.

The ground was a heap. There was an ash track, an uneven ash track. There were no floodlights and we used to train a lot at night due to some players being part-time. I thought running on that track in the dark was bound to cause someone to break a leg one of these days. I went to the board and asked if it would be possible if we could get a couple of 100-watt light bulbs shining from the stand. There was this silence and then one board member looked aghast and says, "That will cost us a fortune. You know what footballers are like, they'll be trying to smash the bulbs with the balls." I looked astonished and said, "I'm trying to get them to hit a space 8 yards by 8 feet and they can't do that. If any of them can hit a little bulb from distance then we'll get a fortune for them!"

I had enemies. The secretary and the Chairman were difficult and I said, "Give me X amount of money to buy players and if it doesn't work out I'll sell myself." The papers had been saying how much I was worth and eventually Sunderland came in and spent £18,000 on me, which was a lot of money in those days. I guess I must be the only manager to ever sell himself.

I had a good couple of seasons at Sunderland before joining Manchester City. I loved it at Maine Road. They were great people, but by the time the World Cup had come around I was back in the North East with Newcastle United.

After my debut I wouldn't say I was a regular in the England set-up and it was frustrating. Once you were in, your aim was to go out and do yourself justice. It was wonderful to be involved, but the big factor was that it wasn't run like a club. That's where we fell down if you ask me. Against foreign opposition we came across national teams who had been together for years. Take Hungary, the best team around at the time; those guys had been playing together for years. Most had played together in the army and played club football together and been in a settled national team for many years, which had won the 1952 Olympic tournament in Helsinki.

After making my debut against Austria in November 1951, I played the following April against Scotland. I went on tour that summer, then missed the following season's games against Ireland and Wales, but played versus Scotland. So, I'd been on tour and then missed the winter games, and then come back again. That doesn't make sense to me. How can you play in April, go on tour and then not be picked for the games the next winter? The selection process was ridiculous. Individuals on selection committees were pushing their own players. Winterbottom probably suggested a team, but that team, in my opinion was toyed with by the selection committee. Who were they? They weren't footballers that's for sure. They were businessmen. Looking back it was a joke. A joke, and it affected the team.

My point was underlined in 1953 when the Hungarians came over to England and gave us a lesson in how the game should be played. That day opened everyone's eyes. Suddenly we weren't as good as we, and in particular those at the FA, had once thought.

Our preparation for '54 was a game against Scotland at Hampden where we won 4-2 (Tom Finney and I played well that day) and then we went to Yugoslavia who kicked us to death and won 1-0. Tom got a clobbering that day. He had a history with the Yugoslavs. We then travelled to Hungary and how Tom managed to play that day I don't know. He was black and blue after Yugoslavia.

We got beat 7-1 in Budapest. They were the best team I had seen up to then. They had a deep-lying centre-forward and, whilst we had experience of that having played Argentina on a South American tour, we struggled to cope. Our centre-halves were marking nobody. They destroyed us. Don Revie later deployed that tactic at Man City. In those days, at Newcastle, where I was now playing, they had two men marking the two inside-forwards and didn't bother about the deep centre-forward. There is always an answer to tactics, but that day we didn't do it. I managed to grab our goal, but that wasn't much of a consolation was it?

Despite that set-back, I thought we had a chance in the World Cup Finals. Obviously Hungary were favourites. They had beaten us twice, but to be honest the latest 7-1 win was against a very inexperienced team. Other than Hungary there were the South American teams who are always a threat.

The press, I remember, weren't as optimistic. That didn't bother us. You always had someone on your back. The previous year I can remember getting off the plane in South America at the start of the England tour there. One hack came over and said, "Ivor old boy, you haven't re-signed for City."

"I'll do it when I get back," I said calmly.

"I was going to write that you're not happy there."

"Well you won't have to do that now will you."

"OK. I'll write how happy you are."

"No you won't." That would suggest that I wasn't happy and there's no smoke without fire. I suppose they wouldn't even ask nowadays.

We had been beaten by Hungary of course and the press gave us a bit of stick after that, but in those days we mingled with them all the time. It wasn't long before we were soon all sitting about and I said to one of them, "How would you go about beating them?"

He thought for a bit and then said sagely, "I would get on top from the start and stay there?" He replied. I couldn't believe it. That was one factor in me later becoming a journalist. I can do better than that! "Get on top and stay there." He was one of the top men as well.

We had a great bunch of players. Billy Wright, Nat Lofthouse and any team which houses both Tom Finney and Stanley Matthews has to have a good shout. Stan was getting on by then, but who cared? He was still one of the best. We also had Sheffield Wednesday inside-forward Albert Quixall in the team. He used to greet Stan with a cheery "Good morning, Father". We all would giggle, but my god, Stan could still play. We would arrive at training in Switzerland and when we were going onto the pitch for our light session, Stan was just finishing his own personal drills. He had got there early, knowing what he had to do for himself and had done it. Walter let him get on with that.

Tom, of course, was another. I liked Tom. He was a great player and he made other people play. He made me play anyway. We roomed together some of the time. In Switzerland it was the first time I had played with Matthews. He and Tom, the two old stagers roomed together and I was with Nat Lofthouse. We were in adjoining rooms with a connecting door. We were playing in Berne and were having an early lunch. The four of us dined together and the waiter came round with this platter. Bear in mind that in those days you got different foods to today. Dieticians weren't heard of. You can't help laughing when you hear about all the fads today. This waiter came with steak, potatoes and peas. He passes us all the food and then he gets to Stan. Stan says, "No steak, no potatoes, just some peas." So Stan just has a few peas on his plate. He waits for us all to finish and he says to Tom, "Come on Tom. We're going up to relax."

Reluctantly Tom follows and they go upstairs. Nat and I are curious and decide to creep up and see what they are doing. We very carefully went to our room and crept in, opening the connecting door very quietly. The room was in darkness, the curtains are drawn and Tom and Stan have their heads down, but their legs are being buoyed by pillows and are up in the air. We shut the door close to hysterics, falling about. Later we asked Tom what all that was about? Tom told us he had taken his shoes off and got onto the bed, but was told by Stan that he had to get as many pillows as he could to have his legs elevated. "That's the way to relax," he said.

Stan also had all sorts of bottles with all sorts of concoctions and often went whole days when he only drank tomato juice to cleanse his body of toxins. Who's to argue because he played until way into his 50s? He always had carrot juice and All-Bran for breakfast. Basically he was doing back then what people take courses to do now. He was an incredible fella.

There was a great camaraderie between the squad. I for one liked a laugh. I remember before the Hungary warm-up game some FA official came into the dressing room and said, "Come on, boys. These lot are terrified of you."

"Puskás and co terrified of anybody?" I thought, and lent over to the guys and said, "If they're scared, what about us?" We all fell about. I liked a laugh. If you didn't laugh you would cry. The game was so uncertain and you had to have a sense of humour to get back at the clowns who were running the game.

I was worried about my place because I had actually been dropped by my club, Newcastle, towards the ened of the season, but thankfully the fickle nature of the selectors worked for me on this occasion and I was in.

Despite that loss against Hungary, morale wasn't low as we approached the tournament. After the Budapest hiding we didn't have another game until the World Cup. You can get down, but you have to have a laugh and get on with it. We picked ourselves up. To be beaten by a team like Hungary was no great disgrace. What it did show us, though, was the difference in preparation and organisation. Their preparation was unbelievable. We got to Switzerland and never played anybody whereas Hungary were playing anyone and everyone. They played school teams just to get a run out. They were winning 28-0, but they were getting games under their belts.

It wasn't Walter's fault, mind. Walter did the best he could with the people he had around him on that committee. Whether he would have chosen to have the same people around him I don't know. He did the best he could with the powers that he had. His hands were tied if you ask me.

The way the groups were set-up was odd. We were in a group of four, Italy, Belgium and Switzerland joined us, but being seeded with Italy we would only play the other two nations. Our first game was against the Belgians and it was a tie we really should have breezed through, but we could only manage a draw.

We actually went a goal down after only five minutes, but soon got into our stride and started to dominate. I managed to get us level after good work from Billy Wright when I ran through to thump a shot home, before Nat [Lofthouse] scored a fantastic daisy-cutter diving header from Tom's brilliant centre. That was more like it. I added a third goal after half-time from a deflected shot following Matthews' centre and the game looked in the bag. But then we let them back in.

It has to be said that defensively we weren't great. Neil Franklin had gone to Bogotá and been punished heavily by being banned from international football. Later on I played against Neil for Carlisle. He was with Crewe and by god would they kick you. I said afterwards to Neil, "What do you feed these guys, raw meat?" He said, "If you come off here still walking you've had a blinder!"

He was a good player, Neil, but why was he left out? It was so silly and yet another example of how vindictive these selectors were. Talk about cutting off your nose to spite your face, because Neil was a damn good player and couldn't be replaced. 'We'll show him', was their attitude and it cost us. In games like against Belgium he was so missed and with Neil I think we would have done better in the two World Cups in 1950 and 1954.

They pulled the two goals back and the game went into extra-time as FIFA didn't want any of the games to end in draws. In extra-time I managed to squeeze the ball through to Nat who smashed it high into the net. 4-3. Surely that was it.

But poor old Jimmy Dickinson scored a late own goal and it finished all square.

We were frustrated I can tell you that, but if one good thing to come out of it was that Billy Wright emerged as a late contender for that weak centre-half spot. He replaced a limping Syd Owen at the end of the game and afterwards Walter asked how he felt about filling in there. He did, of course, and went onto play for many years there.

Some of the press blamed our keeper, Gil Merrick of Birmingham City. He had allowed four past him, including fumbling the shot which led to the extra-time equaliser, but we didn't blame him. We knew we had let it slip collectively and we had to look at it as a team. You don't go looking for individuals. It has to be a collective thing and we all accepted responsibility. I felt sorry for Gil because the cracks had shown up in front of him during that Belgium game. As a keeper you have to live with the fact that you are the last line of defence and people are going to hammer you for any mistakes.

Between games we trained, and relaxed out on the lake nearby which was beautiful. There was an island on the lake that we made for in a boat with a little out-board motor. We would relax over there and have a strawberry tea. It was a little more laid back in those days.

The second game was against the hosts, Switzerland, in Berne in a match that obviously generated a lot of interest among the locals. Being England, there was always so much excitement when we travelled abroad. As an England team we were mobbed most places we went. You'd arrive at airports and they would swarm all over you. In Italy and Hungary there would be thousands. We would save all our fruit for the kids. An orange was like gold after the war and we would hand them out amid joyous scenes.

It was a boiling hot day, an absolute scorcher. Players are all told not to have salt today, but back then they would feed us salt tablets to avoid cramp. Matthews was out for the game and that was a blow. He was outstanding against Belgium, so he was going to be missed. The two Wolves boys, Jimmy Mullen and Dennis Wilshaw came in on the left, Tommy Taylor played through the middle with Tom and I on the right.

The Wolves boys got one each either side of half-time, with Wilshaw's a superb running solo effort, and we ran out comfortable 2-0 winners. Billy Wright was superb in his first full game at centre-half and all in all Walter was a happy man as we had qualified for the quarter-finals. There was no dwelling on that though and immediately we were thinking about Uruguay, our opponents and reigning World Champions. They had some good players. The giant veteran defender Varela and Andrade in midfield. Up front, Schiaffino was superb. He would shortly join AC Milan for a new world record transfer fee. Still, I was confident that we could get something from the game.

We had watched them murder Scotland 7-0 in their second group game. The Scottish manager, Andy Beattie, had decided to change his system and tried to man mark the Uruguay forwards. Willie Cunningham at right-back had to follow their winger whenever he went deep and, of course, left a huge gap behind him. I said to Tommy Docherty about Cunningham that it was the only time I had ever seen a fella with a sunburnt tongue. Tommy uses that on his after-dinner circuit.

There was some disquiet amongst the press about Tom Finney's form, and Tom actually confided in me before the Uruguay game that he thought he might be left out. Nonsense. He felt he was out of sorts, but you just can't leave out a player like Tom, however he is playing and I would imagine that he and Stan would have been the first two names on the sheet.

The press, though, have their thoughts. A lot of them were frustrated would-be players and didn't give us much hope. One of them, Howard Palmer, even came in and joined in sessions. He'd fall over taking a corner, mind.

Whatever anyone else thought, we went into the game confident that we could do well, win and progress in the competition. After only five minutes, that didn't look likely at all as the Uruguayan outside-left raced through and scored after good work from the brilliant Schiaffino.

Our heads weren't to drop though. We picked ourselves and got on with it. Fortunately we had our great captain Billy Wright geeing us on. "Let's get at them," he'd cry. He wasn't one to go daft and shout his head off, but he was a leader by example. He had a bit of everything, Billy, and as he proved he could do a job all over the pitch. He could have played anywhere. He got on with things at centre-back. There was no moaning. He wasn't the tallest fellow, but he could climb and did a great job. In a way it put years on his career.

With Billy urging us on we got at the Uruguayans, and had the world champs on the back-foot. Eleven minutes after going a goal down we were back in it. Stanley Matthews was having a wonderful match, and it was he who changed defence into attack with a clever pass behind their back four for Dennis Wilshaw to run on to. He in turn squared the ball into the penalty box and Nat Lofthouse didn't miss those too often. 1-1.

For the rest of the half it was seemingly all us. Nat had a good shot saved and Wilshaw shot wide, although it looked as though he had been fouled. Suddenly though – and it's a cruel game isn't it – we were once more trailing. Two minutes from the break, poor Gil in goal failed to read the flight of a shot from distance by Varela and in it went.

We couldn't believe it, but we didn't dwell on it in the dressing room. Walter told us to get on with how we'd been playing. He believed we had been the better team. So out we went, but immediately we were 3-1 down. It was a shock. And it was very controversial. Roger Byrne fouled Ambrois and Varela took the free-kick quickly, but instead of placing the ball down, he drop-kicked it like Jonny Wilkinson out to Schiaffino who raced clear to put the ball past Gil with our defence looking non-plussed at the referee, who had been running away with his back to the incident and so didn't see what Varela had done.

Back then it wasn't the done thing to protest like they do these days. We just got on with it really. Referees rarely change their minds. I can't honestly remember anybody who felt at that point it was all over. In fact, once more we really got at them, probably stoked by the injustice of it all, and made it 3-2 through Tom Finney, who followed up after Lofthouse's shot was parried. Our tails were up then. They were struggling and Stan hit the post. We really could have got back in it and won it. With ten minutes left, though, Gil made another error to allow Ambrois' cross-shot to beat him and at that point it was looking hard. Poor Gil. He had played 23 consecutive games up to then and after that match he never played again. You had to feel sorry for him. It's a long way back from 4-2. With a single goal there is a chance, but now with time running out, we were beaten.

You don't point fingers, but over a pint there might be some friendly banter. "What was that big so and so doing there?" That kind of thing. Gil certainly copped the blame in the press though. He never played for England again.

And neither did I. I felt I had done OK. But I accepted the system. I had no choice. As I say, it wasn't like a club team. I didn't expect to be part of future plans anyway. There were calls for changes because really we hadn't done as well as some would have hoped. We beat Scotland in 1954, but that was it really. You also had youngsters like Johnny Haynes coming onto the scene in readiness for 1958. These were guys who were going to last a long time and I would have been 36 by then, so my time was coming to an end.

Walter Winterbottom must have been very disappointed afterwards, but there was no hair dryer treatment in those days. He would come alongside you and have a quiet word. The press would say he was too much of a gentleman, but I would sooner be talked to as an equal, and international players don't need to be screamed at. If you couldn't play, you wouldn't be there.

Walter had played himself at Manchester United and he knew the psychology of players. I found him a very intelligent man. You'll always get people who – and this will never change – interpret Walter's quiet attitude as a sign of weakness and try to get away with something. I can't understand anybody who pulls on that England shirt and doesn't give 100%. In fact I don't think anyone does.

I don't think any of us had jacked it in even at 4-2. South American teams are very good and even better at niggling fouls. They could kill a game with a few body checks. Don't get me wrong they had some great players, but South American football in those days was very rough. They would stop at nothing and could be crafty.

We stayed after and watched the Brazil v Hungary match that became known as the Battle of Berne. It was a physical and often violent match. Afterwards though the Hungarians milked it and got bouquets of flowers and all of that. The Brazilians were waiting for them in the tunnel and as the Hungarians walk down there the next thing we in the crowd hear on the tannoy is POLIZEI, POLIZEI! It was mayhem down there by all accounts. The Battle of Berne.

The strangest thing to come out of the whole 1954 tournament was the cleverness of the Germans. They had it sussed. They got stuffed, but still won through to the next round by winning a play-off against Turkey and then progressed to the final where they played their first team and turned the tables on Hungary to win 3-2 in a game known in Germany as 'The Miracle of Berne'. You have to admire that.

We didn't return home as failures. You didn't get very much in the way of attention when returning in those days.

Looking back that summer of '54 means the world to me. It was the pinnacle and was the best thing that ever happened to me. Anyone starting out wants to play in a World Cup and I have done. Tremendous.

SIR BOBBY ROBSON
INSIDE-FORWARD

SWEDEN 1958

BORN   18th February 1933, Sacriston
CLUBS   Fulham, West Bromich Albion, Fulham
INTERNATIONAL DEBUT   November 1957 v France
ENGLAND CAREER   20 caps, 4 goals
INTERNATIONAL FAREWELL   May 1962 v Switzerland

Best remembered as a legendary manager, Bobby Robson was also an accomplished and hard-working inside-forward, who scored twice on his international debut and only finished on the losing side on two occasions in his international career. As well as being involved in the incredible goings on during both the 1986 and 1990 tournaments, Robson was intrinsically involved in the controversy which surrounded England's participation in the 1958 World Cup.

ENGLAND 0 v BRAZIL 0

World Cup Finals – Pool IV
Wednesday 11 June 1958

Ullevi Stadium, Gothenburg
Attendance 49,348

England become the first team in the tournament's history to keep a clean sheet against the eventual World Champions – but fail to score with a forward line including three Second Division players

Teams

	Managers	
Walter Winterbottom		Vicente Feola
Colin McDonald	1	Gilmar
Don Howe	2	de Sordi
Tommy Banks	3	Bellini
Eddie Clamp	4	Orlando Peçanha
Billy Wright	5	Nilton Santos
Bill Slater	6	Dino Sani
Bryan Douglas	7	Didi
Bobby Robson	8	Joel
Derek Kevan	9	Mazzola
Johnny Haynes	10	Vavá
Alan A'Court	11	Mario Zagalo

Scorers

Referee: Albert Dusch (West Germany)

DESPITE MY PERSONAL disappointment with failing to win a game, and that of the England team at failing to progress beyond the group stage once again, I fell in love with the World Cup in 1958. To be part of this festival of football, with game after game and the eyes of the whole world upon you, was a very special feeling, something I can't fully explain. Although I would get to taste this atmosphere twice as England manager in 1986 and 1990, little did I know this would be my only World Cup finals as a player.

People very rarely ask me about my playing career. I think most of those who know me well know a bit about it – who I played for, that sort of thing – but not in any great detail. That's understandable, because when you play professional football for 18 years, more often than not that will take up the majority of your time in the game. If you go on to become a manager, you'll be lucky if you last that long, but I've been a manager for twice as long as I was a player. Yes, it's been that long – 36 years. As well as being a manager for a long time, I was also a successful manager, winning a lot of trophies, which gives people reference points to my career. When you add to that the fact that I finished playing nearly 40 years ago, it's only natural that my reputation is as a manager above all else.

That said, the best part of your career is your playing days, no question. Most managers will tell you that and I would agree with all of them. It might be different for some, but not many. When you're a player you're young, you're fit and you can't wait to play on a Saturday afternoon. The thrill, the excitement, the crowd, the responsibility, the kudos… you can't beat it.

I think it's fair to say I'm very patriotic. I loved playing for England and I loved managing England – every minute of it. People ask me what my proudest moment as a footballer was and I always say it was being asked to play for my country for the first time. In fact, I would say it was the most thrilling moment of my life. It doesn't get any better than that; that's a once in a lifetime experience.

They also ask me what my biggest thrill as a manager was and, despite all the great clubs I've managed, all the great experiences I've had, all the trophies I've won, again I would say it was being asked to become the manager of England. It's almost like being asked to be Prime Minister. Someone once said being England manager is the second most important job in the country, and in some ways they're right. Of course some would say it's the *most* important.

Of course, playing for England when I was a player and leading England when I was manager don't even compare. When I was first selected, I didn't even have a car, so I used to walk to training at my club, West Bromwich Albion. And when I first played for England, I had to get the train down to London to report for duty. After the 1958 World Cup finals, when Ron Flowers, the Wolverhampton Wanderers midfielder, started getting selected for the England squad as well, he used to pick me up in his car and we would drive down to London together. These days when players are selected they have chauffeur-driven cars picking them up and dropping them back at home. They also travel by specially chartered aircraft. We didn't have chartered aircraft in my day; we had to take scheduled flights like everybody else.

I first found out I was being selected to play for England in the newspaper – that should tell you how different things were back then. In those days it was just the team and replacements who were announced. Squads came later. It was November 1957 and I'd been to Wolverhampton races with some of my West Brom team-mates. I knew the team was being announced that evening and, on leaving the track, I thought it might be worth buying a copy of the local paper. And there was my name – R. Robson. As I mentioned earlier, it really was the biggest thrill of my life – but I couldn't share my excitement with my wife because we didn't even possess a telephone back then! I had to wait until I got home to tell her.

These days, the England manager picks the team. Back then the team was still picked by the FA's International Selection Committee, whose members comprised club chairman and board members. They were no mugs, these guys, and they always picked very good players, but for political reasons you often ended up with a couple of people from each of the half a dozen or so clubs who were represented on the committee! Major Wilson Keys, the West Brom chairman, was an influential member of the committee and doubtless put in a good word for me and West Brom's other England players, Don Howe and Derek Kevan.

It wasn't until Alf Ramsey took over in 1962 that the manager had the final say over selection. It was basically these men in suits who picked the squad and Walter Winterbottom had to work with those players the best he could – he wouldn't be able to dictate to them who he wanted in this team.

I absolutely adored Walter Winterbottom. He had a terrific knowledge of the game – and not just the English game, but European football as well. Nobody in this country knew very much about what was happening on the continent in those days. There was very little television, no videos, no archive footage. But Walter was one of the few coaches who used to travel and watch teams abroad.

The trick with Walter was he could impart that knowledge to his players. He was an academic and came from an educational background, so he was obviously used to speaking in front of groups of people, but it was never education-gone-bananas, he never talked above anybody. It was good, simple, football language that all his players understood. I've been on UEFA coaching courses and to all sorts of football conferences and seminars, but I've never seen a better speaker on football in my life than Walter Winterbottom.

He was also my mentor as a coach. It was Walter who saw myself and Don Howe as future coaches and managers. He was the one person who asked us what we were going to do when we stopped playing. We didn't know, we hadn't even thought that far ahead. "Well, I want you to come to Lilleshall," he told us. "Come on courses and get yourselves qualified as coaches. Somebody has to take the game forward, somebody has to be the coaches of the future, and it has to be you players." He really pushed us. Without Walter, I probably would never have been a manager.

I can remember everything about my England debut. I was excited, of course, but I was also a bit nervous, I have to tell you. Even the greatest of players must question whether they're good enough to play for England when they make their debuts and I was certainly a bit apprehensive.

Funnily enough, I was at a dinner with Sir Tom Finney recently and we were talking about that day. He was an established England player by then, a top, top international performer. Anyway, I sat next to him at lunch at the Hendon Hall Hotel on the day of the game, before we left for Wembley, and I was getting nervous. "Tom, what's it going to be like?" I asked.

"Ooh," he said, stoney faced, "it's going to be quite difficult, I tell you."

"Oh," I said, now even more nervous. "Why's that then?"

"Well you've got to remember, you'll be playing against the best players in France," he explained. "There will be no weaknesses in their team, so it's gonna be a difficult game… but remember, you're going to be playing with the best players in England, so that should even things up a bit!" He was smiling by now. "Anyway, if you get worried at all, just give the ball to me and I'll keep it for ten minutes until you get your confidence back!" He was a lovely fella, Tom. Absolutely hilarious, and if he was trying make me feel better by making me laugh, it worked.

My nerves soon settled and I scored twice in a 4-0 win – my international career could hardly have started better. Two hours earlier Tom was telling me how difficult it was going to be, and there I was with two goals on my debut.

The next game was against Scotland at Hampden Park. I probably expected to keep my place, but instead it went to a young fella called Bobby Charlton. Of course I was disappointed, but I was fine about it. Bobby was the emerging prodigy back then and you could already see that, barring injury, he was going to be a world-beater. After the World Cup we would play together many times for

England. As it turned out, being dropped for the next game proved to be the least of the tragedies associated with my England debut.

That game against France was the last game the Busby Babes would play for England. Three months later Roger Byrne, Duncan Edwards and Tommy Taylor were among eight Manchester United players killed in the Munich air disaster. David Pegg, a young winger who had just forced his way into the squad as under-study to Tom Finney, also died. In fact, of Man United's England contingent, only Bobby Charlton survived.

I can remember vividly where I was when news of the crash came through. I always took a keen interest in European club football, even though it was still in its infancy back then, and I was watching on a television I'd hired from radio rentals when they made the announcement. I found the news appalling, distressing, tragic. "How on earth did it happen?" I remember thinking. I was shocked, upset, just part of the whole country's bereavement, I suppose. A great Manchester United team had been decimated in tragic circumstances and it took me a long time to get over. I don't know whether it was because my generation had been brought up in wartime, but you just got on with it. And Man United? Well, they had to completely rebuild, and rebuild they did, becoming a great team again in the 60s. Life goes on.

The Munich disaster affected our chances of winning the 1958 World Cup considerably. Considerably. For a start, we lost three of our best players, three world-class players. Roger Byrne was our captain – a great captain – and a fantastic left-back. Even in 1957 he was like today's modern-day full-back; extremely quick, always overlapping. Tommy Taylor, who scored England's other two goals on my debut, was a top, top centre-forward, the best in the country at the time. And Duncan Edwards was a colossus, a phenomenon, well on the way to becoming one of the best, if not the best player this country has ever produced. He was that good, the complete footballer. He was a Black Country lad, Duncan, and even though Wolves and West Brom couldn't stop him joining Man United, he was a hero where I lived, and his loss was felt particularly strongly.

With the benefit of hindsight I suppose it's easy to say we would have won the World Cup or gone close, but losing those three was a cruel blow and made a marked difference – how could it not? It would be like Sven-Göran Eriksson losing Ashley Cole, Wayne Rooney and Frank Lampard for this year's World Cup finals. Imagine how much of a blow that would be. You can't just replace players like that. We also lost Bobby Charlton for that World Cup too. Bobby was part of the squad, but Walter felt the mental scars of Munich were still too fresh for him to be able to cope with the pressure of a World Cup, so he didn't play any part..

Given that he'd replaced me against Scotland, people think it might have felt strange for me being in the team, but it wasn't strange at all. I wasn't a left-back, I wasn't a central midfielder, I wasn't a left-sided midfielder, so I probably would have made the team anyway. I was more concerned at how we would get on without three, possibly four, top, top players than I was about my own position.

The FA Selection Committee controversially picked a squad of only 20 for the 1958 World Cup finals, even though they were permitted to take 22. Don't ask me why they did that, but Stanley Matthews and Nat Lofthouse were the two who missed out. Stan was still going strong at 42 and Nat would return to the fold after the tournament. They were still two of England's finest players, but for some reason they were left at home. It was controversial and prompted huge debate around the country. But when you're a relatively young player and new to the squad as I was, you accept decisions far more easily than you do with a bit of experience. It was a management decision and as long as I was in the squad I had no reason to question it.

On the way out to Sweden, I sat next to Bobby Charlton on the plane. We knew each other quite well, even though I'm five years older; we're both from the North East and were both new to the squad. As we made our descent into Gothenburg, the plane was coming through thick clouds and it was a bit bumpy. Have you ever been on an aeroplane when that's happening? You can't see where you're going and you think you might hit something and only when you see the ground and the lights and what have you, do you start to feel a bit better, a bit relieved. "We're alright now," you think.

In the Munich crash, Bobby was thrown from the plane still strapped to his seat. As we came down in Gothenburg I could see he was a bit nervous, a bit tense. He was holding on tight to the arms of his seat and starting to sweat a bit. "You alright, son?" I said – because I call everybody who is younger than me "son".

"Yeah, I'm alright," he said. "I just wish this bloody plane would land." What was going through his mind after what he'd been through I can only imagine. How many people would survive a crash like that and get back on a plane? A lot of people would never fly again, but he did, and has done ever since.

The format for the World Cup finals changed in 1958. Again, there were 16 teams, but this time four groups of four would be followed by a straight knockout competition, with the four group winners playing off against the four runners-up in the quarter-finals. Things would stay that way for quite some time, until 1982 if I remember rightly, when the number of teams was increased to 24.

The 1958 World Cup was the first time there had been no withdrawals, so all the best sides in the world were taking part, making it very open. As a player, I had nothing to compare it to, so I don't know about it being the first 'proper' World Cup. But to suddenly go from reading about previous World Cups in the newspaper taking part myself meant that it was definitely the biggest World Cup to date from my point of view. Representing my country was always special, but now we were playing in the World Cup against 15 of the best international sides in the world. We knew how important it was, the responsibility we had to the country, and we felt special. There were no European Championships in those days, so you only got this sort of opportunity once every four years, possibly once in a lifetime.

Preparation for the tournament was nothing like it is now – there's not even a semblance of similarity between the two. The season ended and we had few weeks' rest. With the finals being staged in Sweden, we didn't need to acclimatise, so we met up for a few days in London Colney, before flying out three days before our first game. That was all there was too it. We didn't think anything of it because everybody did the same. I just couldn't wait for the whole thing to start.

I hoped I would make the starting line-up for sure, and yes, I suppose I did think I would. We had a squad of just 20 players, two of whom were goalkeepers, and only so many inside-forwards, so it's fair to say I thought I had a decent chance of getting in the team.

Whoever played, we were in for a tough time. FIFA did away with the previous seeding system and, because there were four teams from Latin America, four from Eastern Europe, four from Western Europe and four from the British Isles, they decided to seed the teams geographically, with one from each region drawn in each group.

We were drawn in what these days the media would call the 'Group of Death', with Russia, Austria and Brazil the other three teams. Hungary were a shadow of the team that finished runners-up to Germany in 1954, so Russia, who were the Olympic champions, were now the strongest team in Eastern Europe. Austria had finished third in 1954, so they were no mugs and Brazil, well, they were always going to be the pre-tournament favourites. Throw in England, the reigning British champions, and you arguably had four of the strongest teams in one group.

The FA cried foul. I don't remember the controversy myself, and I certainly didn't suspect anything untoward. What I do remember is thinking, "blimey, we haven't been given an easy group here…"

Our first game was against the Soviet Union. Only three weeks earlier, we'd played them in Moscow. It was only my second game for England, but in a 1-1 draw, we were much the better side, so the selectors sent out the same 11 for this game, with me at inside-right. Unhappy with their performance in Moscow, the Russian completely changed their forward line. Their new-look attack took us by surprise, and they took an early lead before doubling their advantage in the 56th minute. We just couldn't get a foothold in the game.

Ooh, they were tough, the Russians. I wouldn't say they were dirty necessarily, but they could certainly put it about a bit and didn't lose many 50-50 tackles. Tom Finney was singled out for some particularly special treatment, but they were quite clever in that respect – they knew what they could get away with and played right on the edge. Sure, they were strong, competitive, athletic – all of those things – but they also had a fair amount of ability, and for an hour they were the better side.

Then, on 64 minutes, Derek Kevan, my West Brom team-mate, headed home from a Billy Wright free-kick and all of a sudden we were a different side. I missed a decent chance, but soon after, I did have the ball in the net.

The goal was disallowed – wrongly… Tom Finney swung the ball in from the left, towards the near post. Seeing that Derek Kevan was going to get there before him, Lev Yashin in the Russian goal stretched out an arm to stop him getting the ball, but only succeeded in pushing it into my path. I couldn't believe my luck. All I had to do was make sure I got there before the covering defender and I'd be left with nothing more than a tap-in. I smashed it in from six yards out. "That's it," I thought, "we're level". I had scored in the World Cup Finals…

But the referee blew up for a foul on the goalkeeper. It wasn't a foul, no way – Derek never even touched him. There was some controversy after the game, because the referee was from Hungary, which was part of the Russian domain at the time and the feeling was he leaned towards the Russians throughout the game. Now, I can't tell you if that was true or not, but I can tell you it wasn't a foul. Had that goal stood, I think we would have gone on to win the game. There was only one team in it after that, but we eventually had to wait until five minutes from time to get an equaliser, Tom Finney scoring from the penalty spot after Johnny Haynes had been brought down. I suppose a draw was a fair result in the end.

Billy Wright was the first 'Golden Boy' of English football. With his blonde hair and blue eyes, he was a good-looking boy and a fantastic athlete. He wasn't very tall, Billy, but he could leap about 16 foot in the air.

After the game against the Soviet Union it came out in the press that he was courting Joy Beverley of the Beverley Sisters. They were just about the biggest thing in popular music at the time. A sort of Atomic Kitten for the 1950s, if you like. The Press loved it. Football meets showbiz. So what? He was single, she was single – nothing wrong with that. Just like Posh meeting Becks.

But that sort of thing was rare in those days and was even frowned upon in some quarters, and the story got a lot of coverage in the press back home, especially the tabloids. The FA in their wisdom were worried that the story would distract the team's attention, especially our captain's, from the task in hand and banned Billy from talking to the media. What a load of rubbish. It was already big news and by making a meal of it they probably made the situation worse. The players couldn't believe what all the fuss was about. We were like "Well done, Billy. Good lad," you know, but it was an outside issue, it would never have affected our preparation for the game. And, of course, it didn't.

Of much greater concern was an injury Tom Finney sustained in the game against the Soviet Union. The Russians' heavy-handed treatment of Tom meant he could barely walk when he stepped up to equalise from the penalty spot late on. In fact he took the penalty with his supposedly weaker left foot – an incredible thing really. It turned out he'd badly pulled a muscle behind his right knee and it soon worsened, ruling him out of the rest of the tournament.

I've talked about the loss of the Busby Babes and the effect it had on us. And leaving Matthews and Lofthouse at home. Then, to lose Tom Finney, well... that was just as big a blow. You're talking about an experienced, world-class player. So all told we'd lost half a team. But what can you do?

When you lose a big player like Tom – or indeed Wayne Rooney if he doesn't make it to Germany – the quicker you get it out of your head, the better, but that's easier said than done. I had to send Bryan Robson home from two World Cups when I was England manager. That's my captain, my best player, and you do curse your luck for a while. Now, I'm not saying one player makes a team, but in certain cases it makes a hell of a difference. Would Argentina have won the World Cup in 1986 if Maradona had not been playing? No chance.

Liverpool winger Alan A'Court came in for Tom in the only change to the side for the next game against Brazil. Even in those days, there was a certain mystique about Brazil, but that was more to do with the way they played than any tangible success. There certainly wasn't the aura of invincibility around them that there is now. England had beaten them 4-2 at Wembley two years previously and the press and public still expected us to beat everybody. We had taught the game to the world and at home we were still seen as the masters. But football was changing; other countries were producing more technical players and there came a time when we weren't the masters anymore. You hear of pupils becoming bigger geniuses than their professors and that would be the case with Brazil.

We didn't know about Pelé at this stage. In hindsight, it's a shame I can't look back and say I played against him, but at the time I didn't feel any disappointment because I had no idea this supremely talented 17-year-old would take that World Cup by storm and go on to become the greatest player of all time. I knew all about the great Garrincha, of course, but after Brazil had beaten Austria

3-0 in their opening game, both were rested for the game against England because they were carrying slight knocks.

It's probably just as well, because I had my hands full with a fella called Didi – D-I-D-I – who was my direct opponent that day. Phew, he was a good player, easily the best I'd come up against at that point in my career. For eight seasons, I'd played against the best players from the best clubs in England – Wolves, Manchester United, you name it – but I'd never come up against a player like Didi. He had everything. He was quick, had a great touch, a great delivery, a great football brain and he was so technical. He was also a good marker, but still managed to always be looking to get on the ball himself.

Did he do a job on me? He did more of a job on me than I did on him! He didn't run rings around me or anything, but he definitely had the better of things over 90 minutes. And because of that, I felt I couldn't contribute fully to the team, because the best part of my game was going forward. I spent most of the game trying to keep Didi quiet. I was very fit, so I was able to keep close to him, but doing doggies [shuttle runs] isn't the most enjoyable part of football, is it? I came off at the end exhausted, thinking "Jesus Christ, what a player he is!" At the end of the day he just had a bit too much for me.

Overall, though, we put in a good, solid, defensive performance. Brazil always found scoring relatively easy, but they couldn't find a way past us. In fact, we were the only team who kept a clean sheet against them throughout the tournament, quite an achievement if you consider the manner in which they would go on to win it. But we didn't just shut up shop – we matched them going forward too.

They had the better of the first half. Their football took your breath away at times. Their passing, their movement, their invention… well, it was from another world. Our goalkeeper, Burnley's Colin McDonald, had a busy first half, saving well from Dino, Mazzola and Vavá. He was another great player, Vavá. He orchestrated them from midfield, a bit like Johnny Haynes did for us, and he hit the bar with one stinging effort. Eddie Clamp, the Wolves half-back, cleared another effort off the line and Mazzola also hit the post.

But Brazil weren't having it all their own way. Derek Kevan was especially unlucky. First he had a close range shot blocked, then the referee waved away what looked to me like a clear penalty when Bellini brought him down in the box. My only half chance of the game came early on, but I was quickly closed down before I could get my shot away. That blasted Didi again!

"More of the same" were the instructions from Walter at half-time. We were doing well, so why change it?

By the second half, our centre-backs looked to have the measure of Brazil's strikers and it was us who looked more like breaking the deadlock. Johnny Haynes burst forward from midfield several times, but none of his shots could find a way past Gilmar in the Brazil goal. I remember late on one of Johnny's efforts took a deflection and skimmed the outside of the post, but it was just one of those days. How it remained goalless I'll never know, but it was one of the most entertaining 0-0 draws you're likely to see. Again, a draw was probably a fair result.

We didn't really get the plaudits we deserved after the Brazil game. If people had known Brazil would go on to win the World Cup playing startling football, they would have said this was a fine England performance. But because we'd drawn two out of two, we now needed to beat Austria to guarantee our passage through to the quarter-finals, so the press called for changes, and I was one of those whose place was rumoured to be under threat. But after matching Brazil, we were confident of getting the job done against Austria, and after a brief chat with some of the senior players, Walter decided to send out the same team.

Austria had performed well below expectations in their first two games and were comfortably beaten by Brazil and the Soviet Union, but there was no complacency on our part. We knew they'd want to go out with a bang and teams were always up for it against England.

And so it turned out. Again, we were slow out of the blocks and Austria took the lead after 16 minutes when we failed to clear a corner. The rest of the first half was scrappy, which suited the Austrians, and they indulged in a bit of play-acting, presumably looking to waste as much time as possible.

But we came out firing in the second half. Johnny Haynes had a couple of chances before he finally broke his duck from close range and we continued to pour forward in search of a winner. Then, completely against the run of play, Austria took the lead with a breakaway goal 20 minutes from time, but we equalised almost straight away. I fed Derek Kevan, who smashed home from the edge of the box.

Then I scored another 'goal'. Again it was disallowed. And again it was the wrong decision. The keeper came off his line and blocked my initial effort, but it hit my chest and put in the rebound. But the linesman gave handball – the same Hungarian fella who had disallowed my goal against the Soviet Union! I was livid. You could say my own personal misery continued. I wasn't just disappointed for myself, but for the team, because again it cost us a win – and I knew how tight the group was, and this time it cost us a place in the second round. I was looking at the sky by this point, thinking "what have I done wrong?"

Because we finished level on points and had drawn against them we were forced to play-off with the Soviet Union for the right to join Brazil in the Quarter-finals.

I thought changes might be made, but I didn't necessarily think I'd be one of those dropped. That second half against Austria was the best I'd played in the whole tournament. I'd had my hands full with Didi for most of the Brazil game, but this time I had really got my game going and had the measure of my man throughout the second half. I'd also been very unlucky to have two goals wrongly disallowed in the tournament.

But this was a must-win game. Walter had a group of players at his disposal and he obviously decided he need to freshen things up. As a professional you understood and accept that. I had to make some tough decisions at the World Cup when I was England manager, and I knew then how tough it must have been. But you can't afford to have anybody thinking selfishly, you need each other's support, so you just have to get on with it.

I was replaced by a boy called Peter Broadbent, the Wolves forward. He was a great player and he wasn't in the team for the first three games, so I just imagined how he must have felt when he wasn't playing. I just had to tell myself that it wasn't permanent and I may get back in if we progressed.

It's awful watching from the sidelines, especially once you've been part of the action – you're completely helpless. Funnily enough, I can't remember much about the game I watched as I can about the games I took part in. What I can remember is that again we started slowly and again we came out a different side in the second half. Don't ask me why, but that was the pattern throughout the tournament. We lost 1-0 with another goal completely against the run of play, against a team who had nothing we couldn't cope with. We proved that only a few months later when we thumped them 5-0 at Wembley.

It was awful in the dressing room afterwards, one of the most disappointing moments of my career – far more disappointing than being dropped for the game. One minute you're on the biggest stage of all, the World Cup, the next minute you're on your way home. It's difficult to explain what that feels like. It was very sad.

In 1958, I only got into the England team eight months before the finals and was still finding my way in international football, but by 1962 I was a well-established member of the team. The period between those two World Cups was the best of my career, particularly at international level. With Bobby Charlton and Jimmy Greaves also establishing themselves, and Johnny Haynes in his pomp, I was part of a very successful England team. At one point we won six games on the trot, a run which included the famous 9-3 drubbing of the Auld Enemy at Wembley in the 1961 Home Championships, when I scored our opening goal.

I was 25 in 1958 and my biggest worry was "would I be in the same shape in four years' time?" As it turned out I was in better shape and also in the form of my life. But for me personally the 1962 tournament turned out to be even more of a disappointment than 1958.

To acclimatise, we flew out to Chile two weeks before our opening game and based ourselves in Coya, an old mining village up in the hills, away from the hurly burly of Santiago. There wasn't much to do and a few days later, Walter Winterbottom accepted an invitation from a local amateur team to play in a 'friendly' game. Walter asked for volunteers and I immediately put my hand up. Anything to break up the boredom, I thought, and I always loved to pull on my boots whenever possible anyway. But again I was the victim of cruel luck when this guy came straight through the back of me. Some friendly! My ankle blew up like a balloon, and the scans revealed I'd chipped a bone. I was devastated and cursing my bloody luck because I was the only player in the squad who got injured. The physio recommended I stay out there with the squad, as there was a chance the bone would heal in time for the knockout stages – if we got that far. In the end, the injury did heal in time for our quarter-final with Brazil, but I hadn't done any training for two weeks. Although I was clinically fit, I wasn't match fit – but I could have played in the semi-final.

But Brazil won 3-1 and again my World Cup ended in bitter disappointment. I was exasperated by it all, because I feel I would have done especially well in Chile. I was established in the side, knew my game inside out and in terms of form, power and confidence I was at my peak. As it turned out, I'd never play for England again.

I'd moved back into midfield by this point in my career, and my replacement in the team for the '62 World Cup was a 19-year-old 'centre-half' Bobby Moore. Bobby's talent was obvious, but he'd been brought along for experience more than anything and I certainly couldn't have predicted then he would go on to play 108 times for England and become perhaps the greatest defender of all time.

I didn't think for one minute his emergence signalled the beginning of the end of my international career – and I'll tell you why… After the 1962 World Cup finals, I moved back to Fulham and changed my position, going from midfield into defence. It was a position I liked, and I was still a very, very good player. And by 1966, although I was the wrong side of 30, I was still good enough to play for England – in my opinion, anyway – perhaps not in place of Bobby, who was in his pomp by then, but elsewhere in defence. But Alf Ramsey was a very good judge of a player and I wasn't selected, which was fair enough. It would have been great to be part of a World Cup-winning squad, especially on home soil, but I was philosophical about it and got over it.

Did I have mixed feelings? I wouldn't say so. I was there at the final and it was a wonderful, magical experience. I wasn't jealous – I was as elated as everyone else, perhaps more so, because I knew all the players. I'd played against them all for many years and I'd played alongside quite a few of them, so I was chuffed for them and chuffed for the country.

In 18 years as I player I won nothing. Nothing. I joined Fulham and won nothing, went to West Bromwich Albion and won nothing, went back to Fulham and won nothing. Nothing. I didn't even come close.

When I went into management that was definitely on my mind. If I'd been a manager and still won nothing I'd have thought "I've had a good life, a good career, but I've won nothing." That would have been a big regret. But as a manager I was nearly always in the business of winning trophies. I won the FA Cup and the UEFA Cup at Ipswich Town, league titles and cups at PSV Eindhoven and Porto and the European Cup Winners Cup and Spanish Cup at Barcelona. In terms of actual achievement, that is what has given me the most pleasure.

For England, it was a similar situation. As a player I knew I didn't have the international career that I should have had. I won 20 caps, which is still a great achievement, something I'm very proud of, but it should have been more, and as I've mentioned, bad luck deprived me of the chance to play in the World Cup at the peak of my career.

As England manager, I was determined to make up for what I didn't do as an England player – and I got pretty close. We were a bit unlucky in Mexico, because although we were knocked out by the best team in the tournament, we were cheated. And the semi-final against West Germany in 1990, well... that was the most dramatic game in my England career, because it was on a knife-edge and so easily could have gone our way. And because it's so fresh in the memory, it's what people ask me about most... very few people realise I played in the World Cup myself!

JIMMY ARMFIELD
RIGHT-BACK

CHILE 1962

BORN 7th September 1935, Denton
CLUB Blackpool, Bolton Wanderers
INTERNATIONAL DEBUT May 1959 v Brazil
ENGLAND CAREER 43 caps
INTERNATIONAL FAREWELL June 1966 v Finland

Jimmy Armfield captained club and country with distinction. A dashing right-back who overlapped at will, Armfield was a huge success during the 1962 World Cup, being voted into the FIFA team of the tournament. He was also voted Europe's best right-back on three successive occasions. He missed out on the victorious 1966 World Cup finals due to an injury picked up in a warm-up game. He later managed Leeds United to the European Cup final. Now an erudite and perceptive commentator for BBC Radio FiveLive, Armfield was voted the nation's favourite commentator during Euro 2000.

ENGLAND 1 v BRAZIL 3

World Cup Quarter-final
Sunday 10th June 1962

Sausalito Stadium, Viña del Mar
Attendance 17,736

*Once again England fall to the defending Champions at the quarter-final
stage, but this time after having the upper hand in the first half and failing
to beat nine fit men thanks to more defensive blunders*

Teams

Walter Winterbottom	**Managers**	Vicente Feola
Ron Springett	1	Gilmar
Jimmy Armfield	2	D Santos
Ray Wilson	3	Mauro
Bobby Moore	4	Zózimo
Maurice Norman	5	Nilton Santos
Ron Flowers	6	Zito
Bryan Douglas	7	Garrincha
Jimmy Greaves	8	Didi
Gerry Hitchens	9	Vavá
Johnny Haynes	10	Amarildo
Bobby Charlton	11	Zagalo
Hitchens 38	**Scorers**	Garrincha 31, 59, Vavá 53

Referee: Pierre Schwinte (France)

AT HALF TIME the England dressing room was very bouyant. There was real optimism. We were holding the World Champions Brazil and we were buzzing, full of hope and expectation. I for one honestly thought it was going to be our day.

Brazil had a fantastic team, they were World Champions after all, but we were having so much joy against them, especially down the wings where Bryan Douglas on the right and Bobby Charlton on the left were enjoying great success. I was doing what I did best and overlapping and seeing a lot of the ball, so much so that Zagalo, their left-winger was tagged to mark me.

We may have been level, but during that half-time interval I was sure that we'd win that quarter-final and if we could knock out Brazil, who knows...

It was, of course, a false dawn.

I made my England debut in May 1959 in Brazil. We lost 2-0 to a team that included their new young superstar, Pelé . In fact I think I still have his shirt. We were on a summer tour of South America and despite losing three of the four games it had been a learning exercise, in which manager Walter Winterbottom decided to blood plenty some young talent. Bobby Charlton and Johnny Haynes were already in the side, Chelsea's Jimmy Greaves, Burnley's John Connelly, and Stoke's Tony Allen came in as well, so there was a fresh look about the squad.

We were inexperienced, but it was the heat that gave us the real problem in the Americas that summer. We knew it was something we would have to get used to in time for the next World Cup in Chile. In Mexico incredibly, it was 104 degrees.

But the team was changing. By 1960 I had taken over regularly at right-back, whilst Ray Wilson had come in at left-back. To begin with we didn't pull up any trees. We lost in Hungary and in Madrid and it was this that I believe brought a change of attitude. The next season, for the home internationals, Walter Winterbottom took us all away to Lilleshall for a four day get together. He wanted to develop some team spirit, get a settled team, and build up for the impending World Cup.

We had to play World Cup qualifiers that year against Portugal and Luxembourg. Portugal were good and Benfica were at the top of their game, but Walter made his move before we played the home international in Belfast. Ron Springett came into goal and Walter brought in Mick McNeil of Middlesbrough to play left-back.

Our central defenders were Peter Swan, and Ronnie Flowers, Bobby Robson and Haynes were in midfield, Douglas on one wing, Charlton on the other with Jimmy Greaves and Bobby Smith as our strikers. That was to be the team really for the near future at least. The manager wanted it settled and it paid off. We beat Ireland 5-2 in Belfast; Spain 4-2 at Wembley, Luxembourg 9-0, then Wales 5-1, Scotland 9-3 and Mexico 8-0. Next we went to Portugal for a World Cup qualifier in Lisbon and drew one each. We should have beaten them as well, nevertheless, it was a result that would hit their World Cup chances.

We then beat Italy in Rome 3-2. It was a great spell. The team was committed and confident. In seven matches we scored 44 goals. No other England team has got anywhere near that. Both Jimmy Greaves and Johnny Haynes have said that was the best team in which they were ever involved. People say if the World Cup had been in 1961 then we would have won it, but that's a big 'if'. Certainly it was the most adventurous and talented team I ever played in and whichever opposition we played – and we played some good teams that year – we were confident and that confidence factor went right through every player. A year, though, is a long time in football and by the World Cup in 1962 there had been one or two enforced changes. Mick McNeil got injured, so Ray Wilson was back in the team. Before we played in the World Cup we beat Switzerland at Wembley 3-1; a good send off before travelling across the world where we would face Hungary, Argentina and Bulgaria in the group stage.

En route to Chile we stopped in Peru and outplayed them, winning 4-0, the perfect tonic before the big test. For that match a young Bobby Moore came in and naturally was a bit inexperienced. He became a very good player two years later. Don't get me wrong, it was clear how talented he was, even then you could see that, but when he was pitched in he still had to learn the international game.

To add to Walter's problems Bobby Robson got injured and Peter Swan became ill once we reached Chile. Bobby Smith was injured before we set off so the whole spine of that successful team of 1960-61 had been removed. Four years earlier in 1958, after Munich, England had been branded as unlucky, in Chile once again fate had been cruel to us as we lacked a number of important players and frankly it was never quite the same.

Along with Moore, Maurice Norman was another new cap, but he had been around and was a good steady centre-half. He was a big, powerful lad, Maurice and had tasted success with Spurs. Having said that, international football is different to the bread and butter of League football. Even very good club players can find the transition hard. Others – and I include Bobby Moore in this – lift themselves in international football often easier than they do their league football.

Basically, losing Smith, Robson and Swan all at once proved crucial. Bobby Smith was so important to us. He was strong; he had great control and was not only a real powerhouse, but also a fine finisher. Jimmy loved feeding off him and it was obvious he was going to be missed. Peter Swan was a no frills type of defender, but he was very effective. When we arrived in South America Peter was sent to bed suffering terrible stomach problems. He couldn't fight off that bug and incredibly never played for England again.

Bobby Robson had, in midfield, been the perfect foil for Johnny Haynes. It was he who did Johnny's donkeywork and was vital to our attacking instincts. Johnny could get on with doing what he did best, opening up the opposition with a killer pass. Losing the experienced Robson was another setback.

We had to get on with things though and concentrate on the positives. The team worked hard. The squad was made up of good technical players and there was a nice balance. Bryan Douglas was a dribbler and a clever player. He could go past defenders and things would open up for us. With the pace of Bobby Charlton on the left we were strong from wide areas – an important factor.

Away from the treatment room, those of us who were fit prepared in Chile in far from luxurious surroundings, but that wasn't really a problem. You have to remember that my generation of footballers had come through the end of the war and had known the difficult days of the 1950s. We had all done our National Service and so living in basic digs was nothing new. Nevertheless I don't know how Walter Winterbottom found this remote training camp in the Andes at Coya. After flying into Santiago, we got the bus up to Rancagua, then another up the mountain which then took us to a single-track train up to a tiny village built around a copper mine. We all slept in huts. Nearby there was a golf course with parched brown fairways and lush greens. We played a couple of times there and had these young local Chilean lads caddying. Frankly they were useless. Ray Wilson ended up carrying the Caddy and I carried the clubs. They wanted paying too, the cheeky blighters, but we paid up.

As well as golf, there was a mini cinema which showed black and white films. Some people complained about the conditions, but frankly there weren't many options available to the FA. Oddly, it didn't bother me. I was there for the football and we could make our own fun. There were no videos to relieve the boredom in 1962. We'd play cards and games. We'd train and we rested a lot. One night we went to the home of the manager of the Braden Copper Company, an American concern and he laid on a super dinner. We also made trips on the railway to Rancagua and so we filled our time and stayed focused.

Before the competition started the four teams in the group, Argentina, Bulgaria, Hungary and ourselves, were invited to parade in the town square in Rancagua where there was an excuse for a brass band. When you think of our great brass bands in the United Kingdom, they sounded very ordinary, but I suppose they did their best. They hoisted the four flags and the mayor greeted us all in Spanish. The Argentineans were the only ones who knew what he was on about. It was a grey day and we were all looking smart in our blazers. All four squads stood there and sheepishly eyed each other up, looking for weaknesses I suppose. Then we got back on the train and headed back to our camp in the hills – a low key start.

Matchday arrived and we travelled down to Rancagua. It was only a small town, but it was here that we faced what would be our toughest game. Hungary were amongst Europe's best at the time. Not quite as good as the Puskas team of ten years earlier, but they had some fine players. They had beaten us 2-0 in Budapest two years earlier and with virtually the same team as that occasion they proved once again a strong outfit. Florian Albert was a gifted centre-forward, Gyula Gorcos was a survivor from their great 1950s side, and the two blonde centre-halves Sipos and Meszoly were brilliant. It was always going to be tough and to me, they represented a far bigger threat than Argentina.

As I've said, we had the base of a good side, but we lacked that original, strong spine. On a wet pitch – it had rained all day – we were holding a 1-1 score line when a slip allowed Albert to get through and score his winner. I had thought that a draw wouldn't be a bad start and I was right because that late goal proved critical to our hopes.

The Hungarians believed that if they could nullify Johnny Haynes then they could control the England team, but that wasn't true. Not when you have the likes of Douglas, Greaves and Charlton about. Johnny Haynes was a vital player I'll agree, but to say we were totally dependent on him was way off mark.

But we'd lost and that meant we had to beat Argentina, who had won their first match 1-0 against Bulgaria. We went to see them play that match and they scored after 30 seconds. They then defended for 89 minutes. Instead of taking the initiative, they sat back and defended their lead. Argentina, I always thought, ruined their chances by having that negative streak in them. Fortunately we had a few days before we met them and so had time to focus on the job at hand.

I helped in the organisation of the training schedule. I had been a captain at club level since 1958 and had stood in for Haynes as England's skipper against Luxembourg at Highbury a year earlier, so I instinctively become a bit of a talker on and off the pitch. It was automatic. As for my form, I was pleased with how I was doing. I felt fit and confident.

So we faced Argentina. It was a must win situation, against a team desperate to succeed on their own continent and one with a ruthless streak running though them. They would try and get away with things and this game was not going to be different in that respect. They would stand on your heels and nip you. It was nasty, petty stuff really and it set the tone for four decades worth of contests between the countries as World Cup rivals. The got up to all sorts of stuff. One guy tapped me on the shoulder, I turned around and he went to spit in my face, but didn't. It was like that. Little things. They were that sort of team.

It was testing, yet, on reflection, they didn't need to misbehave like that as they had talented players. For all his troubles, Antonio Rattin was a top class defender. He would infamously get sent off against England in 1966, making people forget how good a player he was. He was always around, always involved in the play. But he and his team-mates lost their discipline that day in 1962, just as they did again four years later at Wembley.

It proved to be our finest hour in the tournament. Middlesbrough's Alan Peacock came in up front and did well. We led 2-0 up through Flowers and Charlton at half-time and when Greaves got his first of the tournament the game was ours. They had a spell when we really had our backs to the wall and they did pull one back, but we had too much for them, particularly down the flanks. Walter always encouraged me to overlap and that day it was effective. I got forward a lot and even hit the post with one shot. That was probably the nearest I got to scoring for my country. The other occasion was my last ever kick in an England shirt against Finland, a twenty-five yarder that hit the bar. In Chile I came in from the right and saw the keeper had left a space and hit it. My shot struck the woodwork – another hard luck story!

Yet whilst I hadn't scored I was pleased for Jimmy Greaves that he had got off the mark, because he was important to us and his game thrived on goals. He had been my roommate for that earlier tour to South America in 1959. We had been playing for the Under-23 side together in Italy and were both lifted from that trip into the full squad for the South American tour. We had played in Milan and then flew to London and got another plane to Brazil.

I believe Greaves was the best finisher that England have ever had. We've had some good ones – Lineker, Shearer, these are class acts – but for me Greaves was the most natural finisher of all. He had speed, skill, two good feet, he could even dribble. Whenever I played behind him I could see him go one of his runs and the opposition would seem to open up and he would glide through them on goal. I recall playing against Romania for Young England at Wembley. He scored twice in the first quarter of an hour. Both goals were almost identical, with Jimmy slicing though a mesmerised defence. A true all-time great.

Having won the game against Argentina, the squad was in reflective mood. Spirits were high, but we all realised that if we had won the group we would have stayed in Rancagua and avoided Brazil in the quarter-finals in the heat on the coast. There we would have faced Czechoslovakia, who we had already beaten a few months earlier. All ifs and buts I suppose, but it's the little things in these tournaments that can prove so crucial. I suppose it mirrored what happened to England in 2002. Had they won their group they would have probably played Brazil at night rather than in the strength-sapping afternoon heat.

And in any case we hadn't actually finished second yet. We were now on the same points as Argentina, but they had to play Hungary whilst we had Bulgaria. We only had to draw to qualify, but we desperately wanted another win to maintain the momentum. We travelled back down the mountain for the stadium in Rancagua. It was a strange setting. We played our games with the beautiful Andes as our backdrop, but because of the size of the town we were playing in front of very small crowds. In Santiago they were getting 45,000 people. We were in this very isolated mountain resort, so it was not a natural football setting. Chile, it was alleged, had been handed the World Cup by a sympathetic FIFA following the massive earthquake of 1960. Even so, it did seem a way-out place to hold the finals, even 44 years ago.

Gates at Rancagua averaged at 6,000, and that day many of them were Argentineans who had travelled up to cheer on Bulgaria in the hope they would help their country through. Bulgaria had lost both of their first two matches and didn't want to go home having not won a single point. What crowd there was, was dominated by these Argentinean fans and their blue and white flags. They were all supporting the Bulgarians hoping for an England defeat. The Chileans also had sympathy for the pointless Bulgarians, so we didn't have much backing. That all added to the tension amongst us as players.

From the kick-off it became clear that the Bulgarians weren't in any hurry to get at us offensively. It was the first time I had ever played against a team who only had one and out-and-out striker. European coaches didn't employ tactics like that in those days. Yet Bulgaria did, with the striker assisted only by couple of wide men. The rest of the team were defenders and that made life very difficult for our forwards.

It was damned hard trying to get through them. We had the ball for 90% of the match. I've never had so much freedom in all my football life. We had the ball at the back and they just packed their own half and sat back very deep. To make life even more difficult they had two good central defenders who were strong in the air and who won everything. Douglas and Charlton were being marked tight, man to man, so it was hard to get them into space in order to open them up.

The first half was very tight, but we struggled to find a route through and became a bit frustrated. We wasted two good chances in the second half and that made us even more apprehensive. They had one star forward, Kolev, who towards the end had a shot from the edge of the box which went narrowly past our post. Our keeper, Ron Springett, was rooted and if it had been on target we would have probably been knocked out.

I had always been an adventurous player yet, with ten minutes left, Springett threw the ball to me and there was no one near me for thirty yards. I ran forward and the Bulgarians backed off. I slowed, realising 0-0 was enough, we knocked it about at the back trying to draw them out and make space, but they wouldn't take the bait. They remained deep and unmoved, yet incredibly the crowd started to boo us, blaming us for the inactivity. It was unacceptable; this was after all the World Cup, people had paid good money, they wanted entertainment. Fans should expect the best and it was no wonder they became rather hostile.

Bobby Charlton was urging me forward, but we decided to keep the back four intact. If we weren't going to score neither were they. The ref blew up early I think. He'd probably had enough. It's hard to explain, but I got no pleasure from that game, other than the fact that we qualified. It was instantly forgettable. We sat in the dressing room all feeling the same: disappointed with the way that the group had finished, but safe in the knowledge that we could go further. It was the Hungary game that was key. That initial defeat meant that we had to face Brazil, so it was time to up sticks and take ourselves down to the coast to a lovely place called Viña del Mar and warmer climes.

The locals gave us very little chance against the favourites. Brazil, on the other hand, were thrilled that we had seen off their old rivals Argentina. Whenever these two teams meet, form goes out of the window. It's like England v Scotland. Our Press too seemed to offer us little hope, but we were not deterred. Pelé had been lost to Brazil through injury, but they still housed some of the big names in the football world.

Amarildo joined Garrincha, Didi, Zagalo and the two tough men at the back, Mauro and Zozimo. It was going to be hard, we knew that, but we were up for the challenge. Our spirits had been raised by new, vastly improved lodgings. We'd come down to the coast from 8,000 ft and it was a huge difference to what we had been used to, but it was warm and humid and the Brazilians must have felt at home.

We got to the hotel and I remember the first morning, opening the curtains onto the Pacific Ocean and I'd never seen so many pelicans in all my life. They filled the bay and after the copper company this seemed like luxury.

Walter Winterbottom had found the hotel and done his job. To be frank, Walter was always very organised. A lovely man, he always had the respect of his players. He had a quiet approach, but he was, in fact, one of the most professional managers

I've ever had. He ran the FA coaching scheme and developed coaching programmes for the whole world. The first coaching manuals ever to come out were Walter's. 'Training For Soccer' is the skeleton from which many modern football coaching programmes have been developed. He put it all down on paper before the rest. Walter was really a very professional man.

Against the Brazilians, Walter opted for Gerry Hitchens up front in place of Peacock. Hitchens was a talented striker. I first saw him at Cardiff as a young hopeful and even then he was good on the ball and in the air. He went to Villa and ended up at Inter Milan. He had a good all round game, alert, not over quick, but lively and brave. He lacked Smith's aggression, but he was always a handful for defenders.

We missed at least four great chances on that day in Viña del Mar and Jimmy Greaves, our star turn, was one of the culprits. Bobby Charlton was running at Djalma Santos and giving him a torrid time. Bobby had a great turn of speed and was a wonderful wide player that season. Douglas also tormented his full-back and the Brazilians had a hard time controlling them.

Up front too they were struggling to break us down. The famous five, Zagalo, Didi, Vavá, Amarillo (who was in for Pelé), and Garrincha couldn't find a route through. Bobby Moore found his international feet in this match when I realised that here was a real talent. Maurice Norman played at the back and was keeping Vavá relatively quiet. Vavá was a powerful centre-forward, good in the air, very strong, a bit like Bobby Smith. Not quick, but he had good ball control. Amarildo was clever. Zagalo was never going to sprint or dribble around you, but he was a very astute player. He knew the game inside-out. It wasn't easy to get near him. That's why he became such a good coach.

Didi was skilful, a ball artist, and Garrincha, well he was just a law unto himself. A speed merchant, he was very difficult to play against, but Ray [Wilson] was doing well. It was always said that Garrincha had one leg slightly shorter than the other and that made his ability to dribble that much harder to read. He was also very quick over a short distance, but we were holding him and Brazil as well.

That's why it was such a surprise, on the half-hour mark, when they went a goal up, and what a strange goal to give away. When Brazil score against you, you expect a great free-kick, a dribble or a fantastic, bending shot – but a header from a corner? That wasn't the norm. Our centre-half, Maurice Norman, was a big lad, but little Garrincha leapt above him – proving what a good all-round player he had become – and nodded the ball past Springett.

We had been playing well, so that was a blow, but we knew we could get amongst them and carried on playing the way we had started by attacking them down the flanks. Our reward wasn't long in coming. Seven minutes later, we were awarded a free-kick and it was the skipper, Johnny Haynes, whose immaculate right foot floated the ball into the Brazilian penalty box. It was Greavsie who rose and nodded the ball toward goal, his effort struck the post, but fortunately Gerry [Hitchens] was on hand to bury the rebound. It was the least we deserved and I sensed they were shocked.

With the half-time scoreline at 1-1, I thought that this could be *our* day. We started the second half strongly as well and I began to really think we could beat them. You say that to people now and they think, "oh yeah whatever", but it was true.

We continued to make chances, but it just wouldn't go for us in front of goal. Ten minutes into the second-half, Brazil won a free-kick on the edge of our box. To this day, I don't think it was a foul. It was in a dangerous position, mind. Just right of centre and only five yards out of the box. Garrincha smashed it goalwards and Springett couldn't hold it and Vava pounced to make it 2-1.

On the hour mark, they killed the game after another Garrincha free-kick again proved too good, this time completely beating Springett and theoretically ending the game. It was a bitter pill to swallow.

We lost the game and afterwards as I sat in the hotel, two or three of the press corps came in and sat with me telling me they thought I had played well. I don't think I have ever been as disappointed as I felt at that moment because as I say, I genuinely thought that we would win the game and go on and win the World Cup. They were the best side in the competition as they proved by going on to lift the trophy. We'd got through that first half against Brazil and the way we were playing I thought the goals were bound to come. In World Cup football once you've got Brazil out of the way, you're in with a chance. I thought we could have beaten Czechoslovakia in any one off situation, but we never got the chance to find out.

There was pride in the performance, but that wasn't enough. I think all the players must have been genuinely disappointed because we had so much of the ball.

I watched the final in Santiago and Brazil dominated the game from the word go. That had never been the case against us and their reaction to the second goal was one of ecstasy. They knew that win against us was their spring-board to World Cup glory.

Yet, when you have talented players like theirs up front, five world class superstars, the chances are one of them is going to pop up and do something special. This time it was Garrincha's day and eventually his World Cup.

Jimmy Adamson was our assistant manager. Jimmy was a football tactician and had been very skilful as a player. He felt we had a genuine chance, as did Walter. Walter was subdued after the Brazil defeat, which wasn't like him as he always knew how to lose and what to gain from defeat. He was upset because he knew we had come so close and that we were good enough to have done better.

He thought like I thought and like Johnny Haynes thought and Bobby Charlton thought; we all believed we had genuine chance. We were very down about it.

Do I think our World Cup was a failure? That might be the wrong way of putting it, but I do think we were disappointed that we only reached last eight. With the players we had we expected more. You can blame the pre-tournament injuries, the misfortune of drawing Brazil in the quarter-finals or the lack of a killer instinct in front of goal. Take your pick. We should have done better.

Taking the positives, if you look at the players who played against Brazil, seven of the eleven were in the 22 for 1966. The most influential player in '66 was Bobby Charlton. Without him I don't think we would have won it. Then you have Bobby Moore and Ray Wilson. They must have learnt from the experience of 1962 and it helped the rest.

On returning home I learned I was voted best right-back in Chile, but I never actually got the trophy. If anyone has it, I'd like to hear from them. The accolade was voted for by the world's press. The plaudits didn't effect me. The truth was, by today's standards it was a low profile tournament. You never see much footage of the 1962 World Cup; it seems almost like a long-forgotten competition. Colour television hadn't quite arrived!

Chile seemed like the end of the world in those days. It was a long way. We had to travel there and back by various routes to play in what was the least glamorous World Cup there had been since the war. In 1954, and '58, the competition was hyped up and, being in Europe, very well covered. Not this one. For Chile, read Chilly.

The normal thing at Blackpool when I returned from England duty was for the manager to tell me to forget all the hype and get down to proper football. Get it all out of your head. It was no different this time so I got on with my everyday stuff.

Looking back though it was my World Cup experience and I'll never forget it. In those days there weren't many Brits going off abroad for holidays whereas these days families trip off to far off spots like the Maldives and Australia.

In the 1950s I remember Tom Finney saying he was going to Majorca and that seemed amazing. We all talked about it and on returning Tom told us you could get a beer for sixpence.

I had been to France with the school, my National Service was in England, but I played some football in Germany and so to travel to South America and see a country like Chile was fantastic. It was a different world back then. The Cold War was raging. Those eastern European nations were controlled by Moscow. Berlin was divided by the wall. Things were different, but thanks to my football I got to see things that otherwise I never would have.

Yet looking back I still think we could have won that World Cup and no one will ever convince me otherwise.

ROGER HUNT MBE
FORWARD

ENGLAND 1966

BORN   20th July 1938, Golborne
CLUB   Liverpool
INTERNATIONAL DEBUT   April 1962 v Austria
ENGLAND CAREER   34 caps, 17 goals
INTERNATIONAL FAREWELL   January 1969 v Romania

'Sir' Roger Hunt as Liverpool fans dubbed him during his stint at Anfield which saw him bag a club record 286 goals, partnered Geoff Hurst at Wembley as England won the 1966 World Cup. His goals saw England safely through the group stages of the tournament. A poacher by nature, Hunt possessed the instinct which all great goalscorers boast, being in the right place at the right time. All the more amazing that he did not finish off Hurst's infamous second goal in the final, which clearly did not cross the line - the one piece of outrageous luck that England have enjoyed in fourteen World Cups.

ENGLAND 4 v WEST GERMANY 2   after extra time

World Cup Final
Saturday 30 July 1966

Wembley Stadium
Attendance 96,924

Geoff Hurst's hat-trick, the Russian linesman and forty years of celebration of English football's finest hour

Teams

Alf Ramsey	**Managers**	Helmut Schön
Gordon Banks		Hans Tilkowski
George Cohen		Horst-Dieter Höttges
Ray Wilson		Willi Schulz
Nobby Stiles		Wolfgang Weber
Jack Charlton		Karl-Heinz Schnellinger
Bobby Moore		Franz Beckenbauer
Alan Ball		Uwe Seeler
Geoff Hurst		Helmut Haller
Bobby Charlton		Wolfgang Overath
Roger Hunt		Siegfried Held
Martin Peters		Lothar Emmerich
Hurst 19, 100, 120 Peters 77	**Scorers**	Haller 13, Weber 90

Referee: Gottfried Dienst (Switzerland)

I OFTEN WORRY that people must be sick of hearing about that amazing summer of 1966. So much has been written and broadcast about it, but I guess it remains the yardstick by which all England players and managers since have been judged. For us guys, however, who were there and who took part, it seems a long time ago. A lot has happened since, but as the years go by what we achieved is still sinking in and still fills me with such pleasure. It was, quite simply, the most amazing time of my life.

I can remember the moment when a Swiss referee called Gottfried Dienst blew the final whistle after 120 minutes of topsy-turvy football. You'd expect the emotion to be unprecedented joy, but with my socks falling around my weary ankles all I could feel was relief, pure relief as I sank to the turf. Having nearly won it and lost the lead at the end of normal time, and then going 3-2 up before clinging on to win with that famous last minute goal, had me emotionally and physically shattered. Slowly it sank in; I've got myself a World Cup winners medal.

That medal seemed a long way off as I battled constantly through the early 1960s to get a place in the national team. In 1962 I had been playing well for Liverpool under their new manager Bill Shankly in the old Second Division. I was scoring a lot of goals and got picked to play for the Football League against our Scottish counterparts at Villa Park. That was in March 1962 and, although we lost 4-3, I scored two and impressed a few people.

In April that year, just weeks before that summer's World Cup in Chile, I was selected for my international debut against Austria at Wembley. I wasn't the only one winning my first cap. I was joined by Ray Crawford of Ipswich and Stan Anderson, who went on to manage Bolton. We beat Austria 3-1 and I scored again and got into the squad for the Finals in Chile on the back of those goals. I think we only took 19 players and maybe I was fortunate to get in. Jimmy Greaves was the main man and despite Bobby Smith getting injured I didn't get on. I loved every minute of it though.

The next few years were a little frustrating. I got the odd cap, and because I hadn't had any Under-23 experience I was, initially, just so pleased to be involved. Soon though, with Liverpool winning promotion to the First Division and doing well, I obviously wanted to play as much as I could. But when you're understudy to a player like Jimmy Greaves, chances are always going to be hard to come by.

Anyway, I went on the 1963 summer tour to Czechoslovakia, East Germany and Switzerland. I got one game against the Germans, we beat them 2-1 and once more I scored. I managed to score quite regularly, but never felt confident of keeping my place. Alf Ramsey, newly installed as England manager, used to encourage me like he did everyone, but the bottom line was I was in and then out, in and then out. Looking back, I'm not sure Alf was too sure about me or his team for the World Cup three years later.

Alf had immediately set about revolutionising how the England team was run. Walter Winterbottom had stepped aside after 16 years in charge. Walter was a great guy and a real football man, but I don't think he had a full say in how the team was picked. Alf was never going to stand for that. When he came in he insisted that he had full control when it came to team matters.

I had, of course, become used to playing for one exceptional manager. Bill Shankly had come to Liverpool and carried out his own revolution. When it came, however, to his players' England careers he wasn't the slightest bit interested. Being a Scotsman, he couldn't have cared less. Most managers only have eyes for their club fortunes. They have the blinkers on when it comes to international stuff and Shanks was especially uninterested in England's progression. He didn't stand in our way, but I think he would have rather we were training or resting at Melwood

In the summer of 1964, England travelled to Brazil, for what was deemed the mini-World Cup. We faced Portugal, Brazil and Argentina. The two South American sides pummelled us, but I only managed to play against the Portuguese, and scored, once again, in a 1-1 draw.

Those defeats against Brazil and Argentina further persuaded Alf that he needed to change the side's tactics before the World Cup. When he picked his first team in 1962, they were beaten 5-2 in France. He had played the traditional five forwards and must have begun to have reservations in that time-honoured formation. He continued to experiment and use wingers, with my team-mate at Liverpool, Peter Thompson having a great tour in '64 on the right wing.

The following summer I was left out of the England tour. I was upset as I'd won the FA Cup with Liverpool that year and scored in the final. The team went to Europe and Alf began to play a 4-3-3 formation. It was a frustrating time for me. I recall doing a TV interview and saying that every time I played and scored I was left out of the next game. It didn't go down too well with Alf.

Shortly afterwards, Danny Blanchflower, who had a column in the *Daily Express*, wrote about whether England could play with both Hunt and Greaves. He stated that the team *could* fit both of us in, which on the surface was nice of the great man, but when I looked closer it was obvious that he wasn't being the most flattering about me. He said Greaves is 'Magnificent and mercurial, while Hunt is 'Painstaking and persistent.'

When I started at Liverpool, I classed myself as an inside-forward, but as the game changed I was being pushed infield and becoming a centre-forward. It was fine, though, as Ian St John and I worked well together and we had two fantastic wingers in Ian Callaghan and Thommo. As a striker that was fabulous as you just had to make a good run and you knew those two wide men would provide great balls in from wide areas.

With England, Alf started to experiment and settled on that 4-3-3 system and I was concerned. If you imagine I'd always had two good wingers knocking the ball in from either side, which was how my goals had come, but now they've gone. All of a sudden you're thinking, "Where's the ball going to come from?" It was so different. Alf encouraged the full-backs to overlap and we did have good players such as Cohen, Wilson and Armfield who could do that, but it took some getting used to. Today it's taken as read; full backs are expected to get forward and are often better at attacking than they are defending. It was very different back then. The game turned around and it was all due to Alf and the '66 World Cup.

I managed to get picked again late in 1965 and scored in a 2-0 win in Spain. I played alongside the Arsenal duo of George Eastham and Joe Baker as Alf experimented while Greavesie was injured. The Spaniards, I recall, were a little lost when it came to marking us. As a threesome up front, we moved around a lot and they struggled. That night convinced Alf he was on the right lines. The formation was often criticised as being quite defensive as our midfielders were really more like defenders. I remember Nobby Stiles being asked to do a job in front of our back four and he kept the Spaniards totally quiet. Nobby only made his debut a year before the World Cup Finals, as did Jack Charlton and Alan Ball. Slowly Alf was assembling his team, building from the back. It was effective. Less fun, but very effective.

Into 1966 and our form was patchy and we were struggling to get a flow going. Alf, though, remained very upbeat though and famously, of course, stated that we would win the competition. I think that might have been a bit of kidology on his part. With the Finals being held in England, he had to talk it up and there was no point in him being pessimistic. He'd have been crucified in the papers.

The press and the punters were pessimistic enough as it was. We beat West Germany 1-0 at Wembley and got booed off the field. The fans were finding it hard to get used to the new system. You can understand it. They were used to seeing the likes of Tom Finney and Stanley Matthews flying down the wings before floating in perfect crosses for centre-forwards to leap majestically and head home. That wasn't happening anymore and many of them weren't happy.

Unlike me, who was delighted to be included in the initial squad of 27 that Alf selected for the Finals, who went to Lilleshall for a training camp at the end of the regular season. We would be whittled down to 22, so there was a lot at stake. We were all in it together, but the training was very intense and very competitive. It was non-stop, morning noon and night. Alf was very thorough. If we weren't on the pitches we were watching films of the opposition. There was never any animosity, but you could sense that everyone was out to get into the squad.

I didn't think I was near the first team. We would have practice games and it wasn't clear what Alf's thoughts were. Jimmy Greaves had got a virus in the build up to the World Cup and didn't play for maybe two months. I played a few games on the spin alongside Geoff Hurst and things went well. We'd beaten Scotland 4-3 at Hampden in April. Bobby Charlton scored, Geoff got his first for England on only his second appearance and I got two. After that I thought, "I've got a good chance of making the 22 now."

Then I hurt my ankle and was struggling. Liverpool got beat in the final of the Cup Winners Cup (ironically by German opposition) and I wasn't right. I had been playing with this injury and so when I got to Lilleshall I had to work at getting the ankle better without making too much of a fuss. You didn't want Alf to think you were a liability and so I quietly nursed the injury. The coaches were great. Les Cocker, Harold Shepherdson and Wilf McGuinness. And after training they secretly worked on my ankle. I was particularly worried as Alf seemed to like the look of young Martin Peters, Hurst's West Ham team-mate, who came into the team as an attacking midfielder for the run of friendlies just before the Finals.

Alf named his squad and you could only feel sorry for the five who missed out. Two of them, Gordon Milne and Peter Thompson, were my great mates from Liverpool. It was soul destroying for them. Ian Callaghan got in ahead of Peter. I was made up for Ian, but on that tour to South America in '64, Peter had been England's best player and looked a definite to not only make the squad but the team. Two years is a long time in football, though.

There wasn't anyone who made a big show of how disappointed they were. The players concerned just weren't like that. They were quiet, but they were respectful and dignified. There were no scenes, no histrionics, just reflection. I was sad for my mates, but I was also ecstatic to be in.

So, the 22 were soon off to Scandinavia with a World Cup to prepare for. Jimmy Greaves and I got a couple of starts together and began to play well. We played Finland first and won 3-0. We then played Norway and won 6-1 and Jimmy got four. I didn't play against Denmark, but was pleased with my form and felt I was a good foil for Jimmy. Alf didn't give anything away, he wasn't making noises about his team and maybe he didn't know himself. The last game before the tournament was in Poland and I scored the only goal of the match from 25 yards. I was pleased with the timing of that one.

We were back in England with our opening game against Uruguay looming. Still, there was no clue about what Alf was thinking. I haven't discussed this in detail, but I do feel that the squad numbers reflected Alf's initial thoughts about his starting line-up. 1 to 11 were probably the eleven he was going to go with and it was only myself and Martin Peters who played in the final who were outside of that. I was 21 so presumably well down the pecking order! Greaves [number 8] and John Connelly of Manchester United [number 11] were the two who missed out.

The night before the game, there was a good buzz about our team hotel at Hendon Hall. We were all so excited and confident. The defence was very steady and had played a lot of games together. The full backs were exceptional, Bobby Moore was Bobby Moore and Jack Charlton was getting stronger and stronger. There were only a couple of positions that were in doubt really. One of them was mine, of course, but it was great to hear from the manager that I would be starting.

Alf was wary of the South Americans. We knew they were technically very gifted, but also very cynical and would resort to all sorts to get their way. They would be difficult to beat, they weren't very ambitious and that meant we would have to work very hard to break them down and that proved exactly right.

We drew 0-0 and the crowd weren't happy. They were singing 'We want goals', but Alf was unperturbed. There was a lot of hype surrounding our opening game and suddenly we hadn't won and it's all doom and gloom. A bit like England started both the 1990 World Cup and the Euro 96 tournaments which eventually turned into heroic competitions for the national team. For Alf, though, a 0-0 draw wasn't the worst result. We didn't look like getting beat at all and as long as we didn't lose the opening game, things could always turn around.

The following game was against Mexico, five days later, again at Wembley. There was plenty of pressure on us that night. As an England player you're expected to win most games and having drawn the first, we had to put on a show. Luckily the Mexicans were a little bit more ambitious than the Uruguayans, but still, we couldn't find a way through in the early exchanges and the crowd were again getting frustrated. Then Bobby Charlton popped up and leathered in our first goal; a cracker, and suddenly there's relief. The crowd are excited, we've finally scored a goal and we're on our way. I got the second goal after good work from Greavesie who cut in from the left, hit it and I followed up to score the rebound. Thanks Jimmy!

Our final group game was against France who needed to win 2-0 to qualify. Despite that, we tried to play our normal game. We didn't go gung ho on attack, mind. We were a bit tentative to begin with and were not putting much together until we scored. My goals were often far from classics - that long range effort in Poland aside. Against France, Jack Charlton got his head to a free-kick, it hit the post, came out and I was on hand to knock in another rebound from close range. The French claimed offside, but I don't think so. Jack thought the ball was already over the line, but no chance! I always follow up just in case I can pick up the scraps - well, almost always!

Suddenly we were relaxed and got going. Ian Callaghan set up my second. Alf had played a winger in all three group games. John Connelly had played against Uruguay, Terry Paine had played against Mexico and now Cally. This goal had a tinge of controversy about it as Nobby Stiles flattened a French player, Simon, who'd been orchestrating their attacks in the second half. As he lay injured, the referee allowed play to carry on and we broke forward and Cally laid the ball into me. I didn't hit it that well, and in fact it went pretty much straight to their keeper, but he fumbled it into the net. The French moaned about the goal and the FA told Alf after the game that he had to drop Stiles, but Alf told them that if they insisted he would resign. We knew then that he would back any of us and it filled us with confidence.

It was a wonderful feeling to get the two winning goals, but the big news to come out of that match was the injury to Greavsie's leg. He went down on the pitch, but it didn't seem like much. In the dressing room he pulled his sock down and revealed this massive gash to his shin. There was immediate concern because it was such a nasty cut and it became apparent that he would miss the impending quarter-final against Argentina. It was like Wayne Rooney's injury before the 2006 World Cup it was that devastating a blow to England's chances - or so the press and public felt.

As for Alf, he was never happy or satisfied. He was a perfectionist. He was after improvement. We hadn't played brilliantly, but we hadn't let in a goal in three games and we never looked like getting beat. It was slow progress. The flowing, fantastic football wasn't there just yet, but it can be best not to peak too early. These tournaments are all about improving as you go along and it is rare that the winners' group games are ever remembered. Look at Brazil in '58 or later, Italy in '82. They peaked at the right time.

When not playing we were watching games and had seen a lot of Argentina and we all agreed that they looked quite formidable. They were physically imposing, but also very skilful. Everybody thought these were going to be our toughest opponents. They had won the mini-world cup in '64, their players had been around and were experienced, they could mix it and were right up there among the favourites.

The game began and immediately I was conscious of their, somewhat mischievous tactics. A defender called Marzolini was at it. I was strolling out of the penalty area when I felt a right whack on the back of my leg. The ball was nowhere near us and so I've spun around and he's looking at me with his arms outstretched as if to say, "That's what we do." I couldn't believe it.

There had been a few heavy tackles going in and Rattin, their skipper was getting at the ref. Rattin was a superb player, but very mouthy. He was so confident in himself that he began trying to run the show and the ref, a Mr Kreitlein, lost patience. Rattin was shown the red card and he couldn't believe it. To be fair to him, in South America captains do talk to the ref constantly, but this was Europe and so he was off. Famously, he wasn't having it. It took over 11 minutes for him to leave the field.

Some of us were sitting around waiting for the game to get going again when suddenly a roar went up around Wembley. I looked up at the scoreboard and it read, PORTUGAL 0 NORTH KOREA 3. The crowd went berserk. Here's the Argentinean captain refusing to walk and the crowd are cheering on the Koreans. That was surreal.

Rattin wanted the game abandoned, they all did. One of the FIFA guys came on and got the message across that very soon, we would be awarded the game. That got things moving a bit. So, we were now up against ten men, but that made little difference to the match. Argentina remained very organised and very tough to break down.

But we finally made a break through and what a goal it was. It showed the understanding between our two West Ham forwards. They had obviously worked on it in East London. Geoff took his marker to the far post, spun to the near post and headed a perfect cross in from Peters who hadn't even had to look up. He just knew where Geoff would be. There I was sniffing for rebounds, of course.

I was with the lads recently and they were saying that the Argentineans didn't have a chance, but I disagree. I recall a couple of chances falling to the winger Mas and later Onega. Banks saved one and the other was missed, but it was a game of very little opportunity. There was nothing clear-cut, but we got our noses in front and that was enough.

There was to be no swapping of shirts. Alf made sure of that. I hadn't got round to taking my shirt off when I saw Alf run on and stop George Cohen. We all saw that and thought better of it. That was a massive win, but Alf didn't show any elation. He must have been very satisfied inside, despite the Rattin nonsense. It had been a major obstacle and we had hurdled it. We heard in the dressing room that Eusebio had got four and the Portuguese had won 5-3. Now we had to play them in the semi and were quietly confident.

After the Argentina game, the talk amongst the press and onlookers was just how cynical the tournament had been. Pelé had been kicked out of the World Cup, there had been the Rattin incident and plenty of other dirty fouls. We, though, had to concentrate on ourselves rather than worrying about what people thought. Alf had converted to a 4-4-2 formation for the Argentina game with Bally going out onto the right. Maybe he was aware of how physical things had become and was compensating for that.

The semi-final was scheduled to be played at Goodison Park, which really excited me. I may have even got a cheer at Everton! It was common knowledge that the game would be held there, but at the eleventh hour there was a change of heart and once more we were going to Wembley. I don't know the reasons behind that, but it seemed a little unfair on those fans from the north of England. I know all of us players from up north were a little upset as we were all looking forward to the occasion. Who knows who made the decision, but I guess you could argue that Wembley was the right place and that the semi-final of the World Cup had to be there.

We were looking forward to the game. We were aware of how good Portugal were and the players they had, but they played open, attacking football and that suited us. We felt we would be able to play are usual game, but at the same time we had to look out for not only Eusebio, but also Torres, Jose Augusto and Coluna.

It was an evening game and under the floodlights the atmosphere was wonderful. It had been building up and now we had the crowd on side. The initial concerns had gone and you could sense that.

Being so close to the Final, it was tense, but Bobby Charlton soon put us one up and the nerves were calmed. I played my part in that goal. Ray Wilson played me in, but the keeper rushed off his line to thwart me, I managed to knock the ball against his body and the ball rebounded out of the box where Bobby was on hand to calmly side foot in from about twenty yards. Bobby was always very cool in those situations.

The second goal was legendary. Geoff did very well to hold the ball and lay it off for Bobby, who hit it like a thunderbolt into the top corner. Bobby was incredible that summer. I still don't know which was his best foot and you can't say that about many players. He worked very hard for the team. He had all the skills and scored great goals, but he worked hard and he always made time and space for himself and others. He could surge forward and batter defences and that suited the system. His midfield parter, Nobby Stiles, could man-mark - like he did against Eusebio that night - or he could just sit in front of the back four and allow Bobby Moore a freer role.

Three minutes later, though, and with time running out, Portugal scored a penalty. I won't lie, I was terrified that they would equalise. It became very open and could have gone either way, but we held on and were in the final. It was a terrific game that one and a match that salvaged the tournament's reputation after all the cynics and the dirty tactics. It was played in a very good spirit, had good goals and good skills. It was the perfect antidote to the Argentinean game. We were all on such a high in the dressing room, but Alf was on hand, of course, to dampen our spirits, "Don't get too excited lads, we have to win it now." Typical.

I, for one, had more than Alf's pragmatism to keep me on my toes. I was aware that Jimmy's leg was better, and feared for my place in the team. If you look at my England career up to that point, it was very on and off. But in the finals I had played every game, which was rare. I had been heavily involved, but still, there was a major doubt in the back of my head. What you must remember is that Jimmy was England's main man when it came to goals and was the all-time top goalscorer for the country.

If you had said before the tournament that Jimmy Greaves wouldn't be playing, nobody would have believed you, they would have laughed. His name would have been going down first on anyone's team sheet. I thought that Geoff had come in and added something to the team. He was strong, could hold play up, had scored a fantastic goal against Argentina and generally done very well. The press were screaming for Jimmy to get back in and that meant someone had to go, and that someone could be me, despite the fact that I had played all five games up to that point and bagged three goals.

The defence must have known they were in. They are modest guys and wouldn't admit it, but they must have been confident of their place in the final. Banks, Cohen, Jack Charlton, Moore, Wilson, Nobby, Bobby; they were in. Bally might have wondered, as would Martin Peters, as they hadn't played all the games. I was a little insecure. The press, especially the London-based guys, weren't sure about me at all. You read the papers and were aware of what was being said and I was getting stick all the time.

I couldn't do much about it, could I? And I now realise that half the people writing about me really didn't know much about the game and certainly weren't aware of my role in the team. I was being asked to do a job and I was doing it. Having said that, when I was reading that Hunt should stand down, I couldn't help but be concerned.

England were in the final of the World Cup, but you must remember that there was hardly the sort of hype that would surround such an occasion today. The media frenzy that there would be now didn't exist, so we could just go walking down Hendon High Street. Someone might walk past and say "Good luck Saturday lads," but that was it. Today it would be mayhem. I got a telegram from Shanks and everyone at Liverpool, which gave me a boost.

The night before the game we took the coach to the cinema and, as we were getting off, Alf came over to me and said quietly, "You're playing tomorrow." That was that. I couldn't believe it. What a thing to be told. Wooof! He didn't tell me not to tell anyone, but I thought I'd better not. I was rooming with John Connelly and so might have told him, but from the moment that Alf told me I was in a daze. Don't even ask me what film we went to see.

That night I wasn't sure if Jimmy would be up front with me because Alf didn't name the team until the following morning. I think, and this is only my opinion, that after the Argentinean game the balance looked right and improved against the Portuguese. I think he had his team set in his head. Whether Jimmy was fit enough or not I don't know, but I'm sure he would have been had he been selected. I felt for him. He'd been instrumental in England's fortunes for so long, scored so many goals and here he is missing the final.

Of course in those days there were no substitues so Greavesie had to sit on the bench and watch the biggest game in England's history knowing he would not be taking part. Amazingly he would barely play for England again, scored just one more goal and finished with international football at the age of 27 the following year. Just think how many goals he would have finished with if he'd played for three or four more years. Certainly more than Lineker and Charlton who are the only players ahead of him in the all-time England goalscoring charts. Greavesie was an incredible goalscorer, probably the best ever, and here he was sitting out the Final. But that was Alf's call to make and his mantra was all about the team, not the individual. And frankly, I was in. That was what mattered to me.

I didn't sleep that night, I reckon most of us were tossing and turning and the morning was spent in meetings and just trying to relax. I went for a wander to clear my head and I remember not wanting to eat much. It was important to try and not to think about it too much, but that was impossible. The morning of the World Cup final, and you're trying not to think about the match!

Alf officially named the team at Hendon Hall. Those not playing kept us relaxed. I had my mates from Liverpool, Callaghan and Gerry Byrne, who kept the jokes flowing which helped.

Alf had put his faith in Geoff and I, and went through with us how he wanted us to play the game. The Germans played a man-for-man marking system at the back with a sweeper behind. Wolfgang Weber was to mark me, with Karl-Heinz Schnellinger on Geoff. Alf went through this and said to me that I was going to have to take Weber all over the pitch. He wanted the ball to be put onto the sweeper, Willi Schulz and then he couldn't sweep. He'd be forced to defend rather than dictate and that would cause them problems.

I remember arriving at Wembley and feeling quite calm. It sounds strange because it was a much smaller scale, but I had played in the FA Cup final there the year before with Liverpool. That was massive for us and was a fantastic occasion and I think that might have settled me as we arrived. I was used to the place, I had scored there in a final and felt I could cope with this occasion.

The dressing room was calm, but focused as Alf ran through our plans and then we were out onto the pitch amid all the Union Jacks and an atmosphere that took your breath away. There's a lot of razzmatazz that goes on before a final like that, but to be honest you want all that over with; the team-talk, the national anthem, meeting the Queen, you just want to get out there and get playing. Meeting the Queen should be a highlight of a person's life (I had met her the year before when she awarded me my FA Cup winners medal), but I was itching to get on with things.

It seemed ages before I got a touch. In any game you want an early touch, but mine seemed to take for ever. Because I was working Weber out of position it meant that I was not part of play. It was frustrating, but I was there to do a job.

I don't know if I'd even had that touch when the Germans scored. What a shock. This wasn't in the script. Our defence had been magnificent, letting in only one goal in five games and that was a penalty. We'd never been behind and now, in the biggest game of all, that's exactly what we were.

We didn't panic, though, and Bobby Moore wasn't the sort of skipper who needed to scream at us to gee us up. He led by example. It wasn't the most of vocal teams to be honest. Jack would bark, Nobby would cajole and Bally of course would scream in that high-pitched tone, but as a team we knew we just had to get on with things.

Luckily we weren't behind for long and that helped. Like the effort against Argentina it was another goal made at Upton Park. Bobby knocked a quickly taken free-kick into space and Geoff read it perfectly to head home.

At half-time, Alf wasn't pleased with Geoff and I. He thought we weren't putting enough pressure on Schulz. We were trying to drop off and receive the ball and that wasn't helping. When you're man-marked you have to work that marker and make space for the team. You have to be unselfish and not expect much of the ball. It was hard, but we had to try and make space for Bobby Charlton and Martin Peters to exploit.

I think we were fitter than the Germans. We got on top. It wasn't a hot day. We had rain, sun and then rain again. I was getting a little more room as the game went on and felt we could win this. It was a strange half. They had fantastic players who were so dangerous in front of goal. Uwe Seeler was a terrific player as was Lothar Emmerich, but what I remember thinking was that Bobby Charlton and Franz Beckenbauer were cancelling each other out. It seemed a waste really as they were the two such great players.

Twelve minutes were left when Martin took his goal and there's elation. Pandemonium! Martin took it so well with a controlled volley. We all huddled together and you can hear the lads saying, "We're going to win the World Cup!" We were that close.

With only a minute or so left, Germany won a free kick that we disputed. As we organised the wall, they took it, the ball went into the box and bobbled around.

It all happened in slow motion. A German shot, it rebounded off Cohen. Another German shot, Banks saved it and Weber knocked the ball in at the far post. Disaster, they've scored. I stood on the halfway line, waiting to take the kick off thinking, "How near can you get without actually winning the World Cup?" It was going to be very hard to get back up and try and win it again.

Alf - who must have been devastated - didn't show his disappointment; instead he concentrated on getting our minds back on the task in hand. He gave his famous speech saying we'd won it once and now we would go and win it again. It was rousing stuff. He told those who were sitting down to get up, not to let the Germans see that we were tired, because they were knackered too.

Strangely, I felt stronger in extra time and was now getting more space. Weber was tiring and I was seeing a lot of the ball. Alan Ball slowly became a winger as the game went on and we started to exploit the space. We were more or less playing 4-3-3 with any original tactics going out of the window.

Our third goal must be the most talked about goal in history. I'm constantly asked about it and all I can say is that I was a goalscorer. I absolutely loved scoring goals, be they from distance or from one yard out. It didn't matter to me how they went in. In fact, I loved a rebound because the pleasure for me came from seeing the ball hit the back of the net. It was selfish, but you have to be like that. Look at Lineker, Shearer, Ian Rush; they all had that trait.

Geoff received the ball in the box, turned and hit a great half volley and I'm on my way in. If you look at the picture Weber is behind me and he has no chance of getting it. I am inside the six-yard box desperate to get the winner in the World Cup final. It hits the underside of the bar and I've seen it bounce over the line thinking it's going to bounce into the roof of the net. Look at my reaction; I've screamed "Goal!" before it's even come out. I was convinced it was over the line and then bounced away. People have said "Why didn't you knock in the rebound?", but I couldn't have. The ball bounced away from me and I wasn't going to get it. I still feel it was in.

Recently I met the German goalkeeper, Tilkowski who was adamant it wasn't and I guess we'll never really know. Every so often someone analyses the film and 'conclusively' proves that is was or wasn't over the line. The important thing was that then linesman gave it. It still gets quite heated, though. To this day, the Germans are quite serious when they talk about that incident. But for all the cruel luck that has befallen the England team in World Cups before and since that day, I think it's the least that the fates could bestow on us.

You get a second wind because you are defending a lead and you don't want to let it slip for a second time. We were the better team and definitely the stronger team fitness-wise. We'd worked hard at Lilleshall months before, on tour and in London. We were very fit and very strong. If you look at the team, everyone was a strong man. Even Bally, he was so fit. Equally, everyone was an ordinary bloke. Alf wanted players who would give the same performance whatever the occasion and who were honest. He had that in his XI. He didn't go for players who *could* be great, but would go missing when it suited them.

With seconds left, Bobby Moore strolled out of defence like only he could, looked up and picked out Geoff, who was haring into the German half. We were screaming for Bobby to launch it anywhere, but any game plan from the Germans had gone out of the window as they poured forward desperately searching for another late equaliser, and he saw that his West Ham team-mate was in acres. Geoff ran through onto the ball and instead of heading for the corner to kill time, strode towards the box. He still maintains that he just wanted to clear the crossbar with his shot, but into the top left corner it went and suddenly we are the Champions of the World. Geoff was doing a book years later and sent a letter around to all the lads asking us to describe exactly where we were when that goal went in. I replied, "I was helping back in defence where you should have been instead of goal hanging and taking all the glory."

We were the Champions. Jimmy came on and congratulated us all, but he was down, you could see that. Who could blame him?

I just remember thinking that the day had gone past way too quickly and it's hard to recall much about the aftermath. Back-slapping and singing is pretty much all I can remember amidst the haze.

We had a night in the Royal Garden near Hyde Park. That was a good do. We had an official meal with the FA, the Germans, and the 3rd and 4th placed teams. That was nice. The hotel was full. The press, fans, celebrities, Harold Wilson, the Prime Minister. Some of the lads escaped into the West End, but I couldn't get out. It was too chaotic outside!

I was back at Anfield in less than a week as I had the Charity Shield to play in against Everton. Shanks looked at me and said, "Come on lad, you've got more important things to worry about now." He wasn't that happy being a Scot, of course.

As the years go on it means more and more. To be the best in the world is the ultimate accolade. I got back to playing at Liverpool and scoring in front of the magnificent Kop and winning things for the best of managers. It felt like the World Cup in '66 came along, happened and then afterwards we just got on with our club stuff.

But as the years go on and I reflect, that's when I realise what we achieved and how much of a privilege it was to play for my country and to win the World Cup.

BRIAN LABONE
DEFENDER

MEXICO 1970

BORN 23rd January 1940, Liverpool
CLUB Everton
INTERNATIONAL DEBUT October 1962 v Northern Ireland
ENGLAND CAREER 26 caps
INTERNATIONAL FAREWELL June 1970 v West Germany

A giant in defence, who lifted the FA Cup as captain at Wembley in 1966, Labone replaced Jack Charlton as Ramsey's granite centre-back post-66. Having missed out on the squad for the World Cup that year, he became an integral part of England's defence of the title in 1970. He partnered Bobby Moore in the centre of a defence which conceded just one goal during its group games. The quarter-final, however, would once again prove a step too far. This interview was the last he gave as he sadly died returning from an Everton fans' function a fortnight later.

ENGLAND 2 v WEST GERMANY 3   after extra time

World Cup Quarter-final
Sunday 14 June 1970

Estadio Nou Camp, Guanajuato, León
Attendance 24,000

Montezuma's Revenge accounts for Banks, while Ramsey's concern for an ageing Bobby Charlton and the indiffferent form of Banks' replacement account for England

Teams

Alf Ramsey	**Managers**	Helmut Schön
Peter Bonetti		Sepp Maier
Keith Newton		Karl-Heinz Schnellinger
Terry Cooper		Berti Vogts
Alan Mullery		Klaus Fichtel
Brian Labone		Horst-Dieter Höttges
		(Sub. Willi Schulz)
Bobby Moore		Frank Beckenbauer
Francis Lee		Wolfgang Overath
Alan Ball		Uwe Seeler
Geoff Hurst		Hannes Löhr
Bobby Charlton		Gerd Müller
(Sub. Colin Bell)		
Martin Peters		Reinhard Libuda
(Sub. Norman Hunter)		(Sub. Jürgen Grabowski)
Mullery 31, Peters 49	**Scorers**	Beckenbauer 68, Seeler 79
		Müller 109

Referee: Angel Norberto Coerezza (Argentina)

To MOST ENGLISH fans, the World Cup in 1966 remains the most unforgettable World Cup. Ask fans around the world, however, and they will tell you that the tournament in 1970 is by far the most iconic and memorable of them all. That summer arguably offered fans globally the most memorable images; images that remain as vivid today as they did then. Brazil, Pelé , Gordon Banks' save, Bobby Moore's tackles, his embrace with the greatest player in the world. These are all memories that will never fade and to be involved in that summer is something that I will never forget.

Of course, I would have loved to have been involved in 1966, but for various reasons that I'll go into later, that wasn't to be. By 1970 I was far more settled into my football, was captain of Everton, the club I have supported all my life and felt comfortable taking on not only the best forwards in the world at the time, but of all-time.

As a very young man, football, World Cups and Pelé were not exactly at the forefront of my adolescent mind. I went to Grammar school and I suppose 50 years ago I was looked upon as a bit of a clever clogs. I was going to go to University rather than play professional football, but while I was reasonably clever, who knows how I would have done at University. My father was always very keen to for me to have something behind me in case I failed at football. Some Liverpudlians might say I did.

Even when I signed at Goodison, my father had me doing a correspondence course in Accountancy at a local office. I was training twice a day, though, and when you're physically tired you're also mentally fatigued and so it was football all the way. I signed for the Super Blues in 1957 and that was that. I had always supported the club and to this day am a very biased Everton fan. I was once quoted as saying one Evertonian is worth 20 Liverpudlians, so I'm well popular with the Everton mob.

Back then clubs had 40 or 45 pros on the books, so as well as the first team and the reserves, you had A, B and C teams. As a young player I was prepared to learn my trade in those lesser teams, but I was fortunate enough to impress early on and never looked back. In a public practice game between the first team and the reserve players I marked Dave Hickson, an Everton legend, and did very well. I was trying like hell – he might not have been – but that helped me get straight into the reserves and jump all the A and B teams.

My first team debut was at Birmingham when I was 18, which was young for a centre-half back then. My home debut was against Tottenham in a game in which I had to mark the England centre-forward Bobby Smith. Looking back, Bobby did me a favour that day, as I made a couple of ricks and got punished by him. It's not like the reserves. You make an error against someone like Bobby and the ball is in the back of the net. We lost 4-3 and Bobby gave me a bit of a whipping. I then got dropped until the end of the season, but gradually learnt from my mistakes and became more of a regular.

I was a fairly confident young man, but that day against Bobby taught me a thing or two about how to play the game in defence. I had grown up being an inside-forward, so I always tried to play with the ball. Sometimes, though, a centre-half can be too cultured and, as in the case with Bobby Smith, if you take your mind off the defensive duties a good player has mugged you and it's a goal. Rio Ferdinand's suffered with that kind of lapse of concetration over the past few years. I did back then. Sometimes you have to know when to kick the ball into row z. Everton's main stand was one of the highest around, so I knew I had done well when I reached that one.

Into the 1960s I became a regular in Everton's side and showed my willingness to my country's cause by travelling across Europe on my own accord to meet up with the Under-23 squad. Everton had won the league title in 1963 and, as a reward, the club had taken us off to Torremolinos as way of a thank you. Tony Kay and I were contacted and asked to play on the Under-23 tour of Eastern Europe. Some of the lads thought it funny that we were leaving the sun and the beach, but that's what we did. We travelled to Gibraltar, and flew to Warsaw before playing in Poland and East Germany. I think that attitude stood me in good stead with Alf.

I'd already made my full debut under Walter Winterbottom in a 4-0 win against the Welsh in late 1962. England's next game was to be Alf Ramsey's first as England manager and I was retained at centre-half. We were to travel to France, but that winter was so atrocious that most of us had not played regular football for weeks and weeks.

We got beat 5-2, so Alf must have been very impressed with his centre-half! It was a hard game to forget that one. Bobby Moore played, as did Ron Springett. We would have liked to have used the fact that we hadn't played regular football for three months as an excuse, but we couldn't. After that I lost my place for a while and was out in the wilderness. I had to knuckle down at Everton, which I did and was eventually made captain in 1964, and lifted the FA Cup in 1966. We had a great team at Goodison Park and fortunately I began to get noticed again by those picking the England side.

It seemed too late for me and the 1966 squad, though. Jack Charlton was clearly Alf's number one choice whilst Wolves' Ron Flowers, a superb veteran of the game, was also in the squad. I was at Goodison one afternoon and Harry Catterick, the manager, comes to me saying Alf Ramsey is on the phone. Alf had picked an initial squad of 27 players, but I wasn't in it. I was choked about that, but no matter, I had instead arranged to get married. Alf's on the phone, however, and says in that posh voice of his, "Brian, there's been a change of heart and we'd like you to join the 22 for a tour of Scandinavia."

Well, what do I say? In the back of my mind I'm thinking "England aren't going to win the World Cup" – you should see me picking horses at Aintree, I'm a plonker at that too! – and whilst most men are afraid of their wives, I was scared of my wife-to-be. She wasn't the most understanding of women when it came to football and so I told Alf I had arranged to get married and, while I told him I was honoured, I said that he had better look elsewhere.

Then England only go on and win the bloody thing! My very good mate, Ian Callaghan lives next door to me now and with it being the 40 year anniversary this summer, he's getting invited to all these great parties – including a big do in Germany – to commemorate the win. I'm choked because I missed out. I've been divorced for 26 years, but I have got a lovely daughter from that marriage, so I can't complain!

After England's glory in 1966, I became somewhat disillusioned with the game. Players were making very little money at the time, and, while I would have played for Everton and my country for free, I had bills to pay and other options I could fall back on. Back then, my father had a successful central heating business and he was forever pestering me to come out of football and to work with him. I could earn much more money doing that and eventually, in late '66, I went to Harry Catterick to say I was retiring. Effectively I was giving them 12 months notice, which didn't seem to bother anyone too much as I wasn't playing particularly well anyway.

As soon as I had come to that decision, that form picked up significantly. Maybe I was that bit more relaxed, but I was soon playing the best stuff of my life, enjoying it more than I ever had and suddenly my father's central heating business isn't looking as appealing as it once was.

I changed my mind and was soon back in the England fold. In 1966, the country's defence had been the foundation on which Alf built his World Cup glory. That, though, had changed. The two superb full-backs, Ray Wilson and George Cohen had to be replaced, while a place as the partner for Bobby Moore at centre-half was also up for grabs. Big Jack Charlton wasn't going to let it go easily, but I felt confident that I could break into the starting XI.

In 1969, we went on a tour of South America and managed a draw with Mexico and a win over Uruguay before taking on Brazil who had built a new team and were preparing to try and win another World Cup. We actually went one up through Colin Bell, but playing against that Brazil team in the Maracana wasn't easy. I remember, before the game, sitting on the toilet in the dressing rooms reading the programme and going over the names in Brazil's line-up.

You shouldn't be overawed but there I am and each name is a world-beater. Pelé, Jairzinho, Tostao, Rivelino, Gerson, and there are 150,000 fans in the stadium. You're thousands of miles from home, you're looking at their forward line and you think, "Bloody hell!" All I can say, is I'm glad I was already on the toilet!

They beat us 2-1. I didn't have a spectacular game, but banged my head and claimed concussion. Despite that, I felt that going into 1970, I was Alf's number one choice at centre-back; I don't care what Big Jack says! That confidence was helped by the fact that my Everton team won the title again that season. I joke that we were the only three-man team ever to win the title because in Alan Ball, Colin Harvey and Howard Kendall we had a fantastic midfield trio.

England travelled across the world in just as confident mood. People say we had a better squad than the 1966 bunch, but I guess they can always say they won the bloody thing. We felt strong, though, and truly felt we could retain our crown. We were, however, away from home and had to deal with the fact that thousands of the people we came across hated the English. Alf had called the Argentineans 'animals' in 1966 when Rattin was sent off and so, when we arrived, the Mexicans had heavily sided with the South American countries.

Those problems had reared their head in Colombia, where we stopped before travelling to Mexico. We were playing well and beat both the Colombians and Ecuador, but it was off the pitch that we had our first hiccup. Notably the incident with Bobby Moore and the bracelet. I'm always getting asked about it. All I know is that we arrived at Bogotá airport, went to the hotel, checked-in and came back downstairs an hour later to hear about this incident involving Bobby and a supposedly stolen bracelet from a foyer shop. I couldn't believe that Bobby was in any way involved and, if truth be told, we had been warned that Bogotá wasn't the most savoury of places. If you had a nice watch on your right wrist and signalled right, someone would have your hand off with a machete!

Bobby was very calm because he knew he was innocent. His old mate Jimmy Greaves turned up as he was driving in a car rally across the area having retired from international football sometime earlier. Jimmy arrived to find his pal under arrest!

There were all sorts of rumours, such as Bobby covering up for a younger member of the squad, but to me that was nonsense. When you play for England, when you played under Alf, you didn't step out of line. You wouldn't think of doing something like that and I believe the whole thing was a set up. I was worried for a while. Our captain and one of the best players in the world was under arrest and might miss out, but in general we didn't let it bother us.

It was aggravating, but we had to focus and Alf wasn't one to let us become side-tracked. Preparation was always meticulous. We arrived a month before the finals which seemed early, but you had to remember that the kick-offs were at noon in blistering heat because of the demands of European TV and it took some getting used to. The heat and the altitude didn't effect us too much eventually because Alf had us so well prepared. He took us to this British club in Mexico City initially which had marvellous training facilities and we didn't fail to retain the World Cup due to any problems on that side.

What I recall about the heat was how the lads had to think about their hairstyles. Back then a big head of hair and those infamous side-burns were all the rage, but it was just too damn hot. I have a hairdresser in Liverpool that I have been using for 40 years. I have only ever had two haircuts anywhere else in that time and both of them were in Mexico!

With our shorter hair and new, specially made lightweight kit, we went into our opening game against Romania in Guadalajara in a positive mood. It was bloody hot, though. Stupidly you weren't allowed bottles of water during the game and either had to go off injured or wait until half-time. It was a ridiculous ruling, which massively favoured the Latin countries. I suppose it was just them getting back at us for all the supposed English bias which they thought had gone in the '66 Finals.

Romania weren't a bad team and always do well in World Cups. It wasn't a classic, but it was a good start. Geoff Hurst carried on where he had left off in '66 and got our goal and we were pleased to have played Ok, won three points and dealt with the conditions. Geoff lost about 12 pounds, but it all goes back on after a couple of pints of water.

There was a skip full of ice in the dressing room, which we all covered ourselves with, but Martin Peters and I were called in for a random dope test. Martin was a clever player, who was always said by the press to be ten years before his time. He filled his bottle straight away. It took me about 20 minutes and I think the poor Romanian lad must still be there.

It could get boring between games, but we had TV and could see the other games to see what everyone else was doing. I roomed with Tommy Wright, my Everton team-mate and Emlyn Hughes. He was courting his wife back then and would be on the phone all the time. The poor Mexican hotel receptionist would have Emlyn and his strong northern accent saying loudly, "I want to make a call to Barrow-in-Furness. That's B-A-R-R-O-W!"

Our next game was the big one against Brazil, who as I say were exceptional, but we had a good side and were confident that we could give them a game. We didn't do anything special. Alf briefed his back four about Tostao, Jairzinho, and of course Pelé, but you can't let it get to you. You have to go out and play your normal game, be aware, but not overawed.

We were confident despite a terrible night's sleep. As I say, we weren't the most popular bunch in Guadalajara and the night before the game outside the Hilton there was an almighty racket. Cars were blaring their horns, the locals were screaming, there were drums, the works. Big Jack and I had soon had enough and began throwing cartons of milk down at them, but that only encouraged more noise. I'm not saying that's why we lost, but we didn't sleep all that well at all.

The game kicked off and, while Alf didn't want us to get bogged down by worrying about their stars, he had decided to give Alan Mullery the unenviable task of tracking Pelé. Their Number 10 wasn't the only threat and I recall from an early stage knowing I was going to have my hands full with Tostao up front. He was fantastic.

I had a solid game rather than outstanding. Bobby was fantastic, as was our right back, my mate Tommy Wright. He never had any nerves, Tommy. We had a comfortable start, but after ten minutes it took a miracle to stop the Brazilians taking the lead. That miracle's name was Gordon Banks.

Jairzinho beat Terry Cooper – who had played brilliantly against Romania – and got to the bye-line before pulling it across for Pelé who, despite being fairly small was great in the air. He out-jumped Alan Mullery and headed towards goal with a fine powerful downward header that looked to all as if it was in. I had been drawn to the near post by Jairzinho's run and my reaction was, "Oh well we're one nil down." I actually thought that as soon as he headed it. Just as Pelé famously shouted, "Goal!" as soon as he connected with it.

But Banksy had other ideas. In a flash Gordon has scurried across his goal-line and tipped the ball over the crossbar. I went over and patted him on the back. 'Where the hell were you?' he said.

'I got here as quick as I can,' I replied.

Gordon is very modest and says that he was helped by the firmness of the pitch. The header hit the turf and bounced up, meaning Gordon could get the ball on the up and tip it over. I think he is too modest, of course. It was a fantastic save, maybe the best of all time.

The sun was beating down on our backs. I think it exceeded 100 degrees and that isn't right. The organisers had to please the European television audience, but to make us play in that was hard. Even so, with the aid of sodium tablets and great preparation, we managed to battle on and cause them some problems of our own. Geoff ran through, but I think he thought he was offside and that affected his finish, whilst Franny Lee headed straight at their keeper after more terrific work from Tommy Wright.

We came in at half-time pleased with a goalless score-line and our own endeavours. The second-half continued to be tight and, while I was playing well, it was Bobby Moore's form that was frustrating them. What a great player. His tackle on Jairzinho was incredible. Talk about timing.

Fourteen minutes into the second half, Brazil produced one of their magic moments that proved you could never take your foot off the gas when it came to their forward line. Tostao did well on the right, beating three players before knocking the ball into the box. When it arrived at Pelé's feet I thought I'd just push him out to the right, taking him away from goal. My interest was in getting the ball away from goal, but he just nudged it to Jairzinho who smashed it home. It didn't look like a goal-producing moment at first glance, but with Pelé's eye and the movement in that team, you could never be sure. People say that Maradona was better than Pelé, but I can't see it myself, Pelé was out of this world.

We gave it a go and really should have equalised through substitute Jeff Astle, but he missed a sitter. His club, West Bromwich Albion had beaten Everton in the 1968 FA Cup final and Jeff had smashed home a similar chance for the winner, but on this occasion he hurried it and put it wide.

It's become an iconic game that one. The images of the saves, the tackle, Bobby and Pelé, they are still so fresh. I can't recall whose shirt I got, but I sold it for charity. I also gave a Gerd Müller shirt after the quarter-final to some kid in a Liverpool hospital. I hope he bloody kept it. It's probably gone on Ebay!

Alf was pleased after the Brazil game, as he knew we had tested them. He let us go and have a night off in the upstairs bar at the hotel. That was a great night. I remember buying the most expensive drink I have ever bought. £35 it cost me for one glass of champagne! Suzanne Moore, the singer who had a hit with *Bobby's Girl*, came in the bar with her boyfriend. We were all enjoying ourselves and Suzanne came over and was taking pleasure in the team's company. She was a northern lass, a real cracker, Suzanne and so I go up to the bar and order this really expensive bottle of champagne. "Put it on room 154, the England football team," I said. I'm pouring out the champagne for everyone and get just one glass to myself. We had a great time that night, but once I got home to England there was a bill from the FA, £35 for a bottle of Champagne at the Guadalajara Hilton. I reckon if we had won the bloody thing they might have overlooked it.

The final group game was against Czechoslovakia, a game which I would sit out. I was 'rested' and Jack came in for me. I didn't want to miss out, but I knew I hadn't been dropped. There was rivalry between the two of us and I was aware that

Bill Eckersley, Wilf Mannion, Roy Bentley, Billy Wright, Eddie Baily and myself stretch out during our preparation training camp at Dulwich prior to flying out to Brazil

Bert Williams barely touched the ball during the game. Here he picks up a long stray through pass as Neil Franklin (third player from the left) covers, but just about the only other time was when he picked it out of our net

The famous photograph of the USA's goalscorer Joe Gaetjens being carried off shoulder high. I didn't go to see that film about the game when it came out

Jackie Milburn heads for goal in the vital game against Spain. The fact we lost this match was just as important as the defeat to the USA, but no-one remembers that anymore, just the humiliation of losing to such huge underdogs

IVOR BROADIS
1954 FINALS – SWITZERLAND
ENGLAND 2 V 4 URUGUAY

I took this photo of Gil Merrick (standing) and skipper Billy Wright as we sailed across the lake to our favourite hideaway where we'd have strawberry tea in between the matches

And with eight other members of the team relaxing with afternoon tea in the grounds of our hotel. From left Roger Byrne, Bill McGarry, Tommy Taylor, Albert Quixall, Billy Wright, Nat Lofthouse, Tom Finney, myself and Jimmy Dickinson

Billy Wright and Gil Merrick attempt to keep Uruguay at bay, but poor old Gil copped a lot of the blame for our early exit. What is it with England goalkeepers and the World Cup?

Tom Finney didn't have a particularly good time in World Cups and that continued against Uruguay as this effort beat the goalkeeper and covering defender, but bounced agonisingly past the post

The big moment of controversy in the first group game against the USSR was
my disallowed goal given for a foul on their legendary keeper Lev Yashin

Brazil captain Nilton Santos and Billy Wright shake hands before kick-off

I win the ball from Mazola of Brazil. The goalless draw was a
triumph of sorts for us

Colin McDonald is beaten for what turned out to be the winning goal for
the USSR and we were on our way home, dumped out after a play-off

JIMMY ARMFIELD
1962 FINALS – CHILE
ENGLAND 1 V 3 BRAZIL

Johnny Haynes (white shirt) sees Hungary's Grosics save during the group game

The team which faced Brazil, with myself (bottom row second from left), Jimmy Greaves (back row second from left) and a young Bobby Moore (back row extreme right) and Bobby Charlton (back row second from right)

Garrincha was on fire that day. I was glad he wasn't playing on my side of the
field. Here he takes on my fellow full-back Ray Wilson

Maurice Norman puts in a crunching tackle on the genius Brazilian winger,
but he still managed to score twice to end our dreams

ROGER HUNT
1966 FINALS – ENGLAND
ENGLAND 4 V 2 WEST GERMANY

I scored the first against France with a tap in from all of two yards.
That win really set us on our way on the road to glory

My moment of truth. I swear it was in – and as the linesman said it was,
it must have been!

This was the beginning of quite a night of celebrations

A winner's medal, struck in Switzerland, but mine takes pride of place
in my home on Merseyside

Jeff Astle places a record on his damn portable record player which kept us annoyed and his room-mate Peter Osgood up all night. You can be sure that this would have been an Elvis record rather than our very own classic *Back Home*!

Things went very well for us in the first hour of the quarter-final, Bobby Charlton ran the show. Here he takes on Der Kaiser, Franz Beckenbauer

Contary to popular belief it wasn't
all Peter Bonetti's fault.
He showed some pretty good
handling at times. Here he denies
Gerd Müller while I am the meat
in the sandwich

Bobby Moore cannot believe we
have lost after being 2-0 ahead.
Neither could I

And it was all because of the German fightback which culminated in
Müller 's acrobatic volley

It means something to defeat the World Champions. And we found out
the hard way. These Mexican fans couldn't contain themselves and ran
onto the pitch to help the Germans celebrate

Alf faced quite a lot of criticism after the defeat, especially when he
controversially said that we didn't have anything to learn from
Champions Brazil. Given that we didn't qualify for another World Cup
for 12 years, I think we probably did

NORMAN HUNTER
1974 QUALIFYING – WEMBLEY
ENGLAND 1 V 1 POLAND

If you make two mistakes in a row like we did then it's bound to lead to a goal at international level. I missed my tackle and Shilts misjudged his dive. 1-0 Poland

I could barely contain myself after that error. I might have had a reputation as a hard man, but at that moment emotion took over as the enormity of what I had done hit me

Even when we did manage to get the ball past Tomaszewski the clown, the woodwork came to Poland's rescue, so we could only draw and failed to qualify for Germany

Different people show their emotions in different ways. Peter Shilton, like me, couldn't hide his dejection...

...while Sir Alf remained as inscrutable as ever. It was the beginning of the end for him though

My QPR team-mate, Dave Clement (left) and I were over the moon when we heard we had been selected in the team to face Italy. So over the moon in fact that we grabbed the nearest traffic cone and celebrated!

Trevor Broooking leaps with keeper Dino Zoff as we desperately search for an equaliser that was just never going to come

That Claudio Gentile really was a prize ✳✳✳✳. I never stood a chance as
he kicked me, bit me and abused me

At least Elton John & I were able to smile about things afterwards

Trevor Francis puts us ahead against the Czechs as we seal automatic
qualification with two wins in the first two games

German full-back Manny Kaltz was a huge obstacle for me to overcome.
Here I get the better of him with my cunning trick of playing the ball one
side of him and running round him on the other side

From the left: Ray Clemence, Kevin Keegan, Glenn Hoddle and Trevor Brooking. A tremendously talented bench, but one riddled with injuries and other niggling problems…

…which showed when they finally did get onto the pitch and an out of touch Keegan and Brooking conspired to miss the best chances we had and we went out without having lost a game

PETER REID

There was never any doubt as to the level of animosity between England and Argentina. We tried to play it down, but when graffiti like this started appearing outside FIFA headquarters you knew it was just about the biggest game you're ever likely to play in

Diego Maradona was pretty much untouchable that day. Here I and Steve Hodge (right) fail to rob the ball off him

Everything has been said about Argentina's first goal. But what really annoyed me…

…was how the little git had the balls to celebrate such a blatant handball as that. I say blatant, but I didn't actually see it!

I still have nightmares about this moment. Every time I think I'm going to get there and hack him down this time round!

You've got to hand it to the little man. He might have been a cheating ****, but the goal he scored after that incredible run was genius. And yes, that is me way out of picture trailing in his wake…way out of picture

Gary Lineker's header gave us some hope, but we couldn't find another goal and we had to go home, knowing we'd been cheated out of the cup

David Platt's winner in the last minute of the Belgian match was a fairytale goal to set us on our way

Gazza made an unbelievable impression on the whole nation during that tournament. 'Daft as a brush' Bobby Robson called him. About right!

The moment that stung me to my core. When Brehme's free-kick flicked up into the Turin air off Paul Parker it sailed over me and I couldn't get back in time to stop the Germans going one ahead

Gary and Peter Beardsley celebrate the equaliser with just 10 minutes left of the semi-final

Paul is such an emotional fellow. He couldn't really cope with his booking which meant he missed the final and then when we lost on penalties the floodgates openedl

The homecoming to Luton airport was unbelievable. We knew we had done well, but we had no idea how much we had captured the nation's imagination until that bus ride through the teeming mass of fans

Ronald Koeman brings me down when I was clean through on goal.
A simple decision you would think

But first I had to suffer as the referee failed to implement the new FIFA
rules and send Koeman off for denying a goalscoring opportunity…

...and then as I discovered we hadn't even been awarded a penalty

So when Koeman scored from a free-kick to put Holland ahead you can
understand us all being just a little bit pissed off...

The manager, however, was more than a little bit. He did not like that at all

Bergkamp guides in the second Dutch goal and to all intents and purposes
we are out of the 1994 World Cup

TONY ADAMS
1998 FINALS – FRANCE
ENGLAND 2 V 2 ARGENTINA

Training was the root cause of the problems in our camp in my opinion. Often David Beckham was isolated…

…while the coach, Glenn Hoddle, showed off and belittled him. I believe it lead to Beckham's frustration that got him sent off against Argentina

Michael Owen's goal was undoubtedly one of the greatest ever scored by an Englishman, but my first thought was how weak their defence had been against him. Once a defender always a defender I suppose!

And then everything went horribly wrong. Beckham got himself sent off…

…and Sol Campbell had what I thought was a good goal disallowed…

…while Roa saved David Batty's spot-kick and we were out of the tournament

Michael Owen puts us 1-0 ahead against Brazil…

…and the celebrations for that goal will live long in my memory

But Ronaldinho's chip caught David Seaman unawares and we just couldn't raise ourselves in the heat to find a way back

And when you lose in the World Cup it doesn't matter who you are – fan...

...or the most famous player in the world. It hurts like crazy

he was the winner from '66, but I was confident that Alf had faith in me. I was quite a different player to Jack. He had quite an ordinary game against the Czechs and I wasn't unduly upset about it. We won 1-0, but hadn't played well. Those of us who had been dropped would be lying if we said we were all that concerned.

Alf, though, was very loyal and wasn't one to knock his players publicly. In 1969, we were playing the Scots in the Home Nations tournament and we were all in the hotel in Hendon as a team. We were watching the television the night before the game and ITV had their panel of experts discussing the following day's match. Alan Gilzean was playing up front for the Scots and these pundits who included Brian Clough and Joe Mercer began to say just how bad a game I was going to have against the Tottenham man.

There I sat, in front of all my team-mates as these guys dissected my game. I'd had a terrible game before I even got on the pitch! "Gilzean is too clever; too good in the air and poor Labone is going to have a nightmare." They finished and I stood up and apologised to my team-mates for the stinker I was going to have the following day. Anyway we won 4-1, Gilzean was substituted having not had a touch and as I walked off Alf called me over and said, "Some mistake I made picking you, son!"

Ray Wilson used to say Alf was a cockney gypsy who had gone to elocution lessons. He used to act very posh and I'll never forget he would wear these sock garters. Every now and then though he would drop those H's, especially when he got angry.

W e were in the quarter-finals and once more it was West Germany, who must have been hell-bent on revenge after the '66 final. We had to get the bus down to León a few days before the match, but again felt well prepared, or at least we did until our goalkeeper, the best in the world, got sick and was immediately declared unfit to play.

I don't know what really happened to Gordon. He ate the same stuff as us, but was laid very low. We couldn't understand it, but he was far too ill to play. In reserve we had Chelsea's Peter Bonetti, famously nicknamed The Cat due to his being very agile. If you were going to have an understudy for Gordon, Peter was as good as you could get as far as we were concerned..

Losing Gordon certainly didn't seem to bother the team and we got amongst that very good German side from the off, taking the lead after 30 minutes through Alan Mullery, another player having a very good tournament. It was a fine finish to a move that Alan himself had started and set the tone. We were all over them.

Five minutes into the second-half we doubled that lead through Martin Peters, who was showing his form '66 and from there we looked to be in the semi-final.

All we had to do was kill the game and we'd be through. For an hour they hadn't given us any problems at all, but then Alf started to think about the semi. It was in a few day's time, so given the intense heat he had to think about resting some players. I wouldn't say all our minds had drifted to the semi. I know mine didn't. As a defender your mind can never stray from the job, especially with someone like Müller about, but I guess Alf was thinking ahead when he brought off Bobby Charlton and then Martin Peters and replaced them with more defensive players. He had to think about keeping Bobby fresh.

The Germans had actually pulled one back before Bobby went off, through a lucky goal that on any other occasion The Cat would have stopped. But the firm pitch meant that Beckenbauer's long-range effort bobbled over his outstretched arm.

With Charlton off, Beckenbauer came more and more into the game, but it is too easy to blame either Alf or Colin Bell, the man who replaced Bobby, for what happened. We all started to wilt under the heat of León and with the German sub, Grabowski, tormenting Terry Cooper on the wing, we became more and more under pressure.

The equaliser by Uwe Seeler was a header at goal like I've got two holes in my arse! The Germans were applying constant heavy pressure and I cleared the ball rather hurriedly to Schnellinger at left-back. He crossed it, Seeler got his head to the ball and if you ask me just tried to head it back across the area. The Cat had come out and the ball lofted over his head into an empty net. 2-2.

We had to go into extra-time, but there would be no fairytale ending like four years earlier. Geoff Hurst had what looked a perfectly good goal disallowed, but they were looking strong and once more it was Grabowski who caused all the problems. He tied a few of our lads up on the right, crossed it goalwards and the ball sailed over to Keith Newton who was marking Löhr. Keith always said that he jumped for that ball and got a touch which actually took it onto the German's head. The ball bounced in the six-yard box where Müller, like all good forwards, was sniffing and he acrobatically leapt and buried it. Suddenly we're losing and we'd nothing left to give. We were out.

That was one of the most heartbreaking moments of my life. Whenever I recall it, it hurts that one! Nearly 40 years on and I can't exorcise the ghost!

We were all so devastated and went out and got pissed. Personally, I held myself responsible because their centre-forward – my man – had got the winner. It was a shame because we were the only side that might have beaten Brazil. I'm not saying we would have, but Italy were pulled apart. It was a walkover. There was no way we were going to lose 4-1. That adds to the frustration. Brazil were brilliant, perhaps the best of all time, but we gave them a good game in the group stage and in a final, who knows.

Back home, we weren't given much stick. Alf got plenty, though. We all said, don't be blaming him because his was a tactical decision based on the heat and the conditions. If you're two up and looking comfortable, defeat doesn't enter you head. These were still top class international footballers he was bringing on, so it was wrong to blame the boss.

While it still hurts, that was a wonderful World Cup; probably the best of all time. I was lucky enough, due to my football, to visit Mexico and to see the Inca pyramids. Alf took us all and it was brilliant. He even got us all playing cricket out there. Alf was adamant that we were *English* and we would be proud of that. He used the fact that we weren't too popular to motivate us, but in the end I think we returned home with more friends than we had when we'd arrived.

NORMAN HUNTER
DEFENDER

GERMANY 1974

BORN   29th October 1943, Middlesbrough
CLUBS   Leeds United, Bristol City, Barnsley
INTERNATIONAL DEBUT   December 1965 v Spain
ENGLAND CAREER   28 caps, 2 goals
INTERNATIONAL FAREWELL   October 1974 v Czechoslovakia

Norman 'Bites Yer Legs' Hunter was not just the legendary hatchet man in Don Revie's hard-nut team of the 60s and 70s. He was also a cultured footballer, capable of competing at the highest level. His plethora of domestic honours reveal a fierce competetive edge, which Hunter also took into international football. His tackling often took opponents to the cleaners and when the Poles broke clear in a vital qualifier for the Germany World Cup, English fans would have put their house on Hunter stopping them in their tracks. Norman still can't believe he didn't.

ENGLAND 1 v POLAND 1

World Cup Qualifying Group 5
Wednesday 17 October 1973

Wembley Stadium
Attendance 100,000

*Cloughie's 'Clown' denies England a place in the World Cup finals and costs
Sir Alf Ramsey his job*

Teams

Alf Ramsey	**Managers**	Kazimierz Gorski
Peter Shilton	1	Jan Tomaszewski
Paul Madeley	2	Antoni Szymanowski
Emlyn Hughes	3	Jerzy Gorgon
Colin Bell	4	Adam Musial
Roy McFarland	5	Miroslaw Bulzacki
Norman Hunter	6	Henrik Kazparczak
Tony Currie	7	Grzegorz Lato
Mick Channon	8	Lewslaw Cmikiewicz
Martin Chivers	9	Kazimierz Deyna
(Sub. Kevin Hector)		
Allan Clarke	10	Jan Domarski
Martin Peters	11	Robert Gadocha

Clarke (pen) 63	**Scorers**	Domarski 57

Referee: Vital Loraux (Belgium)

I'VE HAD SOME disappointing experiences in my time. I was on the losing side in three FA Cup finals and missed out on winning the league title on the last day of the season. In Europe, I was part of the Leeds United side that lost the Cup Winners Cup final in Salonika in 1973 – when the referee was later banned for life for taking bribes – and in the 1975 European Cup final again we were robbed by the ref.

Those bitter memories stay with you for a very long time, but drawing with Poland and not qualifying for the 1974 World Cup finals ranks alongside any of those disappointments. It was an awful feeling. Awful.

After years of waiting in the wings, I finally got into the England side, on merit, ahead of probably the greatest defender of all time, Bobby Moore, and I blew it. It was my mistake that led to Poland's goal and ultimately cost us a place at the World Cup and that upset me more than any other experience I've ever had – let alone with England. It's my one regret in football.

I wouldn't say my international career was 'stop-start', because once I'd first been selected in 1965, I was in every squad for the next nine years, winning 28 caps. But I was never really going to be first choice because I was understudy to the England captain, Bobby Moore; one of the greatest players I've ever had the privilege to see. I knew that somewhere along the line, if something happened to Bob, I would get in, but he didn't miss many internationals and he never missed the really important games. And the bigger and the more important the game, the better he played.

When you first get into the squad, you're young, you're full of yourself and you just want to play. Initially, I'd look at Bobby Moore and think, "I should be in there," but gradually, I'd look at the situation, watch him play, and think, "No chance." I soon became aware that I wasn't gonna play.

Many people might become more and more frustrated as they become more established in the squad and develop into a top First Division player, but I actually became more understanding of the situation as time wore on. I'd watch Bobby, learn from him and I ended up with so much admiration for him that I never begrudged the fact that I didn't get many games as a first choice centre-half.

Bobby wasn't very quick, but the way he could read the game… well, he didn't need to be quick. And when he got the ball, oh he could pass it. Look at our first goal in the 1966 World Cup final. He won the free-kick, picked up the ball, Hursty made the run and BOOM, Bobby put it right on his head. Back of the net.

Even though I knew I wasn't going to play much, I never even considered not joining up with England. Not once. I loved being in the England squad – I wouldn't have swapped that experience for the world. I never used to defy my club manager Don Revie in any way, shape or form – except when it came to England. He used to try and persuade me not to go. "Go on, son. Tell him you're injured," he'd say. "No, gaffer. I'm going," I'd say.

By being part of the squad I was still representing my country, I loved the social side of it, and I also went to see Alf Ramsey, because I thought he was an absolutely superb manager. He picked me when a lot of people were saying, "Hunter isn't this" or "he isn't that" and he stuck by me for nine years. Because of Leeds United's reputation I was probably a bit underrated as a footballer in some circles, but Alf never made me feel like that. Leeds were disliked throughout the country and we had a reputation – which, a lot of the time, was probably justified – but Alf never brought that into it. Ok, so he wasn't everybody's cup of tea, but he was always fair and always picked the best players.

Only once did he bring Leeds United into it. On one of my rare starts I tackled somebody a bit hard. It was a bit naughty, I admit. I shouldn't have done it. He pulled me to one side and said: "What do you think you're doing? Who told you that you could tackle like that? You don't do that with England." Alright, it probably wasn't his place to say that, but I took it on board, because I had such huge respect for the man. He was different class. He knew I probably wasn't going to play very often, so he'd always take the time to come up to me before we went back to our clubs and say, "Thanks for coming Norman, I really enjoyed working with you." That was the measure of the man. If you asked everybody who worked under Alf for England, I don't think anybody would have a bad word to say about him.

People might wonder why Alf didn't play me and Bobby Moore together in central defence. He did once – against West Germany in 1972, when we lost 3-1 at Wembley – but it wasn't a great success, so I had no complaints whatsoever when Alf didn't stick with it. Bobby and I could read each other's movements well and positional play wasn't a problem, but we didn't have enough pace between us – pure and simple. When Bobby played in '66, the rest of the England defence was extremely quick. Ray Wilson could move, Georgie Cohen was ever so quick and Jack Charlton, the big man, was actually very quick too. Bobby would read most situations and he hardly ever got himself into a position where he could be out-run, but on the rare occasions he did get exposed, the others would cover him.

But if the ball was played over the top with both of us in the middle, you could say goodnight. That's why in 1970 Alf partnered Bobby with Brian Labone and, later, with Roy McFarland.

By 1973, I'd already been part of two World Cup squads. I was a 22-year-old with just four caps to my name when we won in 1966 and, although I was never likely to play that summer, it was still great to be in the squad, to be part of it all. I can remember being amongst Alf's initial 27 players at Lilleshall. Nobody was sure whether they would make the cut or not for the final 22, so when he told me I was in, I was absolutely delighted.

Alf said all along that we would win the World Cup that year, even when others were saying we didn't have a chance, and I think his confidence worked its way down to the players. Perhaps not initially when we drew 0-0 with Uruguay, but once we got our first win under our belt, the public really got behind the team and everybody started to believe we could win it.

Overall, I wouldn't have swapped the 1966 experience for anything and the non-playing members of the squad were as excited as anybody when we won it. But it was a bit strange at the final whistle, when Alf told us non-playing squad members to be down on the Wembley touchline. The lads that had played and won the trophy were doing their lap of honour while we stood there in our civvies. At that moment, it felt a little bit deflating that you hadn't been in the team, it was strange actually. My country had won the World Cup, were World Champions, and I felt deflated.

By 1970, any frustration at not being in the team had gone and I was still very happy to be part of the squad that travelled to Mexico to defend the World Cup. We had a good squad then too, you know, but I don't agree with people who say it was better than the one we had in '66, because you can't do any more than win the competition, and we couldn't quite manage that in 1970. We had a chance, though, and with a bit of luck, who knows? The boys had had their luck in '66. We were a bit unlucky to lose 1-0 against Brazil in the 1970 group stage and that meant we had to move from Guadalajara to Leon, which disrupted us a bit.

Again, I didn't expect to play much. I wouldn't say that was more difficult when you're holed up in a hotel thousands of miles from home, rather than being in the Hendon Hall Hotel, but the trip wasn't without its problems. The locals didn't want us to win it – they wanted one of the South American countries to win it – and did everything they could to disrupt us.

For me, one particular incident stands out. The hotel we were staying in, you could drive three-quarters of the way round and, starting about 10 o' clock, the locals drove round beeping their horns all night. Alf moved all the players who were in the team round to the side of the hotel you couldn't drive round. I wasn't one of those players, and can remember hardly sleeping a wink that night.

The not-playing part wasn't a problem, because it's not as if I didn't know everybody in the squad. I roomed with my mates from Leeds, Allan Clarke and

Terry Cooper. Besides, I could get just as much out of training as I could out of playing, so I was ready, just in case I was called upon…

In the end, I did get the call; in the quarter-final. But it was as a midfielder, in place of Martin Peters. At 2-0 up, Alf wanted to replace Bobby Charlton with Colin Bell, but before he could, the Germans pulled a goal back. Being wise after the event, if Alf had left Bobby on, I think we would have won because he was playing so well. We were well in control and the Germans were dead and buried. I came on at 2-1 to shore things up, but I hadn't even touched the ball when they made it 2-2. Once the Germans got the equaliser they starting coming and coming and there was only one team gonna win it.

I didn't really mind playing in midfield. In fact, I quite enjoyed it. It's something different and personally I think there is less responsibility on you because you're not the last line of defence. At centre-back, you can't afford to make many mistakes because there's a good chance it will lead to a goal, whereas in midfield you can misplace a few passes and miss a few tackles, knowing your defenders are behind you.

Besides, I would have played anywhere just to get a game for England. I got my first proper run in the side as a midfielder in the 1972 Home Championships before the start of the 1974 World Cup qualifiers. I was at the top of my game as a centre-back, but I don't think it was a case of Alf accommodating Bobby Moore, Roy McFarland and myself to avoid making a difficult decision. If you looked at Alf's selections over the years, he always liked to have somebody who could win the ball in midfield. In 1966 he had Nobby [Stiles], in 1970 he had Alan Mullery and if anybody got injured, he knew I could have stepped into the breach. Alf always knew the nucleus of his squad – it never changed much – and if he wanted to look at a player in a certain position, he always gave you a good run at it.

There were only three teams in our qualifying group for the 1974 World Cup – Wales, Poland and ourselves – and for the first two games, both against Wales, I wore the number four on my back and played in midfield. We won the first match in Cardiff with a goal from Colin Bell and Alf named an unchanged side for the return fixture. On a personal level, it was memorable for my second and last goal in an England shirt, a 25-yard screamer that flew past my Leeds team-mate Gary Sprake in the Wales goal and won the January 1973 Goal of the Month award. But overall a 1-1 draw wasn't what we wanted or expected at home and it left us needing to avoid defeat away to Poland in our next game.

Another of my Leeds team-mates, Paul Madeley, came into the side at right-back for the game in Poland, with Peter Storey moving forward to take my place in midfield. Even though, in effect, Bobby Moore stood in between me and a place in the England side for many years, I didn't have mixed emotions watching from the sidelines. I'd never sit there hoping that he'd make a mistake. Never. I'm just not made that way. The last thing you wanted anybody to do for England is make a mistake and let the opposition get a goal. But that's exactly what happened in Poland. We fell behind early on when Gadocha hit a free-kick between Bobby and Shilts on the goal-line. They left it for each other and looked a bit silly. But we dominated for the rest of the first half without finding an equaliser. Then, just after the break, Bobby lost possession on the halfway line and Lubanski broke away to double Poland's lead. We continued to press, but there was no way back. We'd now *have* to beat the Poles at Wembley…

I first got an inkling I would be in the team for the return game with Poland a month beforehand, when we played Austria in a friendly at Wembley. I partnered Roy McFarland at the back in place of Bobby and played well in a thumping 7-0 win. But with Bobby being such a great player and captain, I still didn't join up with the squad for the Poland game thinking I would be playing. I thought it unlikely that I would ever get this guy out! But I got the nod and thought, "Right, this is it, I've got my chance here, make sure you make the most of it." Bob was the first one to wish me well. That was the stature of the man.

Nine years is a long time to spend in a squad together and you get to know each other very well. And when you've spent the majority of the time as somebody's understudy, watching him and admiring him, you form a certain bond.

The other changes from the game in Poland saw Tony Currie and Mick Channon come in for Peter Storey and Alan Ball. Bally was suspended after being sent off in Poland in what was a pretty tetchy affair all-round. The Poles employed similar roughhouse tactics in their win over Wales a month before they came to Wembley, but we didn't expect them to adopt a similar approach against us this time – not at our place. We had people in the side who could look after themselves when they needed to, so it was never gonna be that type of game. We had the same referee as we'd had against Romania in Mexico in 1970, when he let them get away with murder, but not many referees would be biased against the home side in those days. Some of the continental referees left a lot to be desired, real homers they were. As it turned out, I can't remember the referee at all in that game, so he must have done a good job.

Did it make it easier knowing we had to win to go through? No, because we always played to win anyway, especially at Wembley, so our approach wouldn't have been any different if, like Poland, we only needed a draw. Poland had shown us nothing to be afraid of in Katowice, even though we lost, and we thought we were going to absolutely walk it. I don't think we under-estimated them, it's just that when you played for England at Wembley you never thought you wouldn't win, no matter who the opposition was. We had a good side, with Martin Chivers, Mick Channon and Allan Clarke a formidable strike-force by anybody's reckoning.

Poland didn't come with a great reputation, but they couldn't be that bad if they'd beaten us in Poland. As it turned out they would finish third at the World Cup in 1974 and again in 1982, so they were a team just coming to the boil. Did we think their goalkeeper, Jan Tomaszewski, was a clown? No way. He was unorthodox, sure, but he kept a clean sheet in Poland didn't he? He was nowhere near a clown as he proved that night. That was just Cloughie being Cloughie.

Alf's approach to games was nearly always the same: do the basics and do them well. He was a stickler for that and rightly so. He always did his homework on the opposition, explained them to you in training and then left it to you to deal with them. By the time the pre-match team talk came around, he just told us to believe in ourselves and believe that we would win the game. He always sent you out with a positive attitude. In fact, not a negative word was spoken.

There was controversy at the time, because the FA refused to rearrange the previous weekend's league games. That wouldn't happen these days, would it? No, and rightly so, but I don't think that played any part in our performance. It's not as if we didn't have the legs...

We laid siege to the Poland goal from the off, creating chance after chance after chance. Mick Channon hit the post, Tony Currie headed over and even when we did hit the target, Tomaszewski was playing out of his skin. Whatever it took, he kept it out. He was a bit shaky at first, but he grew in confidence. He tipped a low drive from Colin Bell round the post, got down low to save a header from Clarkey, and even when Mickey Channon's shot was deflected, he somehow managed to push it clear. I can only think he was inspired by what Cloughie had said.

Even at half-time, Alf was very positive: "This Tomaszewski is out of this world. He can't carry on playing like this. Keep playing, keep working, keep believing and we'll win this game." He was convinced of it, and so were we. As we walked back down the tunnel I remember thinking, "We're bound to get one in." I never once thought we wouldn't win.

The second half started the same way the first half had finished, with us camped in their half. I remember watching the game – because that's what I was doing, standing at the back with Roy McFarland – thinking, "This is unbelievable, we've got to win this. Again, there were great saves, goal-line clearances, we hit the post, the bar, everything. Occasionally, I would pick up the ball, join in the play, make a pass, but other that, I didn't have a thing to do. Nothing. Then, 12 minutes after half-time, they scored...

The ball broke loose over on our right. It was probably the first time they'd been over the halfway line all match. As I'm coming across, I can see Lato coming towards the ball from the left and I'm thinking to myself, "Right, I'm gonna tackle him here, take the ball and the man." It was 50/50 as to who was gonna get there first and I'm thinking, "He's gonna come into the tackle here," but as I got there, he slowed up. It was almost like he was waiting until I got there. Then – and I don't know why I did this, because I always used to tackle with my left foot, my strongest foot – I thought, "I'll keep this in with my right foot and try to knock it past him." Why, I don't know, because I've never done that before and I was right on the touchline. Maybe I was caught in two minds because Lato slowed up. Maybe I just wanted to get us back on the attack as soon as possible, but I changed my mind and ended up doing neither. The ball went under my right foot as I went to ground. I was out of touch, out of the game, and he was off. There was no way I could catch him.

Lato raced clear, cut inside, laid it square to Domarski and his shot squeezed under Peter Shilton. To be fair – and I've never spoken to Shilts about this – Peter should have thrown his hat on Domarski's shot. People talk about my mistake far more than his, but a lot of that was down to me, because after the game I put my hand up and admitted publicly: "It was my fault." I shouldn't have said that, although I still don't think it was a 50/50 thing. Mine was the initial mistake, I should have dealt with the situation and if I could have my time again, I would have just knocked the ball out of play.

Suddenly, we're chasing the game and my attitude has changed from concentrating on doing my job as a defender to wanting to join in with the attack. You do feel responsible when things like that happen. I thought, "Jesus Christ, I've cocked that up." Then you think, "Right, come on. Let's put this right."

Just a few minutes later, we won a penalty, Martin Peters intercepted a back pass and was bundled over in the box. People say it was a soft penalty, but it looked a good shout from where I was standing. I was delighted Allan Clarke was taking the spot-kick because he was so cool. Under pressure, there was nobody like Clarkey – he was never gonna miss. He just passed it into the bottom right-hand corner of the net, sending Tomaszewski the wrong way.

I doubted meself when I messed up for the goal and wondered whether it would cost us the game, but when Clarkey knocked that penalty in I felt much better. I thought, "That's it, we're off, we'll win this one now."

There was half an hour left and I can only remember them crossing the halfway line once during that period. It was a siege on their goal. In a way it would have been better if they'd had a bit more possession and come at us a bit more. That way we might have had to play a bit deeper, bringing them onto us a bit more, which would have given our attackers more space to play. But they just camped in their half and when it came to them they just whacked it clear and stood their waiting for us to build an attack again.

But we didn't panic. We didn't just lump the ball into their box willy-nilly, we played properly, tried to work the openings, which we had to, because they were all behind the ball. But if you look at a video of the game, it's not as if they shut us out defensively. We played brilliantly really. And there were too many good players in our team, too many capable of scoring a goal, for us not to get another one.

Tony Currie had three chances: the first was a shot from 25 yards, which Tomaszewski famously punched out to Mick Channon, whose follow-up shot hit the side-netting; the second was a header, which rolled along the crossbar; the third the keeper parried from close-range. I had a shot with my right foot, which he also parried. He saved one shot from Clarkey with his foot and Colin Bell had a second penalty shout turned down. Clarkey hit another shot from about ten yards out that was going right into the top corner and this guy dived at full stretch and tipped it over the bar. Unbelievable. Saves like that are a rarity in football, but Tomaszewski seemed to produce loads of them in one game. It was as if he was ramming Clough's words back down his throat with every stop that he made.

It might have been the case that we snatched at a few chances, but only late on when we were getting desperate. Clarkey, usually so cool in front of goal, missed a couple from close range, but I still can't believe we didn't score again. It's only when you watch the 90 minutes back that you realise how many chances we created – 39 attempts on goal to Poland's three. You can't play like that, create so many clear-cut chances, and have a goalkeeper making so many great saves if it's meant to be. For us, in that game, it just wasn't.

Alf was criticised for leaving it too late to make a substitution, but I think people make too much of that. They were still a very new thing back then and I don't think it was his style to do it very often. Alright, sometimes it comes off, when a player comes on late and scores, but in my experience it's horrendous coming on late, because it takes you a while to get into the pace of the game. Besides, even though Kevin Hector came on for Martin Chivers very late, he nearly won it for us. From just a few yards out, he met a corner – our 23rd – perfectly with a header, but it hit one of their guys on the line and Clarkey couldn't quite wrap his foot round the rebound. Our final golden chance had gone begging.

Bobby Moore was the first one over to me at the final whistle. He put his arm around my shoulder and tried to console me. What did he say? Not a lot. What can you say at a moment like that? I was absolutely distraught.

That was my opportunity to finally go the World Cup as first choice – and I blew it. Blew it big time.

At the time I didn't dwell on the fact that it would be my last chance to play in the World Cup. That comes later, when you've retired. The beauty of football is, after a few days off you go back to your club and get straight back into it.

There was a lot of banter from the Scottish lads at Leeds, of course. We had Billy Bremner, Eddie Gray, Peter Lorimer, Gordon McQueen, Joe Jordan and David Harvey and they were quite happy that we hadn't qualified, especially as they had. They gave all of the England players dog's abuse, though, nobody actually turned round to me and said: "You didn't qualify because you cocked it up!" No-one was that stupid. They could see how much and how deeply it hurt.

The papers wouldn't let me forget it, though and because of that I took a lot of stick from fans when I visited opposition grounds for the rest of that season, but you expected that with Leeds anyway, so it never ever bothered me. I think it was the first occasion that one individual player was demonised for causing England to go out of the World Cup. Of course, David Beckham suffered a similar fate in 1998 after getting sent off against Argentina, but I was there a quarter of a century before him. It wasn't as intense back then maybe. As well as at grounds on matchdays, I also had the odd one or two people come up to me in the street and say something, blaming me for us not qualifying and what have you, but most of the public were fine. It was the press more than anyone who blamed me.

The England thing could have affected me badly at the time, but I wouldn't have let that happen. I wouldn't have let Leeds down in that way. In fact, we went on to win the title that season and I was the first winner of the newly established PFA Player of the Year Award. I was delighted on both counts, but I wouldn't say it was consolation for costing us the World Cup – they were two separate things.

The Poland game stayed with me for a very long time. I never realised until I sat down a long time afterwards and went through the whole 90 minutes on video how dominant we were. How we didn't win that game about 6-1 I'll never know. I can not believe we didn't win comfortably. It was unbelievable. Unbelievable.

What I also find amazing is the number of times we've been drawn against Poland since – both in the World Cup and the European Championships. And every time we do, 1973 crops up again and they play the clip of that bloody goal. Even though it was over 30 years ago, everybody either remembers or knows about that game and they always want to hear about it. The one consolation is, at least it earns me a few quid from after dinner speeches!

STAN BOWLES
WINGER

ARGENTINA 1978

BORN   24th December 1948, Manchester
CLUBS   Manchester City, Bury, Crewe Alexandra, Carlisle United, QPR,
Nottingham Forest, Orient, Brentford,
INTERNATIONAL DEBUT April 1974 v Portugal
ENGLAND CAREER   5 caps, 1 goal
INTERNATIONAL FAREWELL   February 1977 v Holland

Skilful winger or gambling alcoholic? Stan Bowles' life and career was never short of magical or controversial incident. Recalled by Don Revie for a vital qualifying match in Italy, Bowles was heralded by the press as the type of player who could match the Italians' flair and creativity. In reality he stood out most for being shunned by the rest of the team. In this frank account of the problems which beset English football in the second half of the 1970s, Bowles' honesty is only equalled by the incredible goings on of that era.

ITALY 2 v ENGLAND 0

World Cup Qualifying Group 2
Wednesday 17 November 1976

Olympic Stadium, Rome
Attendance 70,718

Divisions in the England team lead to failure to qualify
for the second World Cup in succession.

Teams

	Managers	
Enzo Bearzot		Don Revie
Dino Zoff	1	Ray Clemence
Antonello Cuccureddu	2	Dave Clement
		(Sub. Kevin Beattie)
Giacinto Facchetti	3	Mick Mills
Claudio Gentile	4	Brian Greenhoff
Marco Tardelli	5	Roy McFarland
Franco Causio	6	Emlyn Hughes
Romeo Benetti	7	Kevin Keegan
Giancarlo Antognoni	8	Mick Channon
Fabio Capello	9	Stan Bowles
Francesco Graziani	10	Trevor Cherry
Roberto Bettega	11	Trevor Brooking

	Scorers	
Antognoni 36, Bettega 77		

Referee: Abraham Klein (Israel)

I ONLY WON five England caps – and they were spread across three years. But in all honesty I wasn't that bothered about playing for my country. I was always happier playing for Queen's Park Rangers, who I was with when I played all my international football. Don't get me wrong, I was happy to take the England caps when they came along, but I treated England selection as a bonus as much as anything, because the squad was very cliquey in them days. You had your Derby County clique of Colin Todd, Roy McFarland and David Nish; then your Liverpool clique of Ray Clemence, Phil Thompson, Phil Neal, Kevin Keegan and all that lot. And in those days you usually had only two or three days together as a squad before an international – even for a competitive game – compared to the week or whatever it is they get nowadays, so you didn't get to know the other players that well unless you're a regular in the squad.

You've also got to remember that when I joined up with England I suddenly had to become a team-mate of the players who I basically took the mickey out of on a Saturday afternoon. Unsurprisingly, they didn't really want to talk to me and when they did, they weren't particularly friendly. I understood that and I didn't have a problem with it at all. At various times I had some of the QPR boys in the squad with me – Dave Thomas, Dave Clement and Phil Parkes – but sometimes I'd be the only one.

Would I have won more caps if I'd played for a bigger club? I don't think so. QPR were one of the best – if not the most fashionable teams around at that time. It's just that none of our England players became regulars, except for Gerry Francis, who was captain for a while and would have won many more than 12 caps if it weren't for his dodgy back. Much more disappointing than only winning five caps was the fact that Gerry and me didn't get to carry our partnership with QPR into the England side. Even though Gerry didn't approve of my lifestyle, within 20 minutes of playing together we knew exactly where the other was coming from. Our understanding was almost telepathic. But for one reason or another we never played for England together, which was a shame because as a pair we were unstoppable at times. He's still my best friend in football and I know it's something we both regret.

I actually made my England debut under Sir Alf Ramsey. He first picked me for an England XI in one of the old Football League representative games against a Scotland XI at Maine Road in March 1974. I scored twice and played really well in a 5-0 win and afterwards he came over and said to me: "I might see you again soon, Stanley."

Believe it or not I actually quite liked Alf. Even though he was quite straight-laced and I was, well, you know. He was always nice to me, always fair. He was also true to his word and a month later I did see Alf again, as I made my England bow alongside five other debutants in a friendly against Portugal in Lisbon.

We drew 0-0 and I did alright I suppose – as well as anybody else. But Alf would never tell you a lot; he wasn't one of these managers who would say, "Well done, good game". He would leave you in limbo as if to say "I might see you again, I might not", but that didn't bother me. Like I said, it didn't really bother me whether I played for England or not, so I didn't lose any sleep over whether he'd pick me for the next match.

As it happens, Alf was sacked less than a month later. His replacement, although only as caretaker-manager, was Coventry City general manager and former England captain Joe Mercer.

I was born in Collyhurst, one of Manchester's roughest areas, and joined Manchester City as an apprentice, much to my old man's delight. City won everything when I was there: League title, FA Cup, League Cup, you name it. They were a good side. I was only 18 when I scored twice on my debut in the League Cup against Leicester City in September 1967, but with the likes of Colin Bell, Mike Summerbee, Francis Lee and all that lot in the team, I was never gonna get much of a look-in.

At the time I started running bets across town for Manchester's infamous underworld organisation, the 'Quality Street Gang'. I was making more money from that than I was from playing football – a lot more – so I didn't bother turning up for training most of the time.

My manager at Maine Road was one Joe Mercer. Joe was a bit of a father figure to me in the beginning, but Malcolm Allison, who was Joe's assistant before taking over as manager himself, didn't like my attitude. Alright, I admit it, I was a bit fiery in them days, and you could say we clashed. There had been a lot of flash points between us, but the crunch came in July 1970 when I had a bit of a 'falling out' with Malcolm in a Manchester nightclub. He took huge exception to me being out late, frequenting one of *his* regular haunts, and after a bit of an altercation he threw a punch at me. I threw one back and eventually we had to be pulled apart. That was the second punch-up we'd had and was probably the straw that broke the camel's back!

City sacked me, they probably didn't have any choice. Indirectly, they actually did me a favour – it was probably the kick up the arse I needed. Suddenly I wasn't earning a proper wage and was told by Joe Mercer and Malcolm Allison that I would never play professional football again. After just five games, I also got sacked from my next club, Bury, and the only reason I even made a comeback was to prove Joe and Malcolm wrong. I had to go to Crewe and Carlisle to sort my head out, which eventually I did, before I joined QPR, where I made my name.

Later on, I made up with both Joe and Malcolm. We all do stupid things when we're young and I was no different. Saying that, they both said I was hanging around with the wrong people then and I'm still hanging around with the same people now!

Joe Mercer picked me for his first squad as England caretaker-manager – for the annual Home Internationals tournament, which was played over a period of one week at the end of the domestic season. To be fair, I had been playing so well for QPR since the last England game against Portugal that there was no way he couldn't pick me. But because he had sacked me from Manchester City, I always had it in the back of my mind that something might happen again. Even though Joe came out publicly and said he didn't bear a grudge, I still felt uneasy.

Nevertheless, I was in the starting line-up for our first game against Wales in Cardiff and I played reasonably well in a 2-0 win, scoring the opening goal – my only goal for England – with Kevin Keegan getting the other.

Keegan was somebody I always admired. He made the best out of his limited footballing ability through sheer hard work and dedication – pretty much the total opposite of me – and I always got on with him Ok.

Joe named an unchanged side for the next Home Internationals match against Northern Ireland at Wembley four days later. It was 0-0 at half-time and none of us were playing particularly well. In the dressing room I heard Joe telling Harold Shepherdson, the trainer, to take me off ten minutes into the second half. And that's exactly what he did. No matter what I'd done in those ten minutes he was gonna pull me off. Funnily enough it was another 'character', Frank Worthington, who replaced me.

Joe could have taken me off at half-time and I wouldn't have minded so much, but to send me back out there for five or ten minutes… what's the point? It was in my mind that he'd done it on purpose to humiliate me and to this day, I still believe that to be the case. I walked straight down the tunnel, got changed and went back to the team hotel. I had the needle, I had the hump. And I still had the hump the following day. I turned to my room-mate Mick Channon and said "I'm leaving, Mick."

"You can't, Stan," he said.

"You watch me," I said. "You see that car outside? That's taking me back to London." – and off I went. That's the way I am. Once I get something into my head, I can't get it out. I didn't play for England again for two and a half years – until a new man was in charge.

Do I regret walking out? Not at all.

Like I said, I didn't really care that much about playing for England, so I think they missed out more than me. During those two and a half years I was virtually unstoppable, especially during the 1975-76 season when Liverpool just pipped QPR to the League title. Obviously, it was Joe Mercer who kept me out originally, but when Don Revie was appointed manager full time, I suppose I did think I would get called up a bit sooner, yeah.

Funnily enough, I liked Don Revie, even though he was known as another strict disciplinarian and, well, I didn't like people telling me what to do. I liked his Leeds team, they had a bit of everything – a bit of skill, a bit of bite – and so did he. Obviously all the carpet bowls and the table tennis and the bingo he made his players play wasn't my cup of tea; it was boring as hell – we didn't even play for money! Unfortunately, it was more or less compulsory on England duty under Revie, but it was only for a couple of hours before each game and I just put it down to being one of Don's little quirks. When it came to football, though, he knew what he was talking about.

The reason he didn't pick me earlier had nothing to do with football. It was more down to my character – I know that for a fact because people who knew Don at the time told me. Even then, I don't think it was down to Don Revie so much as other people at the FA. I'd had a few run-ins with them over the years and they really didn't like me. One time I got banned for eight weeks, which was a record at the time. If it had been anyone else the ban would have been much less, but they hated me and wanted to make a scapegoat out of me. I lived in Paddington at the time, so FA headquarters were only round the corner at Lancaster Gate. I knew what was coming at the hearing, so I thought "Sod 'em", and turned up in jeans and a T-shirt.

In the end it was the press that got me back into the squad, pure and simple. I'd had my run-ins with them over the years, particularly some of the tabloids, but they were in my corner this time, I'll say that much for them. Almost every week for two years they were saying "He's gotta be recalled," but after England only just beat Finland 2-1 at Wembley in October 1976, the newspapers – especially the London press – starting campaigning almost daily to get me back in. Even some of the journalists who had slated me in the past wanted me to play.

But I still didn't think I'd get the call. If they hadn't bothered picking me before, why would they bother picking me now?

When I'd walked out on England two and a half years earlier, I thought I'd never play international football again. And because it had been so long, I'd almost come to terms with the fact. Why did things change? Because they had to. Even though the World Cup qualifying campaign was only two games in, England's next game against Italy in Rome was seen as a virtual group decider. We were both expected to beat both of the other two teams in the group – Finland and Luxembourg – comfortably, so if we got the better of the Italians over two games, we were virtually assured of going through. If honours were even, it would probably go down to goal difference and after two games against Finland, England's wasn't great at +4.

I'd carried my form from the previous season into the start of the next one and I was already on the verge of equalling Denis Law's record for most number of goals scored by a British player in a single European campaign. There's no doubt I was the man in form and Don Revie was under pressure to introduce some fresh blood. I was the obvious choice.

Don didn't have any what-you'd-call old-fashioned centre forwards in his squad, probably because he thought the Italian defenders would be too clever for them. He was probably right. One option was Joe Royle, who had played in the first qualifier; the other was Manchester United's Stuart Pearson, who had played in the second. But United had just been well beaten by Juventus in the UEFA Cup and seven of those Juventus players would be in the Italian line-up. Stuart hadn't got much change out of them then, so Don probably thought he wouldn't get much change out of them now.

The press had it down as a straight fight between me and Trevor Francis for the last striker's spot. As luck would have it, the Saturday before the squad was due to be announced, we had a league game against Birmingham City, who Trevor played for at the time, and the press built it up as some sort of *High Noon* bollocks. But the club secretary at QPR had already told me I'd got the nod, so it was a load of fuss over nothing.

The squad was announced on the Monday and two days later I equalled Denis's European goalscoring record against Slovan Bratislava. Having scored two in the first leg – a 3-3 draw over there that many people say was one of the great performances by an English club in Europe – I got another at Loftus Road in a 5-2 win. That made it nine in four European games and I think the fact that I was doing the business in Europe as well as domestically convinced Don Revie I could do it in the Italy game.

When the squad was announced, I thought I might get on as sub in the second half – you know, if we needed a goal – but as the game got nearer rumours were rife in the press that I'd be on from the start. Two days before the game, the rumours turned out to be true.

The game was on a Wednesday afternoon, but I didn't join up with the rest of the squad on the Saturday, even though Revie had managed to persuade the League to postpone games involving squad players, because I was in bed with a flu bug. I was renting a flat opposite the dole office in Ealing at the time – a hundred quid a week it was, even back then – and that's where I was when the phone rang on the Monday. It was Don Revie on the other end and he said, "if you're well enough to join up with the rest of the squad tomorrow, you're in, you're playing, you'll be in the starting line-up."

My mind went back to a year earlier, when I was on the verge of an England recall for the European Championship qualifier against Portugal, but was ruled out with a groin injury. It was the only time during my two-and-a-half-year international exile that I'd looked like earning a reprieve. It was seven months until England's next game and by then the FA had thought better of it.

I wasn't feeling the best when I took the call from Revie, but I didn't want to miss out again. Like I said, I wasn't that bothered about playing for England, but this was the World Cup. Even I don't say "No" to a chance like that. And when he said I'd be in the starting line-up, I didn't think twice. I got out of bed, still a bit shaky, and flew to Rome on my own the day before the game. I didn't arrive until the evening, so I didn't have time to do any serious training. Don sent me straight to bed to keep me quarantined from the rest of the squad, which suited me down to the ground because they were all playing bloody carpet bowls and bingo at the time! The squad hadn't even been allowed out of the hotel to soak up Rome's many sights. This was a big, big game and the police said they couldn't guarantee the safety of the players – the Italian fans would probably try to lynch us.

I wasn't there that long, but the reaction from the rest of the squad was just the same as before. Cloughie's Derby boys kept themselves to themselves as usual. Mick Channon, Dave Clement and Kevin Keegan were the only ones who really talked to me. I hadn't been in the squad for ages and I think most of the players were a bit surprised that I'd come straight into the team, know what I mean? I don't give a toss if people don't want to talk to me, though. I was there to play football.

Matters didn't improve on the morning of the game, when Don Revie told us he'd got appearance money up to 300 quid from 200 quid. The players had a meeting before the game and Emlyn Hughes got up and said "We should play for nothing to wear the three lions on our shirt." So I chirped up and said "Ok, well I'll have yours then!" Did he see the funny side of it? Did he f***?! Not at all. Nobody spoke to me after that! Ha ha ha!!!

The Italians reacted to my inclusion by changing their starting line-up. Out went their usual centre-half, Mozzini, and in came the faster, nastier Claudio Gentile to do a man-marking job on me. People have said that perhaps I was brought into the side because I was more of an unknown quantity than some of the other strikers, that I would take the Italians by surprise, but I don't know about that. The Italians always did their homework and their manager Enzo Bearzot knew quite a bit about me through speaking to coaches in England. He even talked me up before the game, comparing my finishing to Jimmy Greaves. Denis Law, one of my heroes, had said the same thing, but I didn't feel any extra pressure and I didn't let it go to my head. My attitude never changed because of what people said to me, it wasn't important.

I felt much more like me old self by the morning of the game, but because I'd been ill, I didn't have much preparation time. At that late stage you only do a bit of light work. Then we went through how we were gonna play. Mick Channon would be the main striker, with myself and Kevin Keegan playing just off him and Trevor Brooking as the only midfielder playmaker. This meant I would be playing slightly out of position. I was all left foot – anybody who knew me will tell you that my right foot was a complete waste of space – but I used to play on the right for QPR and cut inside to devastating effect. But this is England we're talking about here – you just have to play where you're told. Looking back, I suppose the thinking could have been that I was the only front player in the country who could beat a defence on my own! I had a few tricks up my sleeve, but beat the entire Italian defence? That was asking a lot, even for me!

The funny thing is, England's two previous games were both against Finland, much weaker opposition than the Italians, and Don Revie played arguably his most attacking teams, which would have suited me down to the ground. But apart from myself and those three I just mentioned, the rest of the team were defenders by trade, which tells you pretty much all you need to know about how we set out our stall. Of course we wanted the win – I think Don hoped than me or Kevin Keegan could nick a goal with a bit of magic – but we certainly planned for the draw. As it turned out, that wouldn't have been a bad result, as had we got a point there we would have qualified, so you can understand his thinking.

We had a police escort to the ground several hours before kick-off and I couldn't see what all the fuss was about; the streets of Rome were deserted. It was like a ghost town. Rome's Olympic Stadium is surrounded by a moat and lined-up along the front of it there were hundreds of stone-faced policemen, with these big Alsatian dogs barking like mad and straining at the leash. But there was still no sign of these mad Italians fans we'd been hearing about. It was only when we went out onto the pitch in our smart England suits to soak up the atmosphere that I realised why we hadn't been allowed out of the hotel…

The place was packed. It was still three hours before kick-off, but there they were: 85,000 hysterical Italians and they weren't at all pleased to see us. There were firecrackers going off, flags waving and giant banners everywhere.

I'd played at the Olympic Stadium before, on the way to helping Carlisle win the 1970 Anglo-Italian Cup, so I knew exactly what to expect. Besides, a hostile atmosphere never bothered me. In fact, I probably thrived on it. Unfortunately, I was in the minority.

"Look at that lot," said Dave Clement. I looked round and he was frozen to the spot, a look of terror on his face. There were others too, players who had all played in loads of big games and in many more internationals than I had. All crapping themselves.

My second game for Nottingham Forest was in front of 120,000 against Barcelona at the Nou Camp and in the dressing room beforehand I remember people like Martin O'Neill and Kenny Burns sitting there absolutely terrified. Frank McLintock would be the same before big games when we were at QPR together. I never understood that. I'd be like, "What are you worried about the crowd for? They can't do nothing to ya." That was the case even more so in Rome, because the crowd were miles away from the pitch. I've never been a nervous person. Pull a gun on me and I'd be nervous, but 85,000 mad Italians? All in a day's work.

He was a total git, that Gentile, and an ugly git as well. The first thing he did was spit in my face. He knew I was temperamental and was trying to get a rise out of me. What did I do? Rise above it? No. I bit, obviously. I always bit, although I had calmed down a bit since my younger days. I wouldn't say it put me off my game because I'd always been the same. It was mostly verbal retaliation with me anyway and the **** couldn't understand me, could he? He was Italian.

They were all at it; spitting, pulling your shirt, standing on your toes – it was non-stop. That's just what they were like. You've got to remember, there weren't so many television cameras back then, so you could get away with a lot more.

As you'd expect, the Italians started pretty quickly, but we weathered the early storm and as the first half wore on we got more and more comfortable. They had a lot of ball, but most of it was in front of our back four, where Trevor Cherry and Brian Greenhoff snuffed out any trouble. There were a lot of fouls in the first half and it threatened to boil over a couple of times. England had come back from 2-0 down to beat Italy in New York the previous summer, but it had been anything but 'friendly'. Dave Clement had nearly come to blows with their veteran defender Giacinto Fachetti and both were in the line-ups again, so there was a little bit of history there. A scrappy game suited us, though. We knew that the longer it stayed 0-0, the more likely it would be that crowd would start to get on their backs – and off of ours.

We didn't offer much going forward in the first half – I hardly saw the ball – but that was the plan; keep it tight, frustrate the Italians and try to nick a goal on the break. They did have a couple of half chances, both of them created by Franco Causio, who was their best player on the day. He was fast and skilful and the only player we didn't really have any answer to.

In the 36th minute, just as we were starting to look like we had things under control heading towards te break, Causio cut inside from his position on the right wing and was brought down five yards outside the penalty box. Antognoni drove the ensuing free-kick hard towards our goal, but Ray Clemence looked to have it covered until it took a wicked deflection off Kevin Keegan and flew into the back of the net. On the balance of play, they probably deserved their lead, but it was a lucky goal and a bit of a sickener for us. It really knocked the stuffing out of us and for the rest of the first half they really put us under the cosh.

For some reason, our approach didn't change much in the second half. Don Revie asked for more of the same. Maybe he thought we could still nick a goal, with a draw the best we could hope for. Maybe he'd settled for the 1-0 and hoped we could make up the goal difference against Luxembourg before beating Italy at Wembley.

Either way, we'd only had one shot on goal all game when the Italians scored their second. Again, it was Causio who started the move, beating a couple of defenders before feeding their left winger. He crossed and Roberto Bettaga, the golden boy of Italian football at the time, soared through the air and directed his header into the bottom corner. It was a bloody good goal.

At 2-0, we had nothing to lose – except another goal – so at last we pressed forward. Brian Greenhoff and Trevor Cherry both went close and I had a couple of shots, but the Italians were experts at shutting up shop, and it was more likely that the third goal would come from them. At the final whistle, I had a row with the officials – you can see the incident on the TV highlights. Flaming Gentile was still following me around, then these other gits started spitting on me as well. I shared everyone else's frustration and decided to take it out on the referee and his two linesmen. Barring a miracle, we were out of the World Cup, so everybody was obviously gutted. I was nearly 28 and I knew this would be my last chance to play in a World Cup finals, and the same went for many of the other players. We didn't take it particularly well. But it was obvious that it would take a miracle for us to overhaul the Italians now.

Even though he would be in charge for two more games, Don Revie cracked open the champagne and announced on the way home that he was intending to stand down. Of course, all hell broke loose when it emerged later that he'd been negotiating behind the FA's back to take over as the manager of the United Arab Emirates, but we were all but out of the World Cup by then, so he might have got the sack.

In hindsight, we were never gonna beat the Italians using those tactics. They were too good going forward to be given that much possession without scoring eventually and too good defensively to concede without being put under pressure. In fact, they were a good side full stop. A lot of those players would still be in the team when they won the World Cup in 1982. In the end, the best team won, so we might as well have had a go at them from the start. We'd have stood a much better chance of winning that way in my opinion.

As for me, I had to be more disciplined than I was used to. If they had let me loose to do what I did for QPR things might have been a bit different. Looking back, I should have just took the law into my own hands, thought "Sod it" and played my natural game. I had a couple of shots late on, but it's difficult when you've got Gentile following you around for the whole game. Never mind the ball, he was only interested in me. If someone is clever enough and fit enough and intent on following you around the pitch, you won't get away from them no matter who you are, even if they have to kick you. The same thing used to happen to me in England. But if your team is set up in a more attacking way, you're gonna have some help, and you're gonna find more space.

Although Don Revie chopped and changed his team more than any England manager in history, I, more than anyone, wasn't used to playing with those players. It seemed like a lot of them didn't want to pass to me. As I said they fair hated me for taking the mickey out of the on a regular basis in the First Division. Add that into the equation and it was asking a lot for me to come in as some sort of saviour after a two-and-a-half year absence, but what can you do?

None of the press blamed Don for including me. They couldn't really as they'd all been caling for him to pick me! In fact, I think he picked the best team that was available to him. Maybe some of those players froze in that atmosphere, but I think the Italians simply had the edge over us – pure and simple.

The reality was that England just didn't have the players at that time. It was a bit like the Graham Taylor era. You can only work with what you've got and if the opposition have better players than you, you're going to struggle.

I suppose you could argue that the Revie deliberately brought me back for a game that wouldn't suit me, hoping that I didn't do much so that he then had a reason to drop me, but I'm not sure that was the case. Ok, I didn't have a great game, but nobody was outstanding. Besides, I was in the team for the next game, a friendly at Wembley against a Holland team including Cruyff, Neeskens and all that lot. In truth, they taught us a footballing lesson. It was only 2-0, but it could have been a lot more.

That was the game in which I wore two different makes of football boots. You've probably heard the story before, but I was contracted to Gola at the time and I got an extra 200 quid every time I played for England wearing Gola boots. The Gola rep would come to the team hotel in the morning carrying cash for the Gola endorsees. You'd even get an extra 50 quid if you had your picture taken for the paper wearing a Gola T-shirt – obviously I was always up for a bit of that.

Later that day, the Adidas rep came to the hotel with money for their contracted players – 250 quid for each game. I caught wind of this and went to see him. He agreed to pay me the same if I wore Adidas boots, so I took the cash. "You can't do that," said Mick Channon again.

"I can and I will," I said. "You just watch me."

Then one of the other players pointed out that I was now obliged to wear both boots. "What are you gonna do?" he asked, so I wore one boot on each foot.

Nobody found out until a few days later, but when they did, needless to say I wasn't contracted to Gola for much longer!

I'm sure my shenanigans had nothing to do with it, but that was the last time I played for England. OK, perhaps they did!

People say I should have won 40 or 50 caps and if it wasn't for my own stubbornness I probably would have, but like I said, I wasn't that bothered. It's not like I set out to achieve certain things in my career, let alone play for England. In fact, I only ended up playing football at all because I was forced into it by my father. And I've never really watched football unless I had a bet on!

Besides, England caps don't put food on the table. Of the five I won, I haven't got any left. When I won my first cap it was a special moment for my parents, so I gave it to my mum to keep as a souvenir. I found out later that her little Shitzsu was sleeping in it. Jim Gregory, my old chairman at QPR, paid 160 quid to have it restored, so I let him keep it to thank him for the trouble. When Jim died, I let his wife keep it as a memento. As for the other four, I sold one of them. They were hand-made in those days – unlike today when they come off a conveyer belt – so I got about three grand for it. I lost another one in a card game and my daughter's got the other two, which she won't give to me in case I sell them! Or lose them in another card game – old habits die hard!

KENNY SANSOM
LEFT-BACK

SPAIN 1982

BORN   26th September 1958, Camberwell
CLUBS   Crystal Palace, Arsenal, Newcastle United
INTERNATIONAL DEBUT   May 1979 v Wales
ENGLAND CAREER   86 caps, 1 goal
INTERNATIONAL FAREWELL   June 1988 v USSR

A model of consistency for almost a decade in an England shirt, chirpy Kenny Sansom filled the left-back slot with great distinction. His cultured left foot and limitless energy made him one of the first names on any teamsheet filled in by Ron Greenwood and Bobby Robson. As part of the solid defence which saw England go through the entire World Cup Finals in Spain without defeat and only conceding one goal, Sansom can rightly claim to be a World Cup legend. Now a renowned football pundit with wit to burn, Sansom can be regularly heard on LBC radio and seen on Sky Sports.

ENGLAND 0 v SPAIN 0

World Cup Finals Second Round Group B
Monday 5 July 1982

Bernabéu Stadium, Madrid
Attendance 75,000

England fail to score for the second game in a row and go out having failed to win the game by the necessary two clear goals to qualify for the semi-finals instead of those pesky Germans

Teams

Ron Greenwood	**Managers**	Jose Emilio Santamaria
Peter Shilton		Luis Arconada
Mick Mills		Santiago Urquiaga
Kenny Sansom		Miguel Tendillo
		(Sub. Tomas Maceda)
Terry Butcher		José Ramón Alexanco
Phil Thompson		Rafael Gordillo
Ray Wilkins		Enrique Saura
		(Sub. Uralde)
Bryan Robson		Joaquín Alonso
Graham Rix		Jesús Zamora
(Sub. Trevor Brooking)		
Paul Mariner		José Antonio Camacho
Trevor Francis		Jesús Satrustegui
Tony Woodcock		Santillana
(Sub. Kevin Keegan)		

Referee: Alexis Ponnet (Belgium)

IT'S NEVER NICE to have regrets and in general I don't have any from my career. The summer of 1982, however is one. While on the one hand the 1982 World Cup was one of the highlights of my time in the game, it also fills me with regret as I truly feel that we had the team, the manager and the form to win the World Cup. Instead we only reached the second phase and came home, despite not losing a game and conceding only one goal.

We went to Spain with two of our best players, Kevin Keegan the skipper, and Trevor Brooking, not fully fit, with neither playing in any of the first four matches. But no matter, we proved we were a match for some of the best teams in the world, Eventually, though, it wasn't to be and when I look back now, that hurts. Ok, maybe not hurts, but if I think about it that certainly frustrates.

By 1982, I had been playing for my country for a few years having emerged as a 16-year-old left-back in the exciting Crystal Palace team that had so many tongues wagging at the end of 1970s. I made my debut for Palace before my 17th birthday party against Tranmere on Merseyside. I remember the train journey up there. I was a nervous little schoolboy, and for the whole journey whenever I looked up, our winger Peter Taylor, who is now the England Under-21 manager, mouthed over to me, "I...LOVE...YOU!" Git. That was that, I had my head down for the whole trip.

Terry Venables came in and took over a very good, young side who had played together from a young age. Terry was great. We were eager with big ears, more than willing to listen. Whatever Terry said went. Those were special days at Palace.

We had some terrific young players like Vince Hilaire, and it was a great club to learn at. I have seen a new book on us all recently and it was strange seeing all of those photos of myself looking so young and so fresh. My wife saw them and said it reminded me of a time when she had the hots for me! Fortunately, Arsenal also saw something in me that they liked and signed me in 1980 in a swap deal for Clive Allen, who himself had only just joined Arsenal. That was a bit of a strange one.

The Gunners were getting an England international when they signed me as I had made my debut in 1979. Terry Venables had Palace playing a certain way and it involved us closing people down very, very quickly. We would rush the opposition into making mistakes by pressing them hard in their half and it worked wonderfully well. Then, here I am playing my first international against Wales at Wembley, and in the first minute the ball is with the Welsh and I'm screaming at Tony Currie to go and press the play. I'll never forget Tony's face. "Push 'em in, Tone," I screamed and he gave me this look as if to say, "Are you mad?" From that moment I knew, in international football things are done a little bit differently. I loved every minute of it, mind, and Jack Charlton, after the game, was kind enough to say that mine was one of the best England debuts he had ever seen.

It was 0-0, a boring game. I think I actually found my England schoolboy debut against Germany a more memorable occasion. I had never been to Wembley in my life. On the Friday night before the game they took us to see the place and I recall thinking "Wow!" The pitch, the place, the history, it took your breath away.

Ron Greenwood, our manager, was totally different from Terry Venables. Both were fine coaches, but Ron was a far quieter and thoughtful character. He was a very clever man and knew how to get the best out of us all. We would meet on a Sunday before an England game on the Wednesday and when we got to the hotel and met up, he would say, "Right you lot. Off to the pub for a team meeting or what?" And that's what we'd do. We'd all go down there for a beer and a chat and that always relaxed the lads. Trevor Brooking would be there. "What do you want to drink, Trev?" someone would ask. "A Coke, please," Trevor would say.

"Yeah. But what do you want in it?" said the bemused team-mate.

"Ice." Good old Trevor.

He may have been quiet, but Ron had firm ideas about how to coach and how to play the game. His one big thing was to let the ball do the work. Knock the ball in front of your team-mate; let him run onto a pass instead of having to control one. Simple things really, but very effective. Let the ball do the work.

Poor Ron never liked dropping people. I think he had to tell Alvin Martin that he wasn't going in 1982 and you could see how uncomfortable that made Ron. The lads could tell when there was bad news coming their way because Ron would walk toward them, and that always meant bad news. You'd be training before a game, Ron would walk toward you, and bang, you knew were dropped. I remember training once, and Ron started to walk towards Glenn Hoddle. "Oh no. I'm not playing," said Glenn and he turns and runs up to the other end of the pitch.

My first taste of a big international tournament was the European Championships of 1980 that were held in Italy. That was a wonderful experience for me. We played against Italy, of course, and lost. I had to mark Causio, which was incredible. With his big moustache I thought he'd eaten a squirrel. What a player though.

It was fantastic to be involved. Maybe more so then for the likes of us than it is for the millionaires today. I was 21 and loved things like picking up my kit. My name was on the tracksuit; we had the bus, hotels and were to spend the summer together in beautiful Italy. What a buzz. We didn't do brilliantly, but I remember coming home and thinking, I want more of that and couldn't wait for the World Cup two years later.

Those hopes were, at one point, looking fruitless, as our qualifying games were a little shaky. We lost in Romania, Switzerland and in Norway. No other England side has lost as many qualifiers and still made it to the finals. The latter defeat had the Norwegian commentator sprouting famously about how Margaret Thatcher, Winston Churchill and Lady Diana had taken a right beating. I didn't play that night, so I feel no responsibility for such famous Englishmen and women being so humiliated.

It wasn't only Scandinavian television reporters getting hot under the collar. The English press began to turn on Ron and questioned whether he was the man for the job. It was unfair stick. Because of his honesty and the way he managed, we were all behind him and so when he came to us and said he was going to step down in the midst of all this hoo-ha, we were adamant that he shouldn't. The senior players such as Trevor Brooking, Mick Mills, and, of course, Kevin Keegan took him to one side and made him change his mind. They told him that the squad had faith in him and that he should just get on with the job. He did. We pulled off a couple of good wins and, after Romania lost unexpectedly at home to Switzerland, we were off to sunny Spain.

By the time the World Cup came around, Mick Mills, who usually played left-back had made way for me and moved to right-back. That meant Phil Neal's place was under threat and I felt for Phil. I think he is one of the most underrated players England has ever had. He was tremendous. He was the master of certain skills that might not catch the eye. Like marking someone at the far post. Now Phil wasn't the best header of the ball – in fact he never won one in his career I don't think. Having said that, he never really lost one either. He would jump with his opponent and put them off and the ball would always go clear. He was an excellent defender.

It was our first World Cup for 12 years. I was young and relishing every moment, but there may have been pressure on some of the older guys. I just wanted to play football, that's all. I wanted to do my best for the team and for myself. I wasn't one to let outside influences worry me.

Instead I got on with enjoying where I was, whom I was with and what I had to do. Our Hotel was magnificent. There had been lots of talk in the winter about what a dump we were going to and that there were dead dogs on the beach. Nothing was further from the truth. It was stunning.

What I remember most was the quality of the food. It was incredible. The place specialised in superb hake fish and we gorged ourselves on the stuff. The wives came out. It was perfect. Smashing. The owner of the hotel took us down to his wine cellar. Whatever year you were born he gave you a bottle from that year. I gave mine to my wife, who only went and put it in the fridge and ruined it. I never forgave her for that! Having said that, I think Terry Butcher opened his right away and said it was the worst tipple he'd ever had. I would have liked to have had the opportunity to try mine.

As I say, I wasn't the sort of player to let the occasion get to me. I could take things in my stride. Yeah it was the World Cup, but that didn't bother me. I don't have memories of watching the finals in '66. I would have been seven years-old, but I didn't even start playing the game until I was 10. We moved house and I was living on an estate, got friendly with some local kids and that was that, I was playing football on the green. We'd watch *The Big Match* with Brian Moore on a Sunday afternoon and then about 28 of us would be out, trying to relive the best moments. The first World Cup I remember was in 1978. Mario Kempes got the goals. What a player.

We arrived with twenty-two of our own great players, and you would inevitably get small groups forming. I would spend a lot of time with Graeme Rix and Glenn Hoddle because of the North London link.

A good game of cards would bring the squad together and whenever possible we would start a game. We'd get to a hotel and it would be, get upstairs, dump your bags and be down in the lobby to start a game in 20 minutes. Peter Shilton never won at cards, but having said that, when he'd go to the toilet on the coach, we'd make sure he had three threes and he'd be chuffed and bet away, unaware that we'd also made sure that someone had three fours!

While Shilts was no doubt unsettled by his poor luck with the cards, Kevin Keegan had more serious things on his mind. The back injury that had hindered him running up to the tournament showed no sign of subsiding. As a squad we got on with things initially, but I guess it became disrupting later when he actually left the camp to get treatment in Germany. It was quite cloak and dagger and I think Ron should have let us all know what was going on. Kevin left surreptitiously at five in the morning and I think that was wrong. Ron may have thought that if he left in broad daylight the press would get hold of it, but we should have been informed because we were all wondering what was going on.

We, though, had other things on our mind, like the opening game to prepare for, and it was going to be tough. France had some of the best players in the world. We were a relaxed confident squad and felt that we could give anyone, even the likes of Michel Platini, a run for their money. As for me, I was confident in my form and felt I would make the starting XI.

We had worked on throw-ins from my side that entailed a delivery to Terry Butcher who would flick it on and set something up. Within twenty seconds we won a throw on the other side. Stevie Coppell takes it, Terry flicks it on and bang, Bryan Robson scores the quickest goal in World Cup history. I think he got a five grand watch for doing that!

It was odd. We were one up and in a way our tactics went out of the window. Despite our good start and the control we had over the match, we let them equalise. A mix-up let Soler score after 25 minutes and I think to this day Terry Butcher blames himself. That's typical of Terry who is constantly worrying and thinking he's in the wrong. Even today he goes on about how he could have stopped Maradona in 1986. No-one was going to stop Maradona that day. Not even Terry!

We remained in control and got two more goals through another Robson goal and a Mariner effort from close range. What a fantastic start to our campaign. You couldn't help but be lifted by that result. As I say they had Tigana, Giresse, Battiston, great players, and, of course, the best of all, Platini. People talk about Pelé, Maradona, Cruyff and Best, but I think Platini deserves to be talked of in that bracket. He is right up with the best. He had a quiet game against us and that shows how well Ray Wilkins and Bryan Robson played.

It had been a boiling hot day and we all lost about 10 pounds in weight. They gave us loads of salt tablets and chocolate bars. Today I think it's wine gums. We all had wet, cold towels over us at half time, but we coped and could look forward to the next game with confidence.

We genuinely thought, after the France game, "We can go and win this." We'd beaten a very good side, coped with the elements, and proved that, as a squad we had gelled. "Why not? Let's go for it!" We had as good a squad as anybody and if we could cope with losing such a fine player as Kevin Keegan against a side like France, why should we fear anyone?

There had been a lot of talk going into the World Cup about hooliganism and a right wing faction of fans who might cause trouble at the tournament on the back of the recent Falklands War. We didn't see any sign of that, but then again we were very sheltered from the outside world.

Remember, we were staying in the Basque region of Spain, a place renowned for terrorist activity and so the security around us was incredibly intense. Our coach would be searched prior to us getting on it every morning, but I actually found that quite exciting. It was quite a buzz. I felt like we were being treated like royalty and it just added to the feeling that we were involved in something very special.

We had the press with us too and had a great relationship with them back then. We would be in the same hotel, having a drink with the press boys, letting them know how things were going. You'd have all the sports writers, loads of them who were good as gold. Then you'd have one or two newsmen coming into the hotel asking the receptionist if any of us had chatted her up or had been causing mischief. It wasn't too bad. Today it's us and them. Press v Players. That's all changed since my day.

It's the same with the fans to a certain extent. We would greet the fans every day and take pictures and sign autographs. Today the coach's windows are blacked out and they seem untouchable. It's a shame because I'm sure most of them don't mind interacting with the supporters.

Our next game was against Czechoslovakia. They were a decent team, but not as strong as they are today. We ran out comfortable 2-0 winners thanks to two scrappy goals, the first from Francis and then an own goal. We really didn't have to impress too much. We were through though and that was the main thing.

We could take our foot off the gas for our last game against Kuwait a little and Ron made a few changes to give other players a game, but we wanted to keep the momentum going. I was 'rested' for the game. I was training, Ron started to walk toward me and I ran away! No, Ron said he wanted to give me a break and give Phil Neal a game. I always wanted to play and was appropriately eager, but I would never have had a go at Ron. I had too much respect for him. He told me I was his first choice and so that was that.

Phil, too, was fine. He was too much of a professional. Of course he was going to be disappointed that he had been left out, if he wasn't he wouldn't be a pro, but he never showed any dissent. He was too good for that.

We beat Kuwait by a solitary Trevor Francis goal. We felt we had options. Francis and Mariner were gelling well up front, well supported by Tony Woodcock, while Wilkins, Robson, Hoddle, Rix and Coppell were in fine form in the middle of the park.

Then the defence was solid as a rock. Butch and Phil Thompson were a great pairing in the middle and Mick and I completed a quality back four. I really couldn't see how we could lose. But that was the problem.

What annoys me about the World Cup of 1982 was how it was organised. Instead of going into a knock-out round, the second phase was another group, this time of three nations. We ended up drawn against the hosts Spain and West Germany. I just feel that we would have beaten both of them, if it had been knockout matches which went to extra-time. We had a better team, no doubt about it in my mind.

Oh well, it was another group scenario and we had to get on with it. We flew down to Madrid where we would play at the Bernabéu. That was very, very special. The pitch was fantastic, it really was. The crowd were right there next to you and when you looked up it seemed to go on and on. I played there three times. In 1987 we played Spain and won 4-2 with Gary Lineker scoring all four.

I remember the crowd throwing full cans of coke at us that night, and it wasn't because we were thirsty.

Up first was Germany and we were all aware that they had some fine players, who would need special attention. I was an attacking full-back and I was on the same side as Manny Kaltz. He was a fantastic full-back for Germany and someone I truly looked up to. Ron was concerned about Kaltz because he would get down the wing and whip in the most fantastic crosses. Ron wanted that threat cut out so I had to curtail his runs. I suppose it stopped my natural game to a certain extent as they also had Pierre Littbarski on the right, so I had a lot to think about.

It was quite a stalemate, but with only minutes left I suddenly had a chance for a very, very rare goal. I don't take free-kicks, never did, for club nor country. But we won a free-kick toward the end of the game, about 25 yards out. Suddenly it's been knocked to me without warning and whack! I've had a go. It whooshed past the post by inches. It's a fact that if we had won that game we would have qualified for the semi-finals to play France again, a team we'd already beaten, and I believe we would have won the World Cup. As I said earlier, when I think about that summer, it frustrates.

I got Karl-Heinz Rummenigge's shirt after that game. What a player. He hit the bar late on. I always thought of him as such a superstar. He was playing in Italy and lived on Lake Como. He used to drive his speedboat to his Mercedes before driving to training. Brilliant. Where did it all go wrong?

Because we didn't want to lose the first game of two, we were defensive and timid. I think that's where we lost it, ultimately. We weren't aggressive enough going forward. You have to try and be positive and concentrate on what you are good at. I think the modern day England team have the same problem. We have the best six attacking players around, but we are too often defensive and timid. In '82, we were a little too negative. That's no disrespect to Ron, or to his assistant Don Howe, who was not as defensive as he is made out. He worked on a lot of attacking training, but deep down he was a defensive coach and with hindsight that showed in the way we played. I think we should have got at them like we did in the France game but, we didn't look like scoring and their defence looked very strong indeed.

Before the Spain game we sat as a squad and watched the Brazil v Italy match. It finished 3-2 to Italy and remains one of the best games I've ever seen. That made us all buzz and we couldn't wait to get out there. It was like being a kid again, watching *The Big Match* and getting onto the local park, except this time it was the Bernabéu!

Even though we had to win the game 2-0 to qualify for the semi-finals as the Germans had beaten Spain 2-1, again we were negative. We were better than the hosts and it mattered little that they were the home team. We didn't suffer from nerves – Ron never allowed that and was such a calming influence – but, somewhere at the back of our minds we were terrified of losing and that hindered our game. We should have been more aggressive, attacked them, won and gone on to win the World Cup, but we played it cagey.

Keegan's injury had hung about and looking back I think it turned out to be quite a hindrance to us all. All the talk was about whether he would play or not and there comes a time when you have to make a decision. Don't delay it, make the decision and then the guy who will take his place is in the right frame of mind.

It affected Kevin. He acted quite strange that summer. It must have been the injury playing on his mind, but he was far from being the best of company. He so wanted to play in the Finals to cap off a wonderful career, and when it looked unlikely he was clearly upset and had a pop at a few people. It was pure frustration I'm sure. Trevor was fine. He is so relaxed and nothing fazed him. He was a total gentleman.

Ron told us to relax and go and play. We needed to win at least 2-0, and we just couldn't break them down. Ray Wilkins began to shoot from further and further out, while Terry Butcher hit one shot agonisingly wide of the post. But it wouldn't go in. Eventually Ron turned to his two injured stars and threw them both on in the hope that they could produce a piece of magic. They'd sat through the whole tournament, but were now on the bench and with the team struggling to break down the Spanish defence, I suppose he felt he had to try something. So he brought them on.

Kevin and Trevor both had half chances to score, but it wasn't to be. Trev jinked round a couple of defenders and had a sight of goal, but his shot flew straight at Arconada. Then Keegan found himself on the end of a tantalisingly juicy cross by Bryan Robson. Mighty Mouse was only about six yards out, but he put his header wide, mis-timing it like a player who hasn't had much match practice – which of course was exactly what he was.

It was fate, we weren't meant to win it. The dressing room was horrible. We hadn't lost a game, but we were out of the World Cup. It was wrong. Cup competitions should be knock-out and as I say, we could have gone on and won it.

We returned home knowing that we hadn't let the country down. We had been very unfortunate, so there was pride amongst that disappointment. You can't shake it though and as the years go by there is a little regret that that particular summer was a lost opportunity.

Losing Kevin and Trevor was always such a blow. Kevin was a natural leader and could upset defenders, while Trevor was such a deft, and gifted player who could create things. You need a bit of luck to win the World Cup and that was our bit of bad luck. If we'd had those two fully fit, would we have won it? I'm going to say "Yes", but the game is not about ifs, so that's that.

It was an emotional send off for Ron, who had decided he would be leaving, as we were desperate to win it for him. He deserved to finish on a high. He was so gracious. There were never any teacups flying across a dressing room, not with Ron. He was far more like Arsene Wenger. He would suggest things rather than tell you. Some players like to be told, do this, do that, but Ron was different. He would suggest you need to work on your fitness and you would respond. Don Howe was the bad cop to Ron's good cop. I got a lot of praise, which was nice. Ron said I had done very well and that pleased me, but really I just did my job.

PETER REID
MIDFIELDER

MEXICO 1986

BORN   20th June 1956, Huyton
CLUBS   Bolton Wanderers, Everton, Queen's Park Rangers
INTERNATIONAL DEBUT   June 1985 v Mexico
ENGLAND CAREER   13 caps
INTERNATIONAL FAREWELL   May 1988 v Switzerland

The engine room of Everton's muti-silverware winning midfield, 1985 Footballer of the Year Peter Reid was taken to the 1986 World Cup by Bobby Robson as a fringe squad player, but starred as replacement for injured skipper Bryan Robson as England progressed to the quarter-final. He became Glenn Hoddle's minder in midfield and ran remorselessly through the mexican heat to win the ball and propel England to that historic date with Diego Maradona's Argentina. But Reid ran out of puff as he chased the midget genius on his way to bag the second of his famous brace and simply cannot forget it.

ENGLAND 1 v ARGENTINA 2

World Cup Quarter-final
Sunday 22 June 1986

Azteca Stadium, Mexico City
Attendance 114,580

England, inspired by Gary Lineker's goals, meet their nemesis in Diego Maradona, who first cheats, and then gloriously dribbles, his way into the infamy books. The quarter-final curse continues

Teams

Bobby Robson	**Managers**	Carlos Bilardo
Peter Shilton		Nery Pumpido
Gary Stevens (Everton)		Jose Luis Cuciuffo
Kenny Sansom		Jose Luis Brown
Terry Fenwick		Oscar Ruggeri
Terry Butcher		Julio Olarticoechea
Peter Reid		Sergio Batista
(Sub. Chris Waddle)		
Trevor Steven		Ricardo Giusti
(Sub. John Barnes)		
Glenn Hoddle		Jorge Burruchaga
		(Sub. Carlos Tapia)
Peter Beardsley		Hector Enrique
Gary Lineker		Jorge Valdano
Steve Hodge		Diego Maradona
Lineker 80	**Scorers**	Maradona 50, 54

Referee: Ali Bennaceur (Tunisia)

AM I MORE philosophical about it now? No, not really. No matter what people say about Argentina being the better side and the genius of Maradona, goals turn games, and that game turned on a goal that should never have been allowed to stand. To go out on penalties – as the team would four years later – must be utterly heartbreaking, but to be beaten by a handball… well, that's even worse. Almost worse than going to the World Cup, getting walloped in the group stages and coming home early. Instead, we fought our way through adversity to reach the quarter-finals, only to be undone by a cheat. I still feel an enormous sense of injustice.

I came to international football quite late – I didn't make my debut until I was 28 – so I knew that my first chance to play in the World Cup would probably be my last. It was always an ambition of mine to play for England, but I had quite a few really serious injuries when I was younger and I think that held me back quite a bit. In fact, a couple of times I did well to even play professional football again, let alone play for England.

First I broke my leg, then I ruptured the cruciate medial ligament in my knee. These days, those injuries can be fixed relatively easily and players are sometimes back playing again within three or four months, but in those days they were career-threatening.

But I was a very determined player, fighting my way back each time, and after moving from Bolton to Everton in 1982, I got called up to the England squad on the back of Everton's success in the mid-80s, when we won major trophies at home and in Europe.

Having just won the First Division title and European Cup Winners Cup in a fantastic campaign in which I was named as the Footballer of the Year, I was called-up to the England squad for an end of season tour to Mexico, exactly a year before the World Cup. As well as playing three games – against Italy, Mexico and West Germany – Bobby Robson wanted to do a bit of a reccie and some acclimitisation ahead of the finals, with qualification almost in the bag.

I made my debut in the Mexico game. The oppressive conditions were like nothing we were used to at home, but at least we knew what to expect the following summer. For me, it was very much a case of making up for lost time as an England player. To be fair, it was a massive bonus to play for my country after the injuries I'd had, so I was determined to enjoy every last minute of it and grab every single opportunity with both hands. But to play in the World Cup finals, well… that's something else entirely.

For me, that World Cup was a Godsend – and not just because I was fulfilling a boyhood dream. I was one of four Everton players who travelled to Mexico as part of England's World Cup squad having just missed out to Liverpool in both the league and the FA Cup atthe end of another epic season. I sat on the sidelines, injured and helpless, as we lost at Oxford United to all but seal our fate in the title race, and for an hour of the FA Cup final we were the better side, before Liverpool ran out 3-1 winners. They took all the plaudits as the first team to do the Double for 15 years, but I thought we were unlucky not to win at least one trophy. I was p***ed off.

After the Cup final, the two teams travelled back up to Liverpool together – could you imagine that these days? – but I was the one player who didn't get on the bus. I'm a Scouser, I love the city and I was a Liverpudlian as a kid, but I wasn't having any of that luvvy-duvvy nonsense, so I made me own way home. I had nothing against any of the Liverpool lads, but I didn't want to get on a bus with them having just been beaten in the FA Cup final.

After those disappointments with Everton, it was great that the World Cup came around so quickly. It was a case of, "Get me out of here, let me train and if I get a game, even better!"

After a few days off, me and the other Everton players flew out to Colorado Springs to join the rest of the England squad. Training at 7,000 feet above sea level, the same altitude as Mexico City, would prepare us for the knockout stages of the World Cup – if we made it that far – but the Rocky Mountains also threw up some much more unexpected weather. I remember during one training session we were wearing these vests especially designed to cool the body down, when this storm blew over and hailstones the size of tennis balls started falling from the sky! It was murder.

Overall, though, preparations went great. The facilities at the US Air Base where we stayed were fantastic, giving us every opportunity to get fit and acclimatise in time for the tournament. For the Everton players, it was just a case of recuperating and keeping ourselves ticking over, because we'd already played about 60 games that season. While the rest of the lads flew to Los Angeles for the first of two warm-up games against Mexico [the second was in Vancouver against Canada] we got ourselves back into the swing of things.

We played our three group games in Monterrey, which was an industrial city in the middle of the desert. They were the most oppressive conditions you could wish to play football in. The heat was searing, well over 100 degrees most days, but unlike the other host cities, Monterrey was only 1,500 feet above sea. In further preparation for the knockout stages – and to keep us away from the noise of the city – Bobby Robson based us at 5,000 feet, up in the hills in a place called Saltillo. For training and games, we had a 45-minute coach ride through bandit country to Monterrey, with an armed police escort for company. Then we'd go back up the hill, have barbecues, play cricket… nothing too strenuous, just a matter of getting used to the high altitude.

I only had five caps to my name when the squad was announced, and only one of those came in qualifying – in a 1-1 draw with Romania. With Bryan Robson, our skipper and most influential player, and another class player, Ray Wilkins, in central midfield, I went to Mexico as very much a squad player.

Although Robbo and Butch had bags more international experience than me, we were all the same age and I knew them from when we are all young lads, when I was playing for Bolton, Bryan was at West Brom and Ray was at Chelsea – where he was already captain. So in a way, we all grew up playing against each other in midfield. Having played against them and done well, I was always confident in my ability to do a job if either of them couldn't play for any reason.

With the amount of games you have to play in such a short space of time, the World Cup is so demanding – physically and mentally – that there's no way you're going to able to use the same 11 players for every match. So you can never go into it thinking you're never gonna play, especially as an outfield player.

I've always thought that competition football is about how good your squad is, not just how good your team is. If you want an example, you've only got to look at 1966, when Alf Ramsey started the tournament with wingers. John Connelly, Ian Callaghan and Terry Paine all started games, then he decided to do away with wingers and Alan Ball and Martin Peters ended up in the wide positions. And look at Hursty. He only got into the team because Greavesy was injured.

With a whole squad to choose from, I firmly believe that the coach has to be very brave in certain situations. Leave some players out in certain games to keep them fresh, change things if he thinks he has to. We'll see if Sven-Göran Eriksson is able to do that if any of his players need it in Germany.

As a player, you're professional enough to understand the situation. You're in the same squad, on the same side, and you know there are only gonna be 11 lucky ones for each game. Players are brought up in a similar competitive environment with their clubs. If I ever dropped a player and he wasn't disappointed, I'd wonder what's the matter with him. It's Ok to show you're disappointment to a certain extent. It shows that you care and that you're chomping at the bit.

I wasn't even a substitute for the first game against Portugal – you could only name five in those days – but as I sat on the bench in the sweltering heat, my mind went back to the warm-up games a year earlier. I remembered running around thinking, "How much longer can this go on without any substitutions?" It was that hot. You'd never sit there wishing somebody would get injured, but with the intensity of the heat, I was even more convinced that I'd get my chance at some point.

Poland were the seeded team in Group F and would play all their games at Monterrey's main stadium, the Universitario. The other three teams had to play each other at the Technologico, which was basically like a Third Division ground. The facilities were poor, the pitch was crap and the crowd was much smaller than we were used to.

I wouldn't use that as an excuse for losing that opening match against Portugal. We actually controlled most of the game, but we just couldn't put the ball in the net. Then they hit us on the break 15 minutes from time and that was that. Obviously it wasn't a great start, but it wasn't the end of the world.

The relationship between the players and the media was a lot more open back then. We all stayed in the same hotel, and we'd sit around the pool chatting to them every day. It was great really, and although I wouldn't say we were all mates, the press would rarely 'turn you over', because everybody knew each other.

But the relationship started to change around that time. You expect it now, with the massive popularity of the game and the media interest that goes with it, but even 20 years ago we took some serious stick, some of it personal, with the manager on the receiving end more than most.

After the Portugal game there were calls in the press for Bobby to leave out Robbo. Bryan had come off after aggravating an ankle injury and his shoulder, having been dislocated recently in the warm-up game against Mexico, was liable to pop out at any time. I remember him telling me it was the most painful injury he'd ever had – and he had a lot! – but he was as brave as a lion, a winner, and he was that focused on the cause that he was willing to risk getting injured.

But I understand completely why Bobby did everything he could to have Robbo out on the pitch. He's a top top player, your captain and most influential member of the team. It's a chance you have to take. And I don't blame Bryan for wanting to play.

As it turned out, everybody's worst fears were realised when Robbo went over on his shoulder just before half-time in the next game against Morocco and out it popped. We were expected to beat the Africans easily, but they proved to be a tough nut to crack even with our first choice central midfield out there. Then things got even worse. Two minutes later Butch was sent off after throwing the ball petulantly in the direction of the referee and picking up his second booking. Ray was usually such a disciplined player, and I think he was just frustrated with the way the game was going more than anything. It was a nightmare couple of minutes.

I don't know whether it was the heat, the pressure of the game or what, but we looked laboured in that first half. And when it ain't going for you, it ain't going for you – what happened to Robbo and Butch just about summed up our luck. As a North African team, the conditions obviously suited them more than they suited us, but to be fair, we pulled ourselves together in the second half and actually played pretty well – better than we did with eleven men – but a 0-0 draw meant there was massive pressure on the next game. Massive.

We were thousands of miles from home, and there wasn't the technology that there is today. No mobile phones, no internet. But we weren't stupid. We knew we were getting hammered by the press and we knew we'd get even more stick if we didn't beat Poland – and rightly so. We had no choice. It was win or bust.

But the beauty of that squad was that the spirit was so good it was almost like a club side and not once was the atmosphere in the camp compromised by the huge pressure we were under. In those circumstances it was crucial that we stuck together and kept a positive mindset.

I remember we had a barbecue at a nearby monastery when Bobby Robson named the team for that last group game. Obviously, we were without Ray and Bryan, so Stevie Hodge and me came into midfield. Trevor Steven replaced Chris Waddle and Peter Beardsley came in for Mark Hateley. Everybody understood changes needed to be made and they all wished us well. As I mentioned, a manager needs to pick the right squad for competition football and needs to make some brave decisions sometimes. It would take a brave man to leave out talent like Waddle and John Barnes, but to be fair to Bobby he stuck to his guns, told us how we were going to play and created a positive attitude straight away.

With Hodgey tucked in on the left, Trevor down the right, and Glenn Hoddle in the middle, my instructions were simple: get it and give it. Glenn was a lovely passer of the ball, but winning it wasn't one of his strengths, so that was my job. I was used to playing a pressing game with Everton, but you can't charge around too much in those conditions, so you have to play in short bursts, accept the fact that the other team will have the ball for periods and win it when you get the opportunity.

It was so tense in the dressing room before kick-off – you could almost cut the atmosphere with a knife. It was eerie, almost. Glenn Hoddle was sitting in the corner listening to The Eagles on his headphones, Terry Butcher was very vociferous as always and Bobby Robson's team-talk was, well, typical Bobby. It was such a crucial game, there was so much at stake, so Bobby went on for about ten minutes, trying to calm us down and keep us relaxed. Then finally he said: "Don't worry about those 60 million people at home who want you to win!" That was just his passion getting the better off him. I don't think he wanted to make us laugh, but it did anyway.

Poland were a very decent side. They'd finished third four years earlier and in Zbigniew Boniek, they had a truly world-class playmaker. But having faced teams who were more used to the hot conditions, this would be more of a straight 'football' contest and I think the pressure we were under and the determination to prove the doubters wrong, just gave us the edge.

Saying that, we started the game very nervously again. Terry Fenwick let in Boniek and Shilts did well to make the save. Had that gone in, who knows how the game might have unfolded? But once we got the first goal, there was only one team gonna win. The move started right down by our corner flag. Glenn clipped it forward to Links on the halfway line and he fed Gary Stevens who was charging down the right. Links continued his run, got across the defender and stuck Gary's low cross in at the near post. It was a great, flowing move.

We began to grow in confidence and six minutes later we scored a great goal. Peter Beardsley fed Hodgey down the left with a lovely first-time pass and there was Links again to crash in the cross.

Now we were in control, dictating the game, playing them off the park really and ten minutes before half-time, Links got his hat-trick when their keeper dropped a corner right into his lap. Gary didn't miss from inside the six yard box.

As we walked off at half-time, I remember looking over and seeing the England fans doing the Conga in the stands. Fantastic. As I looked over I saw this Union Jack with 'Huyton' written on it – that's where I'm from in Liverpool – and an old school pal of mine, Richie Harrison, was holding it. That was bloody weird. You don't want to go over at half-time, because there was still a job to do, but at full-time, when everybody was celebrating, I ran over to see him.

The atmosphere in the dressing room at half-time was fantastic – probably the best I've known. The game wasn't won yet – and Don Howe, Bobby, Robbo and Butch were saying as much – but in the back of your mind, you know it probably will be. It was a bit surreal too, because as it was so hot, literally sizzling, while the management were talking, we were lying down on these towels that had been in an ice bucket – and wearing oxygen masks!

I can't fully explain to you how difficult the conditions were, but to give you an idea… during the second half, Chris Waddle came on as a sub and he was carrying these bags of water. These days, the authorities are sensible, and let you grab a drink of water when there's a break in play in conditions like that. Back then, it didn't happen that much, so everybody was trying to get one of these bags of water off

Chris. I remember the ball going near Hodgey and he could have got to it, but he went for the water that Chris was carrying instead! I remember thinking, "what the hell are you doing?!"

We saw out the second half with very few alarms. Job done. It was a great release at the final whistle. We'd been under such pressure – the most pressure most of us had ever felt. Before the game, even Links was getting hammered by the press and was under pressure for his place because he hadn't scored for half-a-dozen games. The same thing happened when he first joined Everton, and people were asking whether he was up to it. But the thing about Gary is, he wasn't the most gifted player technically, but he was very strong mentally. He didn't worry if he didn't score, because he always believed he would score in the next game. That is a gift in itself and because of that single-mindedness, he always got himself into the right areas. He says his six goals during Mexico '86 only added up to about 15 yards, but that's no accident. That's down to a fantastic, natural instinct.

Gary's always said that was a career-changing game and he's right. It could so easily have been him who was dropped, then he goes and gets a hat-trick and before you know it, he's the tournament's top scorer, on the back of which he gets a move from Merseyside to Barcelona, and we all know what he went on to achieve.

Having been up in the hills, away from civilisation in Saltillo, we now moved to Mexico City, one of the biggest, noisiest cities in the world, for our second round match against Paraguay. In fact, it was so noisy that we had to check out of our first hotel because it was by the side of the motorway and nobody could get any kip. The manager ended up booking us into the Holiday Inn, where Italy were also staying.

I'd done my ankle earlier in the season against Nottingham Forest and it was still a problem going into the tournament, but this is a World Cup, so you try and play it down as much as possible, tell the manager you're fit, and that's all there is to it. To be fair, it wasn't affecting my movement, but it was very painful, very sore. But like Robbo earlier in the tournament, I was so desperate to play, that I just strapped it up and took anti-inflammatories before each game.

Against Paraguay, I took a whack on it before eventually coming off in the second half, hoping it wouldn't keep me out of the quarter-final against Argentina.

Overall, it was a very professional performance against Paraguay. They weren't the greatest side, but they had one very good central midfielder – a silver-haired lad called Romero – and once we nullified him, we were always gonna win. Once Links gave us the lead after half an hour, they lost their discipline – Peter Beardsley scored our second when Links was off having treatment for a whack in the throat – but we kept our heads, played good football and they ended up chasing the game. It wasn't the greatest match ever, but 3-0 tells its own story.

If you think England versus Argentina is a high-profile game now, imagine what it was like in 1986, after what had happened in the Falklands only a few years earlier. The fixture's had a bit of a history to say the least! The build-up to that game was mind-blowing, especially with it being over in Mexico, because loads of media had flown up from Argentina and they all wanted to ask us about the war. We were receiving the English papers a couple of days late, but days in advance of the game they were full of talk about the war, especially the tabloids. But to be fair, we managed to steer clear of the subject on the whole. To me it was totally irrelevant.

The political side of the game didn't even come into the equation for us. We were playing Argentina, the pre-tournament favourites, in the quarter-finals of the World Cup, in front of 115,000 people, in the capital city, at the Azteca Stadium, the venue for the final. Whatever anybody else says, the game couldn't get any bigger. Even though we were thousands of miles from home, you could feel how massive it was to the whole country, just through the media and the fans that were out there with us. I know that sounds ridiculous, but it was that big. It was our World Cup final in a way. I don't know that the pressure was off, but whereas we were expected to win every other game, Argentina were strong favourites for this one and favourites for the tournament as a whole. In a way, we had nothing to lose.

My ankle mended enough for me to be passed fit, but I also had another potential barrier to playing in the game. Ray Wilkins was available again after serving his two match suspension for his sending off against the Moroccans. But I got a great thirtieth birthday present when Bobby Robson announced that I would be in a side which showed just one change from the Paraguay game with Terry Fenwick in for Alvin Martin.

If you think how big the Poland game was and what Bobby was like in the dressing room before that game, imagine what he was like before we played Argentina! This was another example of him trying to calm us down, get us focused, telling us to forget about the politics surrounding the game. Then, his enthusiasm started getting the better of him again, because he badly wanted to win and he ended up going off on one... He started telling us how we'd had good luck messages from the Queen and the Prime Minister, and how Maggie Thatcher had said we'd already won one war and all that... To be honest, we didn't pay much attention. We had enough on our plates with Argentina. We knew they had some good players: Valdano, Burruchaga and, of course, the man everybody had been going on about, Diego Maradona. He came to Wembley as a youngster in the early-80s and he was already an outstanding international player. By now, he was easily the best player in the world. He had an outstanding touch, an incredibly left foot and the ability to produce the unexpected at any moment.

For all the difficulties of playing in Mexico City, with the heat, the humidity and the altitude, there's no denying it's a football-mad place and the atmosphere inside the Azteca Stadium was sensational. As you walk out onto the pitch, the noise, the Mexican wave going right round the ground, the colours – it really lifts you. Looking back, those are such great memories, memories nobody can take away from you, no matter what the result of the game. It was an utterly unbelievable experience, which I shall always cherish.

The game itself was a cagey affair, especially the first half. In fact, until the first goal five minutes inside the second half, I don't remember either side having a proper chance. As for the goal itself, well, everybody who saw it remembers what happened, but I didn't see it! Honest, I didn't.

As Hodgey flicked the ball back towards Peter Shilton from the edge of our area, I remember seeing Shilts coming off his line, and I turned away thinking he would gather it easily. I hadn't seen Maradona at all at that point. Then all of a sudden everybody's just gone up in arms, and I can remember Fen and Butch running past me, towards the referee, screaming, "He's handled it, he's f***ing handled it."

I turned round to someone else – I forget who – and just said: "What's gone on here?"

But everybody just carries on: "He's handled it."

Course, there's nothing anybody can do about it by then, because the referee's Tunisian and he can't speak a work of English – and he's already given the goal.

The second goal, I can remember...

Peter Beardsley and Glenn Hoddle lost it between them just inside Argentina's half and in a split second Maradona's picked it up and swivelled and he's now facing our goal. At that point, I thought, "BOOM! I'll get him here," but once he set off the moment was gone and I couldn't get near him. If it had been a January night at Goodison, pissing it down with rain, I'd have got him, or at least fouled him, but on that day, no chance.

You know when you have a dream and there's a wind blowing against you? Well, I have a recurring nightmare about that goal and it's just like that. Every time I have that dream I think I'm gonna get there – I'm trying harder and harder, running faster and faster – and every time I can't get near him. It's like the wind's blowing galeforce against me.

But I don't blame myself, so to speak, because once he's beaten me he well and truly beats three more players. First Fen, then Butch, and if you look at the finish, Shilts does well, because he stands up big for a long time and narrows the angle. Gary Stevens is coming across from Maradona's left, Butch is coming in behind him, but he just waits and waits and waits, draws Shilts and knocks it in, all in one movement, calm as you like.

Whatever you say about him – and he cheated for the first goal, pure and simple – he was a great player and that was a great goal. You have to remember the pitch was terrible. Terrible. Bumpy, full of divots, and you couldn't just pat them back down, because the pitch was rock hard. I was brought up on some dodgy Sunday league pitches and if you could play a bit, you could actually play on those, but this was like a cow field and Maradona could still play on it because of that touch of his. What a touch.

You must also remember he played against Belgium in the semi-finals and he was up against Eric Gerets, one of the best man-to-man markers there was, and he tore him apart, scored two more brilliant goals, and tore the Germans apart in the final as well. He was untouchable.

We didn't go man to man on Maradona – it was down to whoever was closest to him – and thank God we didn't because I would have been the one who would have had to mark him, probably! Ha ha ha ha ha ha!!!!!! Seriously, though, if you look at the footage, I actually had a pretty good game. My ankle was sore, but that's no excuse for not getting near Maradona for that second goal. Even when I see it now, I don't think about what a great goal it is, because all I can think about is how I just can't get there. I can't get it out of my head.

Even at 2-0, we nearly got back into it. Chris Waddle came on for me and John Barnes came on for Trevor Steven and Barnesy was absolutely brilliant. He just kept beating their right-back and getting to the byline and from one of his crosses, Links got us back into it with a header at the back post ten minutes from time.

A couple of minutes later he had an almost identical chance, but somehow it didn't go in. If that was on What Happened Next? and you played the clip and stopped it as the ball came across, you'd say, "Lineker scores" – no question. Nobody knows how that ball didn't end up in the net – Links included. Gary was in the net, the defender was in the net, the keeper was in the net. Everything except the sodding ball.

On the bench we were all up. "GOAL!... What happened there?... Why isn't it in?"... he must have been fouled." Watching it back, though, you've got to give the defender credit, because he just did enough to stop Gary getting there.

Had we equalised, I'd have fancied us to go on and win it, but overall I think we showed them too much respect. We only really started taking them on when we were 2-0 down, and you saw what happened when we did. But it's very hard to chase a game in those conditions, and in the end we just ran out of time.

The Azteca Stadium has a really long tunnel and it was mayhem down there afterwards. The Argentinians were singing and dancing and all that. I wouldn't say they were goading us particularly, because I think we would have been celebrating massively if we had won too, but they were obviously delighted.

It was extremely quiet in our dressing room. There was just a massive sense of disappointment. We lost our rag even more because we had to wait for ages while Terry Butcher was having a drugs test. He'd also tried to get in the Argentina dressing room to have a pop at Maradona, but Butch was mad, wasn't he? We hadn't seen the replay, but by then word had got around all of us that Maradona had definitely punched the first one in, so we felt we'd been cheated.

I don't take any consolation from the fact that we ran the favourites close. I thought we had a good squad, and having lost two of our better players, I thought we showed great determination to get ourselves into that position, only to be cheated out of it. Could we have gone on to win the World Cup? Who knows? Instead Argentina did.

To those people who say Argentina were the better side, I think if you look at the game overall, there wasn't much in it. Once we started getting at them, they were right on the back foot. Look at how delighted they were at the final whistle – they knew they'd got out of jail.

PETER SHILTON
GOALKEEPER

ITALY 1990

BORN   18th September 1949, Leicester
CLUBS   Leicester City, Stoke City, Nottingham Forest, Southampton, Derby County, Plymouth, Wimbledon, Bolton, Coventry, West Ham United, Leyton Orient
INTERNATIONAL DEBUT   November 1970 v East Germany
ENGLAND CAREER   125 caps, 56 clean sheets
INTERNATIONAL FAREWELL   July 1990 v Italy

A teenage prodigy at Leicester, where he ousted World Cup winning keeper Gordon Banks from the team, Peter Shilton won two European Cups and set an English international appearance record of 125 caps. He captained his country through the latter stages of Italia 90 after skipper Bryan Robson's tournament was decimated through injury once again and played an integral part in England's solid defence that saw them through to the semi-final for only the second time. There England faced up to an old enemy once again. Just don't mention penalties...

ENGLAND 1 v WEST GERMANY 1

(West Germany won 4-3 on penalties)

World Cup Semi-final
Wednesday 4 July 1990

Stadio delle Alpi, Turin
Attendance 62,628

Penalties put paid to England's chances for the first, but not last time, while Gazza's tears spark the revival of modern football as England are beaten by the Champions to be once more

Teams

	Managers	
Bobby Robson	**Managers**	Franz Beckenbauer
Peter Shilton		Bodo Illgner
Paul Parker		Andreas Brehme
Stuart Pearce		Jürgen Kohler
Mark Wright		Klaus Augenthaler
Des Walker		Guido Buchwald
Terry Butcher		Thomas Berthold
(Sub. Trevor Steven)		
David Platt		Lothar Matthäus
Paul Gascoigne		Thomas Hässler
		(Sub. Stefan Reuter)
Gary Lineker		Olaf Thon
Peter Beardsley		Rudi Völler
		(Sub. Karl-Heinz Riedle)
Chris Waddle		Jürgen Klinsmann
Lineker 82	**Scorers**	Brehme 60

Referee: José Ramiz Wright (Brazil)

I DON'T LIKE third-place play-offs – what player does?

You are out of the tournament, you just want to get home and mentally it's very difficult to get yourself up for the game, especially when you're playing against a host nation who still have something to prove. For us, it was a nothing game, played right down in the south of Italy in Bari, in an open, windy, half-empty stadium. After the emotion of our semi-final against West Germany in Turin four days earlier, it was a strange game with which to end my international career.

I knew 1990 would almost certainly be my last tournament and although I'd achieved a lot on the international stage in terms of caps and what have you, I suppose it was my last chance to actually win something. I say 'suppose' because even if you play international football for as long as I did, I think you're very lucky if you end up winning something, because there are only two major tournaments – the World Cup and the European Championships – and a lot of good teams.

Italia 90 would be my fifth World Cup campaign and my third appearance in the finals. We'd been unlucky in the two previous finals, going out without losing a game in 1982 and then obviously being on the wrong end of the 'Hand of God' four years later.

I was particularly looking forward to the 1990 World Cup – for several reasons. Firstly, it would be my last, so I thought, "I'll give it everything". Secondly, it was in Italy, which was a great place to have a World Cup. You knew it would be well organised and because it was being held relatively close to home, you knew we would have a lot of support. In fact, all the European teams would have great support, which would make for a great atmosphere. Thirdly, Italia 90 felt bigger than the previous World Cups I'd played in. Each had felt bigger than the last, in fact, but 1990 really captured the public's imagination. Since then, the amount of television coverage has increased dramatically, which has helped turn football into a truly global game. More teams than ever before are now competing and, in 1990, teams who weren't considered big names, such as Cameroon, qualified and did well. Now it happens all the time. It was a landmark tournament in many ways.

As with every World Cup, the England squad went to Italy feeling we could do well, and as one of the few teams who had a genuine chance of winning it. I think it's very difficult to go to the World Cup with the mindset of "yeah, we're definitely one of the favourites, we'll get to the final", because you will end up looking too far ahead, but as one of the six seeded teams, somebody obviously saw it that way.

Preparation for the tournament was very good. We had two weeks in Sardinia, which was basically a Mediterranean holiday resort. It was very hot and very hard work, but I could think of worse places to have a build-up for a World Cup. For Mexico, we were away for a month before the tournament began, because we had to go to Colorado for altitude training, which made for a bit of a strange, drawn-out process. In Italy, humidity wouldn't be much of a factor.

Before the real business end of things began, our wives and families were flown out to join us for a few days. After a long domestic season that was a nice touch by the management. Bobby Robson wanted us to relax, re-charge the batteries and switch off from football before re-focusing and building momentum with the aim of peaking for the first game. None of the players abused that privilege because everybody realised why it had been done.

Even after our families flew home again, it didn't become too regimented. We definitely prepared correctly and thoroughly, but we weren't locked away, so to speak. As a professional, you know what's expected of you. Saying that, I remember one or two of the lads decided to go up the road for a drink at another hotel where a load of England fans were staying. Probably not a good idea. There were one or two stories about them getting on a boat and Gazza getting up to no good.

Gazza was great, although, to be quite honest, he could be a pain in the backside at times. He was always bubbly, but one minute he's making you laugh so much you can't stop, the next minute you're thinking, "Gazza, what the hell are you doing?" But on such a long trip you need characters like that in the squad. In 1970, they had Jeff Astle, who was one of the funniest people I've ever met. Everybody just accepted the way Gazza was, because as soon as he got on the training pitch he was completely focused, always doing his best. And when he got onto the pitch he could be a genius.

As an experienced player, all you can do is try to lead by example a little bit. In my first England squad there were people like Bobby Charlton and Bobby Moore and I remember watching them, trying to see how they approached the game and applying it to my own preparation a bit. I wouldn't go around giving people advice every two minutes, but if I'm doing the right things, hopefully the younger players will do the same.

At the World Cup, you train for a couple of hours a day, and when you're not training you're relaxing. That's a lot of time to lounge around and put you're feet up and there's only so much sleeping and TV-watching you can do. So to add a bit of variety to proceedings, we'd have a race night, with Gary Lineker and me as the bookmakers. It wasn't big money or anything, five- or ten-pound bets per race, something like that.

Anyway, one night we were a few hundred quid up, taking some of the lads for a bit of money, so – led by Gazza, of course – they came up with the idea of getting their own back. It was simple really: they got hold of Fred Street, the physio, who kept the tapes, and he gave them a sneak preview of some of the races. They didn't bet 'big', because that would have been too obvious, but they were gambling more than normal – 20 quid a race or whatever – and this horse, which was at long odds, about 20-1 I think, romped home.

Initially, we didn't have a clue it was a scam, because they'd done it so well, but the next day there was a raucous atmosphere round the pool, with the lads doing the Conga and taunting us. I remember Links and I sat there looking at each other, as if to say, "What's gone off here?!" Then Links said to me: "This doesn't seem right" – and I agreed. A couple of hours later, the guilty parties came to us and said: "Look, you'd better have your money back, we've done you!" It was all in good fun and was clearly great for team spirit!

So there I am, in the wind and heavy rain, on a pitch with a slight slope, playing against players I faced every week and in a team managed by an Englishman – and a World Cup winner at that. After all our warm-weather training, all our tactical planning, our opening game of the finals just didn't feel like a World Cup game – for obvious reasons. In fact, it felt just like an English First Division game. We knew exactly how Jack Charlton's Republic of Ireland side were going to play and obviously the conditions suited them far more than they suited us. It was a poor game, played in poor conditions and Gary Lineker's early goal pretty much summed it up – scrappy. After such a good start, we didn't play very well and a 1-1 draw was probably a fair result, although it was hardly satisfactory.

You're never surprised by anything in football, so when Bobby Robson decided to change our formation from 4-4-2 to 5-3-2 for our next game against Holland, we just had to get on with it. It was a system he'd never used before during his time as England manager, but obviously there were reasons why he felt the need for change and as long as the players trust the manager and everybody knows their jobs, there isn't a problem. When you go to the World Cup, you've got to have a Plan B – and sometimes a Plan C – because you never know what might happen in terms of injuries and form, and the players coming in might be more suited to a different way of playing.

Personally, I didn't have any misgivings about how it would work, because I was playing with centre-half Mark Wright at Derby County at the time and I knew he was perfectly capable of playing in that system as the spare man. From a goalkeeping point of view, it didn't really affect my approach. If anything, I suppose you're not expecting the ball over the top as much, because the sweeper is there for that sort of thing, but you adapt very quickly.

The system worked a treat, with Gazza really coming of age against one of the pre-tournament favourites. Holland were European Champions and fielded most of the players who were in the side when they beat us 3-1 in 1988, including the famous AC Milan trio of Gullit, Van Basten and Rijkaard, but this time we were the better side.

In the dying minutes I thought we'd got the win we deserved when Stuart Pearce's free-kick from wide on the right went under Hans Van Breukelen and in. My first reaction was one of great joy, thinking we'd got the win, but it soon turned to enormous disappointment and amazement when the goal was disallowed. It didn't even register with me that the free-kick was indirect when it was first awarded, but even then, it is amazing it didn't touch anybody.

It might have been a much better performance than against the Irish, but with two draws in two games – the same as everybody else in the group – we needed a win against Egypt to be sure of a place in the second round. The pressure was really on.

With Egypt intent on defending, it probably looked like a very comfortable game on the surface, but as a goalkeeper you're thinking, "Right, let's get a couple of early goals here," then you can relax a bit. There's nothing more unsettling for a keeper than a one-sided match. Those games when you don't have as much to do can be much more difficult, because you have to keep your concentration for long periods without actually touching the ball. The ball was up the other end so much, that at one point I looked up at the stands and noticed this big group of Egyptian sailors. I remember thinking, "Christ, that's a bit unusual..." before switching back on to the game.

Even when we went 1-0 up through Mark Wright's header in the 58th minute, you know you can't relax, because they can be back in it in an instant. And after we'd dominated from start to finish, they nearly did get back in it right at the end. The fella was only six yards out and he should have scored to be honest. In fact, I shouldn't have even smelt it, but he didn't hit it cleanly and fortunately it was close enough for me to be able to get down quickly to my left and make a smart save.

People tend to forget how close we were to going out. After scoring just two goals in three games, it was our defence that kept us in it initially. We didn't concede a goal in six qualifying games and again we were solid. Obviously the fewer goals you concede the better chance you have of going through, but I had enough to do in most of the games, and I even found the Egypt game very hard because we had to win it to go through.

With Holland and the Republic of Ireland drawing, we topped the group, setting up a second round match with Belgium. It was terrific being on the Italian mainland at last. Initially, we were stationed on the Islands because of worries about England's hooligans, especially potential clashes with their Dutch counterparts. We were shut away from all of that, but it was a bit strange being cut off from the mainland, almost like you weren't really part of the World Cup. I have to say I think moving to the mainland helped us the way it helped in Mexico, when we went from Monterrey, with its Third Division ground, small crowds and bumpy pitch, to the 120,000-capacity Azteca Stadium in Mexico City. This time we went to Bologna: great place, great stadium, great atmosphere.

As a single moment, David Platt's winner in the last minute of extra time against Belgium was one of the highlights of my World Cup career. Had it been five or ten minutes from the end they could have thrown the kitchen sink at us, but they were dead and buried, they barely even had time to kick-off, so you can just celebrate.

As a goalkeeper you're thinking "penalties" at that stage, mentally preparing for them, so it's part relief, part elation to win in that manner. Had I been a bit younger I might have charged up the other end and jumped on top of that pile of players, but I probably wouldn't have made it back in time! Experience tells you to prepare for the restart, even though you know the game is up, but I was obviously chuffed to bits.

Looking back, it's a game that might easily have gone the other way. It was a very good game to play in, end to end, although Belgium probably just shaded it. John Barnes had a perfectly good goal disallowed for offside, while it was probably the most work I had to do in one game in that tournament. They hit the post twice – once in each half – first through Jan Ceulemans, then through Enzo Scifo, but funnily enough I never felt like they were going in. The second one especially I always say in my after dinner speeches, "It was never going in, I had it covered!!" It was a curler which I always felt was going wide, even though it had enough curl on it to hit the outside of the post! We didn't exactly feel our name was on the Cup, we'd had a bit of luck for a change, which you need if you want to do well in any tournament.

After the Belgium game I told the manager I would definitely be retiring after the tournament. There were whispers that the new manager, whoever it might be, would ask me to continue, but there's only a big tournament every couple of years and I wanted whoever was going to succeed me to have a whole qualifying campaign to settle in. I also wanted to finish on a high. Going out in the first knockout round would have been a bit of an anti-climax, but getting the quarter-finals was an achievement in itself and it just felt that the time was right. I told Bobby Robson I now wanted to go on and win it, but after that… He understood and he said "It's kind of nice that you'll be finishing with me." Bobby was great. He made me his number one goalkeeper. Before he came into the job I shared duties with Liverpool's Ray Clemence as Ron Greenwood played us in alternate games and I wasn't happy with that scenario. I was ready to quit international football had Bobby not plumped for me as his number one, but he did. I'll always be grateful for that and I'd like to think – if you look at my record – that I did the business for him.

Our relationship with the press had become increasingly strained as the tournament progressed and after the Belgium game we pretty much stopped speaking to them altogether. Footballers had been making the front pages as well as the back for a while by then, but they took it to ridiculous levels at that World Cup, particularly with Bobby – in fact, it got rather personal – and we decided to make a stand. I don't think that approach does you any good in the long-term, but you develop a siege mentality, especially when you're away from home, and it's a good way of sticking together. It was as if to say, "you've given us that much stick, but now we're in the quarter-finals…"

England 1, Cameroon 2: I was shell-shocked. "Has it turned against us?" I was wondering. "Are we going out?" Looking back, it was such an end to end game that we were always going to get the chance to come back into it, but it all happened so quickly that I had serious doubts.

I don't think we underestimated Cameroon at all. Bobby Robson said it would be our easiest game so far, but we'd seen what they'd done to Argentina, Romania and Colombia and knew we were in for a tough match. They were strong, quick, skilful – very useful – and they played with such a freedom, such a joy, which we soon found out.

They were so relaxed in the tunnel beforehand, singing and dancing and holding hands. I don't think they did it to put us off, that was just their way, but it was very unusual – I'd never seen anything like it before. I think they realised that they'd done exceptionally well to get that far and went in with the attitude that they were just going to enjoy themselves. But at the back of mind, I knew we had more big-match experience than Cameroon and I thought that would see us through.

We knew we were in a proper game inside five minutes when they were clean through on goal. Fortunately I managed to get off my line quickly and Oman Biyik blasted it against my legs, but the danger signs were there early. We took the lead in the 20th minute, when Stuart Pearce's perfect cross found David Platt, who headed in at the far post. Even then, I didn't think, "Right, this is it now, we're going to win comfortably," because it came against the run of play. But drawing first blood certainly gave us confidence, because Cameroon had yet to go behind in the tournament so far, and you do hope they might fold a bit. But they didn't. They were still up for it, they were still confident and they came roaring back at us.

They were in the ascendancy right up to half-time and again in the period after half-time, with 38-year-old striker Roger Milla, on as a second half substitute, a real thorn in our side. On the hour, Gazza tripped Milla in the box and the referee pointed immediately to the penalty spot. I managed to get a finger tip to the resulting spot-kick, but Kunde hit it hard into the top left-hand corner and I had no chance of saving it really. Four minutes later, Milla drew two defenders before slipping the ball through to Ekeke. I ran out to narrow the angle, but he clipped it cleverly into the top corner and we were behind. They bossed the game in that period and we were really under the cosh, even after they'd taken the lead.

It was very hot in Naples, which obviously suited a team from West Africa more than it suited us, but I wouldn't use that as an excuse. We were well used to it by now – they were just playing better than us.

It showed great character on our part to come back and win 3-2, but from their point of view, they probably showed a little bit of inexperience and naivety under pressure. I don't think they really had it in them to change their approach and shut up shop, and although they tried, I think that inability to close out the game allowed us to get back into it.

At this point Gazza and Links really came into their own. Gazza's main job was to try and unlock defences – that's why he was in the team – and Gary was always on the look out for those through-balls. It was a combination that worked well at Spurs and they did it twice for us. They were both definite penalties and again you're starting to think luck is on your side.

For the first penalty, seven minutes from normal time, I was very confident Gary would score, which he did, sending the keeper the wrong way. The second one, a minute before half-time in extra-time, I wasn't so sure. There's an enormous amount of pressure on a penalty-taker in that situation, and to take two in quick succession takes great mental strength. I spoke to Gary afterwards and he said "To be honest, I didn't know where to put it, so I just blasted it down the middle." If N'kono hadn't dived so early he would have saved it. Again, we had that little bit of luck. Again, we so easily could have been going home.

There was a great atmosphere in the dressing room and you celebrate as much as you can at the time, but with the next game coming so quickly and having to change venues, you forget about it very quickly and re-focus.

The FA brought out the wives and families for the semi-final, which was a great gesture. It wasn't a distraction, in fact it probably helped some players, but by that point you're in tournament mode. You've been together such a long time that you're so together and so focused, that nothing is going to distract you from the job in hand.

We only had three days before the game against West Germany, but tiredness doesn't even come into it at this stage. Training is very light, because as a tournament goes on, each game takes a little bit out of you, so you basically have to concentrate on keeping the fuel in the tank. But you don't even think about fatigue – you could get through it on adrenaline alone.

Although we had enjoyed a bit of luck against both Belgium and Cameroon, the press and the public probably still expected us to beat both of those sides. Whereas, although we were confident going into the semi-final, West Germany were the favourites to win the whole tournament, so we were the underdogs. It was a tag that suited us more, as it did against Holland, because we played with a great deal of freedom in those games – had nothing to lose if you like – and one or two of our players really got the bit between their teeth. Everybody was really up for it, but then this was the semi-final of the World Cup against West Germany of all people... Motivation was never going to be a problem.

In the dressing room before a game is always the tensest time, but I don't remember anybody being particularly nervous before the semi-final. Neither were our instructions anything out of the ordinary. All the hard work had been done on the training ground and we knew how we intended to play; now it was just a case of reminding everybody of their jobs.

As a goalkeeper, my main concern is keeping a clean sheet, so I might have a word with one or two players, saying things like, "C'mon, let's keep it tight." Generally, though, I tried to look big and confident, calm and focused and hoped I could transmit that through to the other players. Big Terry Butcher would get a bit more emotional, going around trying to get everybody wound up a bit, but by this stage all your preparation is done really. The rest is in the lap of the Gods. As we walked out onto the pitch and lined-up for the national anthems I remember looking up and seeing what great support we had. In fact, it was a great atmosphere in a great stadium and it really felt like it was going to be a 'proper' football match. All you want to do is get the game started.

It was always going to be a great match. Neither side was set up to defend, so you always knew we would have a go at each other, and that's exactly how it panned out. It was a real end-to-end affair, from the first minute to the last, so it's great to play in, because you're always in the game. Strangely, though, there weren't many chances in the first half. Gazza was at his confident best, making player of the tournament Lothar Matthäus look average at times and it was Gazza who went closest to scoring, his volley from the edge of the box being tipped round the post in the early stages. I was soon called into action, saving smartly from Klinsmann at close range, then just before half-time, Riedle, who was on as a sub for the injured Völler, got up well, but I dealt with his header pretty comfortably. In fact, I felt more and more comfortable as the half wore on.

At half-time the game was finely balanced and knew it could go either way, but we felt confident we could win it, especially if we got the first goal. We were up for it, we were playing as well as we'd played throughout the whole tournament and if there were any nerves beforehand, they'd all disappeared within minutes of the kick-off. What did the manager say? What could he say? "More of the same, lads, more of the same…"

Then, on the hour, the Germans scored…

Stuart Pearce fouled Hässler 25 yards out, just right of centre. It was a direct free-kick and I was expecting a shot, so I treated it as I would treat a shot in open play, standing a couple of yards off my line to narrow the angle, giving them as little of the goal to shoot at as possible.

I was in position, the wall was in position, everything was fine.

Suddenly, Thon knocks the ball square to Brehme and the wall doesn't come into play anymore, except for right-back Paul Parker, whose job it was to charge down any indirect free-kicks. With the ball on its way, Paul is breaking his neck to block the shot and he's only a couple of yards away when it hits his shin and loops up high into the night sky. I felt I picked it pretty quickly and reacted pretty quickly, but I've seen instances where, even from deflections nowhere near as big as that one, goalkeepers have struggled to get anywhere near the ball.

This one ballooned up and arced right over my head, just out of my reach and into the net. The Germans led 1-0 with the cruellest luck possible. I've always said: if it had been six inches higher it would have gone over, six inches lower and I would have saved it. It wasn't that I had my weight transferred forward, it's just that I was slightly off my line, narrowing the angle as I always did. It was that element of luck that often swings big games like this. Even Brehme was quoted as saying he thought it was definitely in as soon as it took a deflection and that he was surprised I even got as close as I did.

I honestly don't think I could have done any more, but the fact that I got so close made it even more disappointing in a way. I was gutted, because you realise that it could be the game. It was so tight there weren't going to be many goals, so it was obviously vital. And after feeling that things were maybe starting to go our way, suddenly you think the opposite.

Bobby Robson immediately replaced Terry Butcher with Trevor Steven and we went 4-4-2 in search of the equaliser. It came at almost the same time as our equaliser against Cameroon and again Links came up with the goods. Paul Parker's right-wing cross caused confusion between Augenthaler and Kohler and there was Gary, always alert in the box. He controlled it on his right thigh and drilled it low past Illgner with he left foot. I was really chuffed because we were back in it and very relieved because I thought "We're not gonna lose to a goal like that!"

Extra time was a bit like the previous 90 minutes: end to end and we both could have won it. Both teams hit the post, but again theirs was a curler that hit the outside of the post and I think I had Buchwald's shot covered as it ricocheted away to safety. Chrissie Waddle's was the complete opposite. It looked in all the way, hit the inside of the post and came out to one of their players. That's when lady luck really turned against us. We had bits of luck against Belgium and Cameroon, but eventually it deserted us. Had Chris's shot gone in, I don't think West Germany would have come back. That was a defining moment. Bobby Robson told me later that he was right behind Chrissie's shot and he thought it was in. That's the margin between winning and losing. Their lucky deflection went in and Chris' great shot stayed out.

As for Gazza's booking… Gazza is Gazza, he can be a bit rash at times and it was a rash tackle on Berthold. Sometimes you don't get booked for them, sometimes you do. He obviously thought it was a bit harsh, as did a lot of the lads, and the Germans certainly made a meal of it, but I've seen them given. Gazza was a bit emotional for a few minutes, but he managed to pull himself together. I wouldn't say he could have gone to pieces – he's an international player. He had the character to get through that sort of thing and his priority would have been to help us get through to the final, so I wouldn't have expected anything else.

I think penalties were, and still are, the best way to decide a game like that. It's not very nice when you get beat, but it's still the most exciting conclusion for the fans, and until the authorities find a better solution, it's the only way to go.

We hadn't practised taking penalties in training and people who say you can are wrong, because it's not the same as taking them for real. You can never replicate the pressure of an occasion like that. I also think it's a bit unfair to say there's no pressure on the keeper, because as a keeper your job is to save penalties, so you always put a certain amount of pressure on yourself.

My philosophy was always to stand big and still for as long as possible. There is a lot of pressure on the player taking the penalties, so you hope that at least one of them isn't going to be right in the corner. If you commit very early and they trickle it down the middle of the goal, you look daft, and as we saw with Stuart Pearce's penalty, if you give yourself as long as possible before diving, there's a chance that it will catch you on the legs.

Unless I'd have gone very, very early and committed myself I don't think I'd have had a chance with any of the German penalties. They were all hit firmly right into the corner and I dived the right way for all of them – I even got my fingertip to one – but unless I'd have taken a chance and guessed, I don't think I would have saved any of them.

You're obviously disappointed, when Stuart's had his penalty saved – it's unfortunate when any player misses a penalty – but it's even worse when you miss the goal completely like Chrissie did. You're gutted for them, gutted for the team, but the Germans hit four perfect penalties out of four and we only hit three out of five, so what can you do?

People ask me what it was like in the dressing room after the game and the truth is, I couldn't tell you. I don't know because I was called in for a routine drugs test, along with Stuart Pearce of all people. I think that pretty much summed up our night really, especially as we were stuck in there for two hours. Two of the German lads were in there with us, Brehme included, but they were very good. Obviously they were full of it at the final whistle, but they'd calmed down a bit by now and they obviously knew how we felt.

How did I feel? How would you feel? Gutted. You're obviously very bitterly disappointed to have gone out, even more so when you've gone so far and come so close. You could be thinking "What if?" your whole life, but as a professional you've got to be philosophical about these things and in time I always tend to remember the positive.

I'll always remember the overwhelming public response on our return to Luton Airport. When you're away from home, shut away for long periods, you can't comprehend just how many people are watching you at home and I couldn't believe the response. To see thousands of people hanging from roofs and lampposts just to get a glimpse of you is the sort of memory that lives with you for a very long time.

In fact, looking back it was a great tournament to finish my international career with. With Pavarotti singing *Nessun Dorma* being used by the BBC, it was very emotional. It was the tournament that took the popularity of football in this country on to the next level. People always remember where they were when they were watching certain games and they always ask me about it. And it's still the best performance by an England side away from these shores – and you've got to be proud of that.

Would we have lifted the World Cup if we'd won that penalty shoot out and faced Diego Maradona and Argentina in the final? I don't know. But I remember Bobby Robson was convinced we would have. He said "I'm not saying we would have beaten Argentina in the final, but my house would have been on it."

DAVID PLATT
MIDFIELDER

USA 1994

BORN 10th June 1966, Chadderton
CLUBS Crewe Alexandra, Aston Villa, Bari, Juventus, Sampdoria, Arsenal, Nottingham Forest
INTERNATIONAL DEBUT November 1989 v Italy
ENGLAND CAREER 62 caps, 27 goals
INTERNATIONAL FAREWELL June 1996 v Germany

Having made his mark with his late volleyed winner against Belgium at Italia 90, David Platt became head and shoulders England's best and most consistent player of the early 1990s. When his former club manager, Graham Taylor, acceded to the England throne after Bobby Robson's departure, many felt that Taylor and his captain could inspire England to great things. Sadly the players available, with Gazza injured and only the likes of Carlton Palmer and Andy Sinton as replacements, weren't up to the impossible job. Platt's record amidst this latent mediocrity is exemplary. But it still hurts that he only played in one World Cup.

HOLLAND 2 v ENGLAND 0

World Cup Qualifying Group 2
Wednesday 13 October 1993

De Kuip Stadium, Rotterdam
Attendance 48,000

*Graham Taylor's reign ends with a blaze of controversy surrounding
Koeman's foul on Platt and a grammatically incorrect catchphrase*

Teams

Dick Advocaat	**Managers**	Graham Taylor
Ed de Goey	1	David Seaman
John de Wolf	2	Paul Parker
Ronald Koeman	3	Tony Dorigo
Frank de Boer	4	Paul Ince
Frank Rijkaard	5	Gary Pallister
Jan Wouters	6	Tony Adams
Erwin Koeman	7	David Platt
Dennis Bergkamp	8	Carlton Palmer
		(Sub. Andy Sinton)
Marc Overmars	9	Alan Shearer
(Sub. Aron Winter)		
Ronald de Boer	10	Paul Merson
(Sub. Ullrich van Gobbel)		(Sub. Ian Wright)
Brian Roy	11	Lee Sharpe

R Koeman 61, Bergkamp 68   **Scorers**

Referee: Karl Assenmacher (Germany)

IT'S ALMOST LIKE the John F Kennedy assassination: everybody knows where they were when David Platt scored the winning goal against Belgium in the second round of the 1990 World Cup finals. It's not even as if *I'm* asked about it much. People mention it more than any other moment in my career, but it's more a case of them giving me *their* story, which usually starts with something like, "You gave me the best night of my life…" It's actually quite humbling for people to describe it in that context. Obviously it's only English people, but everybody watches the World Cup finals, and it was such a pivotal moment – although I didn't realise it at the time, of course – and it happened in such dramatic circumstances… the last minute of extra time. We hadn't played that well, but it was almost like at that moment, the whole nation got behind us.

Then you've got the Holland game in 1993 and the incident with Ronald Koeman. That's the second most talked about moment in my career and completely at the other end of the spectrum. I wouldn't say I cringe at the thought of it, because I'm realistic about such things. I had an unbelievable career and if you hold my international goalscoring record up stands against any English midfielder since Bobby Charlton, so I have no complaints. But it was hugely disappointing, because it effectively knocked us out of the World Cup.

I look back now and wonder what might have been had Koeman been sent-off. Would we have won that game? Quite possibly.

Was I at my peak in 1994? Would I have made the same impact in the USA? I've never really thought about it like that. I was certainly enjoying my football and playing well, but I went to Italia 90 as an unknown quantity and didn't start a game until the quarter-finals. In fact, I probably only started that game because I'd scored the winner against Belgium and was on such a high. But I would have gone to the USA in 1994 as Gary Lineker had gone to Italy in 1990 having won the Golden Boot in 1986: as an established, recognised player. So yes, I probably was at my peak when I had a World Cup taken away from me.

Let's be honest, Graham Taylor was made England manager because he was the best man for the job. This was before the FA even considered hiring a foreign manager and in 1990, when he was appointed, Aston Villa finished second in the league – just missing out on the title to Liverpool – so he was by far the most and best qualified English manager.

People say he played 'long ball' football, but I would say he played effective football. At Watford, yes, it was a case of putting the ball into the corners and turning the opposition round. At Aston Villa I would say Graham played 'direct' football, but it certainly wasn't the 'long ball'-game as most people understand it.

Graham was an exceptional club manager. He was very honest, extremely genuine and players bought into his style of management and way of playing because it brought success. Every day in training he spoke about the way he wanted you to play. It was a case of "this is what we want to do", over and over again. He built clubs up, but it's very hard to build international teams up in the same way. With England, he went in with the attitude: "I've got X number of days with the players, this is how we're going to play... WALLOP!" I think he suffered because of that.

If results don't go for you, the media scrutiny starts to build. Players would go back to their clubs after a poor result, and all of a sudden the criticism's coming at you from all angles and you're on your own. After our elimination from the 1992 European Championships it became a witch-hunt. It began with the 'Turnip' headlines and got progressively worse until Graham left the job 18 months later. I'd been there and seen it before, first with Bobby Robson, then with Graham, so by the time the Holland game came around it was water off a duck's back to me. You still had to go out the pitch and perform and I had such a close bond with Graham anyway that I wanted to perform well and help get the critics off his back.

Maybe there were less experienced players who let it affect them. That would have been no fault of Graham's, though, because he was very good at handling that aspect of the job by himself and shielding the players from it.

I remember one occasion during a training session at Wembley before a qualifying game. We were having a crossing and shooting session. It was Wrighty and Incey versus me and Gazza and whoever scored the most goals won the bet. Wrighty completely missed one of Incey's crosses and, in that Geordie accent of his, Gazza called Wrighty a "turnip head". Nobody said a word, but then Graham, calm as you like, sidled up alongside Gazza and said: "There's only one f***cking turnip head in this squad." It was great, because in front of the whole squad he put a light-hearted tinge on what was a very personal campaign against him. But Graham was a strong individual and he coped with the abuse as well as anybody could have. Not once did he refuse to face the press. He wanted to give journalists what they wanted and because of that he became unguarded. He was too honest if anything.

At club level, one thing Graham did was put enormous trust in his players. Perhaps he didn't have as much trust in some of the players he picked for England because he didn't have as much time to work with them, week in, week out. He just didn't have time to develop a relationship with them.

It's very, very easy for those players to have a pop at him now – and one or two of them have – because he oversaw a few poor performances and we failed to qualify for the World Cup finals. But let's not forget; he stuck by a lot of players when they were getting stick. At the end of the day, Graham picked you because he thought you were an international player. It's easy to turn around now and say, "I didn't play well because I was played out of position" or "his style of play didn't suit me." I think that's crap to be honest. If you were an international player, then your performances would have been up there, no matter how the manager asked you to play. Ok, a tactical decision may stop you from playing exceptionally well, but it doesn't make you play badly. If you're not good enough, you're not going to say "No" to being selected, nor will a player ever turn round and say "he shouldn't have picked me," even though the press were on to some of them straight away, saying "You're never an international." How easy would it have been for Graham not to be his own man and not pick them? Very. But he made them internationals and gave them England caps, so they shouldn't have a pop.

Despite our inconsistency as a team, my own form seemed to thrive under Graham. I carried it through from Italia 90 into the Euro 92 qualifiers, scored our only goal in the finals, and I was the only ever-present during 1994 World Cup qualification, scoring seven goals in 10 games.

I think the reason I thrived is that I was comfortable in myself at that stage of my career. I knew my game inside out, I was reasonably experienced and had developed good mental strength. Without being boastful, you get to a stage in your career when you know how good you are. You go out onto a football pitch and you know no matter who you are playing against that they are as mindful of you as you are of them, if not more so.

I was playing in Serie A, where most of the very best players in the world were playing at the time. If you're pitting your wits against the likes of Gullit, Van Basten, Rijkaard and Baggio – top, top players – every week and holding your own, that gives you the confidence to shine, no matter who the opposition are.

I suppose playing in Italy I was away from the UK spotlight to a certain extent, away from the negative publicity towards the manager. Not that I needed shielding, because it didn't worry me at all. I wanted to qualify for the World Cup for Graham and for the country, but to be a top player you have to be extremely selfish. So with me it was a case of going out there and saying, "There's a goal from David Platt" or "There's a performance from David Platt" – that's all you can do. That wasn't to the detriment of the team, it was actually benefiting the team, because you can only control your own performance really. As a player, it would often go quiet in between England games and then WALLOP: you had to deal with the media attention around the game. Then you'd go away to your clubs and it would all die down again, leaving the manager to deal with the majority of it.

You've also got to remember that Graham was very unlucky with piles of injuries, suspensions and loss of form. In fact, I was the only key player who didn't miss a game for one reason or another. Gazza was injured for one game and then suspended for another, Stuart Pearce only played four games because of injury and Des Walker and Chris Woods both suffered a loss of form. But I'd say the biggest loss was Alan Shearer. He was the natural successor to Gary Lineker and losing somebody who poses such a goal threat was a major blow. You need that to win games and Alan only played three qualifiers.

In any qualifying campaign there are always games on the schedule that you look at and think, "That's gonna be tough" or "That's gonna be interesting". But so much can happen that you never know what the crunch game is going to be, especially, as was the case with Holland away, it's the penultimate game in the group. As we know, that turned out to be the crucial game, but had things gone our way in some of the earlier games, the game in Rotterdam might not have mattered as much.

In truth, we were always stuttering along. The first game was against Norway at Wembley and from what I remember we battered them. We did everything but score in the first half. Then finally I scored a header from Gazza's free-kick in the 55th minute and from there we had every reason to believe we would go on and win the game – Norway barely had a look in. But with 15 minutes left their captain Rekdal equalised with a freakishly good goal – a volley from about 30 yards out, I think it was – and all of a sudden we've dropped two points at home. We never really got going after that.

As expected, we won our next two games, both at home, against Turkey and San Marino comfortably and then we got a good win in Turkey in a typically hostile atmosphere. By this point, Norway had emerged as the surprise front runners in the group, followed by Holland and ourselves.

We played the Dutch in our next game at Wembley and in the context of the whole campaign, it was probably just as important as the game in Rotterdam. We went 2-0 up early on, John Barnes scoring a great free-kick in the second minute before I put in the rebound after Les Ferdinand hit the post halfway through the first half. Dennis Bergkamp pulled a goal back for the Dutch before half-time, but we were bossing the game, and continued to do so in the second half. It all seemed set for an England win.

We should have had a penalty of our own when Frank de Boer fouled Les Ferdinand with ten minutes to go, but five minutes later it was Holland who scored from the spot. Again, we'd dropped two points at home and again it was a game we should have won.

Des Walker pulled back Marc Overmars in the box; there's no question it was a penalty, but he should never have got that far. I'm not having a go at Des, because he was a very honest player, but Overmars picked the ball up just inside our half and Des tried to recover before pulling him down in the box. But if that had been an Italian defender, he would have walloped him much earlier. From playing in Italy I soon realised that we're too honest. It's not cynical, it's pragmatic and it's something that they coach in Italy.

I remember playing against AC Milan for Bari once. I pushed the ball past Franco Baresi on the halfway line and instead of backing away, he just took me out. When I got up, he was still rolling around on the floor. It was then that I clicked: I'm not getting anything change out of him! Had Des done the same to Overmars, they'd have had a free-kick in an easily defendable position and we'd have probably won the game. It was similar to what Ronald Koeman did to me in Rotterdam six months later.

The next two games, a double-header in Poland and Norway, were probably our worst two performances of the campaign. We drew 1-1 in Poland, which wasn't a bad result in itself, but we only equalised late on – when the keeper allowed a shot from Wright to squirm under his body – and were lucky to escape with a point.

We were still unbeaten, but we'd dropped three points already (it was still only two for a win in those days) and our toughest two games – in Norway and Holland – were still to come.

Norway were the runaway leaders of the group by this point. They'd already beaten Holland at home and a similar result against us would leave ourselves and the Dutch fighting for second place.

Understandably, England and Holland were the fancied teams when the draw was made, but I wouldn't say we underestimated Norway. What I would say is we didn't know as much about them as we would if we were playing them today. These days, you could have a 20-minute edit of a team that would show you all you need to know about them. There are more camera angles, more scouts and more of an acceptance that most teams can cause you problems.

Norway had a set way of playing, no matter who was in their team, which was fed down through all the different levels of their football by Norway's manager Egil Olsen. He was a coaching guru in their country and his system was the way of playing in Norway, where outside influences were still minimal.

Basically, it was a 4-5-1 formation, with long, aerial diagonal balls being played up to two tall wide men, whose knock-downs would be fed on by the lone striker and the midfield runners. It wasn't pretty, but it was affective.

Famously, Graham changed our formation to cope with this, going from a 4-4-2 to a 3-5-2. Tony Adams and Gary Pallister were both very tall and really good in the air and as the two 'wide' centre-backs, it was hoped they could deal with the aerial threat. Jostein Flo on their right was particularly strong in the air and at six foot four, Pally was expected to deal with him.

There was a certain logic to Graham's thinking, but the problem was, we didn't have enough time to prepare for what was a pretty dramatic change in formation. For a double-header, you spend the first week concentrating on the first game, then by the time you've travelled to Norway from Poland, we only had a couple of days to prepare. The training facilities were poor and we only really had a proper pitch for one practice game. That wasn't sufficient. Sometimes subtle changes are better but in this instance, everybody's positions changed. I think that was a mistake. Tactically, we could have dealt with Norway better within our original formation. You'd have to ask Graham, but I think if he had his time again, he would have done some things a little differently. This was one of them.

But you can't use that as the only excuse for losing, as some have. The fact of the matter is, it was 11 against 11, and we just didn't perform. We lost 2-0, but it should have been more. With the football season over, everybody headed for the beach with our chances of qualifying for the World Cup hanging in the balance.

During pre-season, Graham flew out to Italy to tell me that Stuart Pearce would be returning as captain for the next qualifier against Poland at Wembley. When Gary Lineker retired after Euro 92, Pearcey was the obvious choice to replace him. He was our most experienced player, captain of Nottingham Forest and a natural leader. But after playing in the first two World Cup qualifying games, a groin injury kept him out of the next five and I took the armband.

Graham told me in private that Pearcey would be returning as captain then asked me if I minded staging the conversation again for the now infamous Do I Not Like That documentary, which they were filming at the time. He knew me well enough to know I wouldn't mind, but some people thought it was wrong to have him telling me on film that I wasn't going to be captain for the next game. Because I'd been captain for a while, scored my goals and done well, some of the media thought I should stay captain, and expected me to react differently to the decision. But it didn't annoy me at all. I said on camera that it was the right decision for the squad – and I meant it. There was no issue whatsoever. I only got the captaincy because Pearcey was injured, so when he was fit again it's only natural that he would return to the role. He was the England captain. Graham knew me well enough to know that not being captain wouldn't stop my captaincy characteristics coming to the fore – being captain didn't make me score more goals.

Later on, I was captain under Terry Venables when Pearcey was in the team and it didn't stop his leadership skills coming through and it was the same when Tony Adams took over from me at Euro 96. Pearcey was made captain because of the way he played and there's no way he'd play differently if he wasn't captain. I know him well enough to know that me being in the team when he returned as captain wouldn't have affected him at all. When you have more than one captain on the pitch you need all your combined leadership qualities to come to the fore.

As it turned out, I did captain the side in Holland after Pearcey picked up a hamstring injury between the Poland home game – which we won 3-0 with a good performance – and the trip to Rotterdam. Quite rightly for such a big game, Graham gave him until the very last minute to prove his fitness, but it wasn't to be.

We'd also have to do without Gazza, who'd picked up his second booking of the campaign against Poland. It was a reckless tackle that ruled him out, but we weren't annoyed with him because that was Paul. He played the game as he saw it. With me there was more of a cold planning. If I had a yellow card, something would trigger in my mind that would make me exercise a bit of caution. If Gazza thought he could make a tackle, he'd just go for it. He was instinctive, and that's what made him such a good player, so you just had to accept it when he got booked.

Despite his absence, Graham tried – unsuccessfully – to get Lazio to let him join up with the squad anyway. I'm not surprised Graham wanted him there, because although Gazza's insecure in his private life, there was no negativity at when it came to football. He had total belief in his own ability and his own performance and that transmitted through to those around him. He had such a positive attitude in training and Graham would have welcomed that in the build-up to the Holland game.

Although we expected Norway to cause us some problems, they took us by surprise to an extent because they didn't have much pedigree on the international stage – they were a bit of an unknown quantity. But when you play a country like Holland, you understand what it means. You don't need to see the video, because you know who their players are and you know how they play. England v Holland is always a big game so the intensity goes up a notch automatically. Players are much more aware, much more focused. The concentration levels are a given. If you could bottle that it would be priceless.

Despite the hiccups, we went into the game level on points with Holland in second place. Their goal difference was three better than ours, but we still had San

Marino (away) to come, so there was a very good chance we would make that up. As a player, especially an English player, sometimes you prefer the situation to be more clear-cut. We fully expected Holland to get a result in Poland in their final game and we didn't want to have to rely on goal difference, so perhaps it would have suited us for this to be 'must win' game.

Graham had reverted to a more familiar 4-4-2 for the previous game against Poland and stuck with it to face to Dutch. As well as being without Pearcey and Gazza, Chris Woods and Des Walker had each paid for a loss of form and were replaced by David Seaman and Gary Pallister respectively. Having missed the previous six games, Alan Shearer replaced the injured Les Ferdinand up front. Carlton Palmer replaced Gazza and was given a man-marking job on the Dutch left winger, Bryan Roy. Just as controversial was the decision to play Paul Merson ahead of Arsenal team-mate Ian Wright. Wrighty was the man in form, but Graham felt two conventional strikers would make us too rigid and gave Merse the license to roam left and right, occupying their defenders that way. He actually had a pretty good game.

Holland were the favourites and quite right too. They were playing at home for a start and although Marco van Basten was injured and Ruud Gullit was out of favour, on paper they had the edge over us. But that doesn't mean I didn't think we could win. Man for man, we had better players than Norway but they deserved to beat us. I went to Rotterdam thinking, "We're up against it, but we can win".

We were much better prepared going into the Holland game than in Norway, in terms of how we wanted to play. Our plan was to keep it tight early on, win our individual battles and try to silence the crowd. The Dutch only have one way of playing. We expected an open game and knew that we'd get goalscoring opportunities at some point and in Merson, Shearer and myself, we had players who could take them. In Tony Adams and Incey we also had resolute characters down the spine of our team, so we were well equipped to deal with whatever the Dutch would throw at us.

It was an evening kick-off and there had been clashes between English and Dutch hooligans outside the ground prior to the game. As players, you're not really aware of any of this because you're locked away from the moment you join up with the squad. You hear about incidents, but it doesn't affect you and there's certainly nothing you can do if people are intent on causing trouble.

Inside the ground the noise was intense. Feyenoord's de Kuip Stadium was chosen especially for its unique atmosphere. The Dutch always provide a good atmosphere with the colour and vibrancy of the orange clothes and face paints, but on that night I remember it being particularly powerful. Everybody knew what was at stake and the crowd reflected that mood.

Other players might tell you differently, but I've never been intimidated by a hostile atmosphere. I actually liked it. I read somewhere that when Jose Mourinho went back to Benfica as manager of Porto, he went out onto the pitch 45 minutes before kick-off knowing that the Benfica fans hated him. He wanted to experience that hatred, soak it up and use it in a positive way. That's what I felt like in Rotterdam. It's great when the crowd like you, and I'm sure it lifted the Dutch, but that doesn't mean it has to have an adverse affect on the opposition. Daft as it sounds, it would be completely different if the crowd could get at you, but you're separated from them by the police and fences. I certainly don't think any of us choked that night.

I think 'focused' is the word that best describes the mood in the dressing room beforehand. I can't remember anybody being particularly nervous, but it was clear there was a lot at stake. Despite what came out later in the documentary, Graham was the same as he always was in the dressing room: very positive, giving everybody final messages. If he was more nervous than usual, it didn't show. He always behaved in the manner that he wanted his players to take onto the pitch, so if he was nervous, he would leave the players to it for 15 minutes and return to the dressing room just before kick-off.

I was a tactical captain, a kind of coach on the pitch, so I'd be reinforcing the manager's positive messages before kick-off, reminding everybody of their responsibilities. Tony Adams was much more animated, geeing players up, motivating them. It was great to have someone like that in the dressing room, because I wasn't that kind of captain. I was someone who took responsibility and players probably looked at me and thought, "He takes thing in his stride", so maybe I inspired some confidence in them that way.

The Dutch were out of the blocks quickly. If you're Dick Advocaat, the Dutch manager, and you're playing at home in that kind of an atmosphere, the worse thing you can do is start off poorly and dampen that atmosphere. We knew they would throw everything at us, so our aim was to be ready for them: stand firm, don't give anything away, weather the storm and then you'll be able to get a foothold in the game and play a bit yourselves. And that's exactly how it panned out...

Marc Overmars was getting a bit of joy against Tony Dorigo down our left at first, but David Seaman remained untroubled. Our approach didn't change as such, but the start cemented our belief that we could get a result and soon it was us who were creating the chances. Merse was starting to cause some problems in his free role and he put me in, but the keeper was off his line quickly to parry the shot. Merse then had a crack himself, cutting inside from the left and shooting just wide.

Midway through the first half, Tony Dorigo came closest to breaking the deadlock, hitting the post with a 25-yard free-kick. Tony Adams got to the rebound first, but they just managed to block his shot. From the resulting corner, I made a run to the near post, but my header was blocked on the line. We could, and should have been in front.

We had the better chances, but the Dutch always looked threatening, especially down our right, where Bryan Roy was really starting to get the better of Carlton Palmer, struggling in his unfamiliar wide role. Just before half-time they did have the ball in the net when Frank Rijkaard latched onto a through-ball and finished neatly. It was chalked off for offside – wrongly as it turned out, but I don't think we deserved to into the break behind.

I've seen loads of players walking around a dressing room before a game saying, "I believe we can win this game", but how often do they really believe it? By half-time, I think everybody believed we could win the game. It was 0-0 and we were still the underdogs, but we were handling ourselves and I remember thinking "this is there for the taking".

Holland, on the other hand, would have expected to be in front, but we'd frightened them a couple of times, fired a couple of shots across their bow, and all of a sudden the tables have turned. It's their turn to start having negative thoughts. It's not that you sense it in the opposition particularly, but having been in that position, you know what would have been going through their minds.

Carlton was taken off at half-time, with Andy Sinton, who was unlucky not to start in the first place, giving us a bit more balance down the right – both in defence and in attack. Despite the change in personnel, we saw no need to change our approach. Although a win would have been decisive, a draw wouldn't have been a disaster, so there was no need to be gung-ho. Do that against the Dutch and they'll cut you to ribbons. At the same time, it would have been counter-productive to be too defensive against them, because as they'd shown in the first half, they'll always give you a chance. At the back, Ronald Koeman was a good footballer, but he had no pace…

Again we expected the Dutch to start quickly and again they didn't disappoint. This time they did test David Seaman, Dennis Bergkamp dropping deep as he always did, before picking up the ball and running 40 yards to unleash a shot that David was equal to.

Then came the incident…

I don't remember us putting together a move as such. All I can remember is the ball going out to Andy Sinton on the right and him hooking the ball forward first time. It was a speculative ball, but and it was one of those balls where it seemed like

I was the only person to react – that was the strange thing. I remember jogging forward as I always did, looking to support the play and then seeing the gap. All of a sudden it just opened up and I went for it. People think you time your runs from 60 yards away, but you don't. You get yourself in the vicinity and when the opportunity presents itself, you react. That was my game really.

At first, I wasn't even thinking about having a shot, because the ball was still bouncing when I got there. The picture in my head has told me I'm going to get there before the keeper, so my sole aim is to beat Koeman to the ball and get across him – which I did. I've chested it down and in that split second all I'm thinking is "I'm gonna score now." Koeman is out of it as far as I'm concerned – he's dead. It's just me against the keeper. He's coming towards me, the ball's sitting up and I know exactly what I'm gonna do – just touch it past him.

If Koeman had just pulled my shirt I might have been able to stay on my feet, but he pulled my arm, which turned me right round and threw me off balance. People ask me why I didn't stay on my feet and the simple answer is that I couldn't. I think most people recognised that, but Jimmy Greaves wrote an article in *The Sun* saying, "He should have stayed on the feet." He's an idiot – it was impossible. I'll be honest with you, in the past I have made a meal of challenges in the box to get a penalty, but I would never go down if I thought I had a chance scoring.

Because of the pace I was travelling at, my momentum means that I'm a good five yards inside the penalty area when I hit the ground, so my immediate thought is, "penalty". As I got up I remember looking back and seeing the referee pointing to what in my opinion was the penalty spot. As the team's penalty taker, everything else now goes out of the equation. I'm not even thinking about the possibility of Koeman getting sent off. I'm just looking for the ball – which has gone out of play – looking to take charge of the whole situation. Having had experience of taking penalties, I'm already thinking about where I'm gonna put it. I took a penalty in 1990 where I changed my mind walking up to take it, and the keeper nearly saved it, so from that day on I vowed never to change my mind again.

I pick the ball up and it's only when I turn around and see this melee of players that I twig that, of course, under the new rules of stopping an obvious goalscoring opportunity, Koeman's been sent off as well – he's gone. My focus is still on the penalty, but now I'm thinking, "Right, score here and they're really gonna struggle."

The thing I can remember next is Incey complaining to the referee. And I'm thinking "Why is he complaining?" Then it dawned on me – it's not a penalty, when in my mind the foul took place in the box. I knew immediately I wouldn't be taking the free-kick, but it was still in a dangerous position and they'd still be down to ten men. It's only then that the ref's produced the yellow card. I'm stunned. All of sudden the whole situation has gone against us. No penalty, no sending off.

As I walked into the box for the free-kick, Koeman turned round from his position in the wall and shrugged his shoulders as if to say "That's all I could do." It's no consolation, but if I would have done exactly the same in his situation, so I just nodded as if to say, "I know." I bore no malice and I still don't. In my opinion, what he has done has been professional and therefore justified. The fact that he hasn't been sent off is totally down to the referee.

I think that decision affected us mentally in the immediate aftermath. It's very easy to say you have to put it out of your mind and get on with it, but it changed the whole momentum of the game. You've gone in at half-time thinking you've got the upper hand tactically, having started as underdogs. You know it's gonna take a monumental effort to win in the first place and that you won't get many decent chances. Then you get a golden one and through no fault of your own, it's gone begging. All of a sudden everything is going against you...

Within two minutes we were behind – and again in controversial circumstances. Incey fouled Wouters on the edge of their box, fair enough. But then Koeman hit the free-kick into the wall and you think the danger has gone. But the referee orders it to be retaken for encroachment. Of course, Koeman then realised that he couldn't get the ball up and over the wall with any real power without hitting over the bar, so he dinked it into the corner the wall was covering and David Seaman couldn't get across in time.

Of all people, it just had to be Koeman who scored. Just to rub it in. Just to hammer us that little bit more.

Now you're really feeling that everything has gone against you. You lose your focus, you're arguing with the referee for the rest of the game, and having been on top tactically, you're now needed a piece of individual brilliance from somebody.

We nearly got it as well. A couple of minutes later, Merse cut in from the left and hit the inside of the post. But instead of going in, the ball flew across the goal line and out. Typical.

As we pushed for the equaliser the game became stretched and that suited the Dutch, especially with their pace out wide. David saved well from Bergkamp, but he could do nothing a couple of minutes later. Dennis picked the ball up just inside our half and seemed to have only one thing on his mind. He was very quick in them days and as we backed off he just keep going, before hitting a low shot in off the post from the edge of the box. The second goal completely knocked the stuffing out of us and from that point onwards you're almost looking for the final whistle to blow.

Little did we know what was happening on the touchline throughout all of this. It wasn't until the documentary came out that we realised how much pressure Graham was under. Like I said, he didn't seem any more nervous before that game than any other.

I didn't know this either, but there was all sort of commotion in the tunnel afterwards. Apparently, Graham had gone into the referee's room to confront him about his decision not to send Koeman off, when Brian Woolnough of *The Sun* burst past and started pointing at the ref, accusing him of cheating. Bearing in mind it was *The Sun* who were responsible the 'Turnip' business, it just goes to show how high emotions were running and the sense of injustice everybody felt.

I was doing a television interview at the time and they showed me the Koeman incident. The referee was right; it was only a free-kick, but he was totally and utterly wrong not to send Koeman off. He was the last man. It was a professional foul. End of story. What bugged me is that he never came out and admitted he got it wrong. If he holds his hands up, fine, because we all make mistakes.

Back in the dressing room it was glum, everybody was very down – not much was said. I've been in dressing rooms where coaching staff have wanted to have an immediate post-mortem and I've been asked for my opinion. But there's no foundation in your opinion at that point – it's too hot. I've never been one to put a defeat – or a win – behind me straight away. It needs to be thought about, analysed – but never in the heat of the moment.

Straight after the game you're emotional. You know, realistically, that the chance has gone, but a positive person then starts to focus on the scraps of possibility – of Holland being beaten in Poland and us scoring enough goals against San Marino. You don't actually realise what it means – that comes later: in my case, at the end of my career. You're disappointed, sure, but I was back playing for Sampdoria on the Sunday. That's the thing about football – before you know it you're pulling for boots on again.

It was an unreal game that one in San Marino, very eerie. You know you're going to win, you know you're going to win easily, and you know it probably won't be good enough. But you've got to keep your side of the bargain and score the seven goals, just in case the Dutch slip up in Poland. Then, within eight seconds, you need eight goals, and San Marino have only touched the ball once. All this at the ground where I'd scored the winner against Belgium three years earlier… only this time it was empty! It couldn't have been more different.

The feeling after the San Marino game was one of deflation, of resignation, a bit of an ant-climax after the emotion of Rotterdam. We'd just won 7-1 away from home, but Holland's victory in Poland had knocked us out of the tournament.

I don't know if the other players knew Graham would soon be on his way, but I did. He'd said "Judge me on the World Cup" and we didn't qualify. He called me a couple of days after the San Marino game and said "My position has become untenable". I wasn't surprised.

It wasn't the end of my England career, of course, but it was my last chance to play in a World Cup. At the time, I was playing well, in good shape and probably thought "There's always '98..." The new coach Terry Venables made me captain and I played every game at Euro 96, when, as in 1990, we went very close.

But I'd had a knee injury in the lead-up to the tournament and I wasn't assured of my place in the team, so Tony Adams took the armband. I managed to get myself fit enough to play in the tournament, but I never got the problem properly sorted. My game was all about dynamism, being fitter than everybody else, being able to still get into the box in the 85th minute and score a goal. I didn't have enough ability to change my game, play in a deeper role and still be as influential.

Glenn Hoddle named me in his first couple of squads, but I wasn't getting into the team and he soon stopped picking me altogether. He probably did me a favour by pulling the plug on my international career, because I was too stubborn to do it myself. It didn't worry me at the time, because I had other big games with Arsenal to look forward to. It's only now when I analyse my career that I think "I only played in one World Cup and had another one taken away from me."

I've never watched the Holland game all the way through, but I have got a video of it and I've put the Koeman incident on from time to time and wondered "Could I have stayed on my feet? Could I have scored?" I wish I could. But I couldn't.

TONY ADAMS
CENTRE-HALF

FRANCE 1998

BORN   10th October 1966, Romford
CLUB   Arsenal
INTERNATIONAL DEBUT   February 1987 v Spain
ENGLAND CAREER   66 caps, 5 goals
INTERNATIONAL FAREWELL   October 2000 v Germany

The dominating personality of English football in the 1990s, Adams made the most appearances at Wembley [60] and captained his country on 15 occasions before being relieved of the post by new England coach Glenn Hoddle during the 1998 qualifying campaign. He was first choice central defender for his country for over a decade and became a lynchpin in Hoddle's World Cup plans despite having lost the captaincy. Having lifted countless trophies with Arsenal, he revealed his drink addiction problems to the world and founded charity *Sporting Chance*, Adams now feels it is time to lift the lid on why England failed at France 98 – and it will make uncomfortable reading for some famous names.

ENGLAND 2 v ARGENTINA 2   (Argentina won 4-3 on pens)

World Cup Finals Second Round
Tuesday 30 June 1998

Stade Geoffroy-Guichard, Saint-Étienne
Attendance 30,600

Penalties cost Englasnd again on the night that David Beckham becomes a a national hate figure and Michael Owen becomes a World star aged 18

Teams

Glenn Hoddle	**Managers**	Daniel Passarella
David Seaman		Carlos Roa
Gary Neville		Nelson Vivas
Graeme le Saux		Roberto Ayala
(Sub. Gareth Southgate)		
Paul Ince		Juan Sebastian Veron
Tony Adams		Jose Chamot
Sol Campbell		Javier Zanetti
David Beckham		Matias Almeyda
Darren Anderton		Diego Simeone
(Sub. David Batty)		(Sub. Sergio Berti)
Alan Shearer		Ariel Ortega
Michael Owen		Gabriel Batistuta
		(Sub. Hernan Crespo)
Paul Scholes		Claudio Lopez
(Sub. Paul Merson)		(Sub. Marcello Gallardo)
Shearer (pen) 10, Owen 16	**Scorers**	Batistuta (pen) , Zanetti 45
Beckham 47	**Sent Off**	

Referee: Kim Milton Nielsen (Denmark)

BY THE TIME the World Cup had come around in the warm summer of 1998, I had got myself into a much better place. On August 16th 1996 I had come clean to the world and to myself that I was indeed an alcoholic and that I was going to do something about it, at last. By 1998, I felt really good and I actually found things then very easy. I'm not speaking egotistically, but I felt very free. I would sometimes come off the pitch without one drop of sweat on my face. After years of abusing alcohol, that was new to me and I would think to myself, "Oh this is good. I can do this without running around with my tongue hanging out." That was very enjoyable and it allowed me to play the game with much more freedom.

I had made up my mind that I was going to work without restrictions, enjoy myself and make up for lost time. It was a wonderful time. I had a life away from football and away from booze. I would go to the theatre; I would go to the cinema and enjoy things that I hadn't done for so long. Football wasn't the be all and end all and because of that I enjoyed it that much more. It was a culmination of a lot of things, but in 1998 I was a very happy footballer and a very happy man.

That happiness was, of course, aided by Arsenal's great domestic form and by the magnificent Double we won that year. Arsene Wenger had arrived at Highbury in 1996, just weeks after my declaration and the timing was impeccable. He was the right person for me at the right time. When he arrived at Arsenal he must have thought "Bloody hell; I've got not only Adams, but also Steve Bould, Lee Dixon, David Seaman." A ready made back five full of international quality and a captain who's actually turning up for training. It was perfect.

What was perhaps not so perfect in my mind was the appointment of my International manager. I have nothing against Glenn Hoddle and to this day we are fine with each other, but I missed Terry Venables. Glenn took over as England's Head Coach, also in 1996 and I had to adjust.

For me, this country simply hasn't produced enough outstanding coaches recently and the best one we have had in years is Terry Venables; so immediately Glenn was following a very hard act. Terry was the last of a good bunch. Men such as Don Howe, Dave Sexton, Ron Greenwood, these men were football men who brought new and good things to English football.

Don't get me wrong, when Glenn was appointed to the job I was pleased, if a little surprised. He had a good head on him, Glenn, but lacked experience for me.

That showed later in the way he eventually had to leave the job. The episode with the newspaper and Glenn's thoughts on religion taught me that you never mix your beliefs, be they political, religious or whatever with your football.

Glenn was an incredible talent as a player and that England squad had grown up watching him play. I had actually played for England with him when I first broke into the national team, so knew him as a team-mate, but there were problems sometimes with others, as Glenn, somewhat immaturely, still wanted to be the best player on the training pitch. Some of the lads actually called him 'Chocolate' because he could eat himself!

I grew close to him at first, though. I was, and still am in the process of going through the 12 steps of alcoholism and was very open to a lot of spiritual things he had to say. I listened to Glenn's opinions on religion – I didn't always agree – and in general we got on very well.

One of Glenn's first decisions, though, was to replace me as Captain with Alan Shearer. I had to disagree with him over that. I felt that was a bad decision. He explained it to me by saying that he felt Alan was a big world name and therefore might win us a penalty or two and could have more influence on a game. I simply said that I respected his decision, he was the manager and I was going to play for him, but I told him I thought he was wrong. There were certain things that I felt I could do as captain in France that summer, but now I couldn't. Off the pitch I mean. On the pitch I would play my normal game.

I won't lie, I had a much better relationship with Terry. We were both Dagenham boys and there was a very real empathy between us. With Glenn it was different. As I say, I knew him as a player. I once nut-megged him in training during Euro '88 which hadn't gone down too well. He'd changed and so had I. That's normal. Ten years had passed. I didn't expect to have Glenn my team-mate back, he was now Glenn my manager and I had to get on with things.

As well as the captaincy I had my doubts about his tactics. Glenn had a preference for 3-5-2. At Arsenal I was strictly a 4-4-2 man, but under Terry we had played a similar formation, known as the Christmas Tree. There were differences, though. Under Glenn it was far more rigid. The two wing-backs were really full-backs so it was almost a 5-3-2. Under Terry, the two wide men were offensive wingers. Darren Anderton and Steve McManaman would do their defensive bit, but these guys were fantastic attackers. In 1998, there was a shift. Glenn put in Gary Neville and Graeme Le Saux and that immediately strengthens you defensively, but how are you going forward and attacking the opposition?

Terry was very advanced and I actually see Sven having similar options available to him this summer. John Terry can play in the middle where I was, with Gary Neville and Ashley Cole either side of him and Rio Ferdinand in front of the back four like Gareth Southgate did back then. If teams play three up, Rio could slip back into a back four. It's crying out for the Christmas tree!

As for Alan and I, there was no problem. He was a fantastic striker and I had tremendous respect for him. He was our goalscorer. He was inches away from being dropped for Euro 96 due to a lack of goals, but look what happened that summer and he went on to be our main goal getter for a number of years. There was no animosity between us, but regarding the captaincy, I do, to this day believe I would have done a better job and it should have been left as it was. Perhaps, like Terry and myself who were very similar, Alan and Glenn were alike and that's another reason why Glenn made the decision he did.

I had got to the stage in my life, though, when I wasn't taking crap. In that respect I can see why Alan got the job. Under George Graham I would have done anything I was told. If he had told me that Alan Smith had to jump over a brick wall, Alan would have gone over it with my boot behind him. I had changed. I had strong feelings about the way I wanted to play and I would have taken issue with a few things that went on.

We did well in the qualifiers, but lost to Italy at Wembley and it seemed we would have to qualify the hard way through the play-offs. Results however went our way and we got a great win in Poland that set us up. Italy could only draw in Georgia and suddenly we're a draw away from the World Cup. Granted, we had to draw in Rome but hey, why not, we felt good and we went as a confident squad.

I loved that trip. Prior to the match I was lapping up the atmosphere of the city, reading *The Celestine Prophecy* in the outskirts of Rome. It was a spiritual time for me, I was on cloud nine and couldn't wait for the match. When it came to the match itself there were no nerves for me. I had stopped playing with nerves. A touch of fear came in from time to time, but I was playing with that freedom I talked about earlier. It was a strange game. I was floating and was aware that the Italians weren't totally on their game and they weren't going to get it going on the night.

Yeah at times we had to hang on, there was a little bit of crowd trouble and Paul Ince went absent without leave for about 25 minutes, but all in all we were in control. The whistle went and there was euphoria. "I've got my World Cup," I thought. Although there was a little tinge of, "Yeah, but Glenn's in charge!"

What I must get across is that it didn't change my behaviour. I tried to do my job to the best of my ability. There was a World Cup coming up, but I could now just get on with things. I went on and won the Double with Arsenal that season as I have mentioned. My point is, that I had got things into perspective. The Double was great, but seemed normal because of all the domestic success we'd had. Going to a World Cup was exciting, but it felt like another high. I could have handled never playing in a World Cup. My feelings were now in check and I could handle anything. Because of that I didn't get too overly excited either. In 1994, when we failed to qualify, I went and got smashed out of my head on booze.

The build up to the tournament was quite intense surrounding whom Glenn would pick for his final squad of 23. He took a larger squad away to La Manga and then onto Morocco for a warm-up match. Then we flew back to Spain where he was to announce who had made the cut and which five players were going to be left distraught.

On the flight from Casablanca I sat next to Gazza, who I knew was struggling in his personal life. He was in a bad way even then and I chatted to him and felt I made some good headway, so I thought, "Eureka, I've got through to him. We can stop all the madness. I've got a chance." I shared my experiences with him, as we're told that is what works. Identification it's called. He listened and realised that is exactly what he did and I seemed to have made a breakthrough. "By Jove he's got it!" I thought. But alas and as ever with Gazza it wasn't to be.

We got back to La Manga where Glenn told everyone his decision and, of course, that meant no Gazza. He didn't take it well. In hindsight, maybe Glenn could have done it differently, but that wasn't to be. What way could you have done it? I got bombed out in 1990 by Bobby Robson. Alan Smith, myself, and David Rocastle got the bad news, went straight to a pub near Burnham Beaches, I got smashed out of my head, drove all the way home, didn't get caught and that was that. People are people and they react differently. Given his psychological state at the time, it was no wonder Gazza went off the rails a bit.

Having said that, I understand completely why Glenn left Gazza out. Absolutely. It was very difficult for Glenn. Especially as he had no empathy with Gazza's disease and no understanding of it. He tried to throw God at it and that isn't always right.

Gazza wasn't performing. If you are consuming that much alcohol, you can't do it. For the last six months of my problem I was spending more time in a pub in Bethnal Green that I was on the training pitch and you just can't do your job. I think that at the time he was abusing alcohol quite badly and there was no way it was going to work out. In 1996, Terry handled things quite differently. He'd had him at Spurs, of course, and he would shove him in the corner with a big cigar in his mouth. Gazza would have his up moments and his down moments, his bulimia would be a problem, but somehow his football was still working. By the time 1998 rolled around, that was no longer the case and his football was suffering.

There comes a point when the drink takes everything away from you. Physically there's nothing left. As Gerard Houllier once said to me, "It's like putting Diesel into a racing car." That's what Gazza was doing. He was spitting and farting all over the place to be fair. If I had been Glenn and I had a player who was abusing himself then decisions have to be made and I think I would have made the same one. These days it's not just booze. Players can be afflicted by all sorts from Internet porn to gambling. They could be up all night on the computer and it affects them in training on the pitch too.

Glenn had made up his mind that we would be in La Manga, he would call everyone in, man by man and let them know the news. Glenn had it set in stone, that was his way and that's how it would be. He didn't realise that he was dealing with a guy who was abusing alcohol.

That afternoon, Paul Merson was with Gazza by the pool. Merse was good at helping Gazza, who was flipping out a bit. "I'm not going to get picked, I'm not going to get picked, I'm out," he was crying and we had to calm him down with a coffee. I would have maybe picked another venue and another scenario to tell him, but I am not criticising Glenn because there is simply no easy way to do something like that and rejection is never easy. A letter is wrong and has been tried before. A phone call is hard too. How do you do it?

Gazza flew home amid many arguments within the press about whether Glenn had made a mistake or not. For us, the matter was closed and we travelled to France wanting to do well. I would have felt more confident if Terry had been in charge if I'm honest. To be fair to Glenn, the team was in transition. Having said that, we had good young players coming through though. Scholes, Beckham, Owen, these were good players, but you expect that from a country like England.

Expectations for the tournament? You know what? I'm not big on that. I did try and reflect on what we had, and being sober and clean my thoughts were clear and peaceful. I was doing my best on the pitch and enjoying it. I could be very forceful, mind. I told Glenn he was making a mistake dropping me as Captain. I could do more off the pitch than Alan could. For instance, Glenn treated David Beckham a little strangely during our time away. He would belittle him too much in training. For example, David, who at the time was just building himself into the great free-kick artist we know and love today, would miss a free-kick or two and Glenn was on him like a shot, showing him how it should be done and making David feel like crap. Maybe Glenn could take a better free-kick, even then but I wouldn't have let that situation get out of hand. I would have done something about it. I had control of the squad in 1996. I knew where Gazza was all the time, I got him to go fishing with David Seaman rather than out on the tiles. I knew what was best for the players and I would have made my presence felt.

Our first game in that World Cup was against the un-fancied Tunisians in Marseille. They obviously had a lot of local support and I recall that day was boiling hot. Strangely I was nervous that day. It was the temperature, there were thousands of fans, it was the start of the World Cup, we're expected to win, and yeah I was a little apprehensive. In the past we've been too offensive early on and things have gone wrong and there was always that possibility that we could slip up against the Tunisians, so my initial fear was not unfounded.

The first game can be tricky, but Scholesy came up trumps for us and got a great goal after Alan had put us one up with a header and we could relax a little bit after it went to 2-0. They weren't particularly great opposition, but you have to perform. People tend to forget that the World Cup is a very tough competition.

I had been involved in the European Championships in 1988 and 1996 and had got used to the long days between games. By 1998, I was a very different person, of course, and would enjoy reading a couple of books. There was an arcade set up at the hotel, but I thought that was for the younger lads. Having said that Merse spent most of his time in there with Michael Owen.

To pass the time we all decided to get as many song titles as we could into our press and TV interviews. I was allocated Madness and had to get some obscure references in. I said something like "School days and baggy trousers." Don't ask me how! I think Gareth Southgate won with a load of Phil Collins titles. It got quite competitive. There we were in some quite serious interviews and the boys are more concerned about getting their titles in. One of us, who had Lionel Ritchie said after the Colombia victory, "They'll be *Dancing on the Ceiling* back home I bet." Terrible.

You watch all the other games. We were in nice places, nice golf courses and all that. I think there was a little too much golf for my liking and I may have cut that out had I been skipper, but Alan likes playing Golf. It disenfranchises those who don't play.

The players who weren't starting games were training hard. Martin Keown complained that the training was tough and stamina led, but Martin loved to moan. I was always reassuring him. For us who were playing, though, it was very relaxed. Plenty of massage, recovery, nutrition, Glenn was very good at that. He had picked up a lot from Arsene from his days at Monaco.

Next up for us were Romania, our true rivals in the group. It didn't go our way and I remember sitting in the dressing room after the Romanians had got their last gasp winner and Glenn walked in. "Do you know what," he said, "I've had a strong feeling for a while we were going to lose that game."

"Bloody hell," I replied. "You could have told us beforehand!"

We had made a poor start to the game. David Beckham was again left out of the starting line-up as was Michael Owen and we were struggling to find the right impetus. Gheorghe Hagi set up Viorel Moldovan to score and it looked like we were well and truly up against it. Glenn had to make changes and he did to be fair to him.

Beckham came on, as did Owen, and we found some new spirit and got at them. Owen was really worrying their back four and it was his opportunism in the box that got us a late equaliser and what I thought was an OK draw. Michael came in and didn't need any sort of coaxing or looking after from older players like me. He was incredibly focused and always has been.

He was right out of the Alan Shearer School of player. Wouldn't offer much in the way of public speaking, but Glenn used him very wisely that tournament. I may not have played him at all, but he was doing so well he just had to be involved. He hadelectric pace and frightened tiring defenders. Glenn did the right thing and used him as a sub, albeit a super-sub. That's how I saw Wayne Rooney being used in Portugal two years ago. I thought Scholes could have played off Michael there at first and Wayne could have come on and surprised everyone. I did an interview with the *Daily Mail* about that and the headline was DROP ROONEY. Bless them. You learn.

We had got ourselves back in the game and Romania got a late winner in the 95th minute or something ridiculous. That was the first time I had to get used to the fourth official letting you know how much time was left. It's used every day now, of course, but it took a little getting used to. I was looking at it, thinking that's interesting and, as I'm doing that, they've crept in behind Graeme Le Saux and scored!

We had to take positives out of the game. Michael had got on and looked so hungry, but Beckham's inclusion in the second half was another bonus. For me David was a natural starter. He was the right age, and I think he was as surprised as anyone about his exclusion from those first two games. In fact I know he struggled to come to terms with it. He sulked a little bit. I spoke to him. Sulking isn't macho enough and I'll give him the benefit of the doubt and say he was disappointed. David is very internal. I don't think he liked Glenn to be honest and has gone on record saying he felt aggrieved about what went on. I tried to mediate between the two even though I wasn't captain. I said, "I'm sure Glenn has his reasons, I played with him, David, and he was very talented and he may have a little issue about you, but hang in there." I couldn't exactly say, "Yeah, I don't like him either," could I?

Glenn was playing Darren Anderton on the right side of midfield, who was also a great player. If he had played the system correctly they both could have played and eventually they did against Colombia and both scored. That was a good win. A lovely evening in Lens and one that holds truly great memories. David scored a wonderful free-kick, the perfect repost to Glenn, I suppose, and we were through to the last 16.

We travelled down to St Etienne and I was really falling in love with the country. I ended up buying a place out there after that tournament. I love the food, the sun and saw a place for sale that summer and said to the lads "I'm coming back to buy that," which I did. I had to get rid, though, because the new wife isn't such a fan of the place.

It was going to be Croatia or Argentina in the Second Round and funnily enough I felt it was best to avoid the Croatians, which we did having come second to Romania. Croatia reached the semi-final that summer and were unfortunate to lose to France, but what a good team and what players. As a country of 4 million people they don't half churn out some talent.

Instead it was the old enemy. By no means were Argentina the greatest team in the tournament, but this fixture goes back years. I am studying anthropology and sport, and it's fascinating to learn about the history of this game. Southampton FC travelled over there in 1901 and the country fell in love with this wonderful game of football. They developed their own game using Tango, their historical dance as the basis for their education. They got on with it without us and did it their way, never looking back. Ever since Argentinians have been brought up as kids through countless generations to beat England. You must beat England. That is drilled into them and is always in the back of their minds.

We're a million miles away and it seems a little stupid, but it is really deep. It's a reflection of their society and very deep rooted. They hate us with a passion and it's part of their historical roots. Not a lot of English people know that. We think we're hated everywhere, Maybe so, but not like in Argentina we're not I can tell you.

As I say, they weren't at their strongest that year, but they had good individuals and I had to prepare to face Gabriel Batistuta. He was very similar to my pal Alan Shearer. He's a god. He got 150 goals in the Italian league and he was a real scorer, a strong player. They had fluidity, though, they always have and that comes from that Tango based game. I think we had that same movement in 1996, but the squad had slightly deteriorated since then. We still had very good players but maybe we weren't as offensively free or tactically aware. It got even worse when Kevin Keegan came in mind.

Man for man, I felt we were level with them, though. It could have gone either way that night. Our defending was a little sloppy and that allowed the equaliser, which made it 2-2. That should have never have happened. People love this game because you can't control it, but I spent my career trying to do just that defensively. David Seaman and I were very disappointed with that goal and could see that things could and should have been done to prevent it.

We had gone a goal down after Seaman upended their forward in the box. Michael Owen, though, was playing with that same hunger and won us our own penalty in a perhaps somewhat South American fashion, and then went on that devastating run that announced his arrival in the world game.

It's funny because at the time I didn't think much of it. I was excited because we'd scored, but I thought it was a weak goal from their point of view. He went around Nelson Vivas, who a year later was thrown out of Arsenal for messing up our league chances at Leeds. Ayala then gave him loads of room, but Michael has done that to numerous players. Back then he was young, enthusiastic and he's kept that and he hurts people. They didn't know who he was back then, but they do now. It's good to have a player you can spring on people in your team at a World Cup. Who knows, maybe Theo Walcott this summer could do the same.

Glenn got stick for not using Michael earlier, but I was in complete agreement with him. He eased him in and then unleashed him on an unsuspecting opposition and it paid off in terms of goals.

Michael scored that wonderful goal, but needed no looking after. By that I mean he didn't need to be brought back to earth. We let them back into it and went in at half time level at 2-2, but Michael was still so focused. It was a great goal, but it was behind him now. As I say, he was always like that and still is as far as I can gather.

As I say, we should have been more aware for their equaliser late in the half, which came from a well-worked set piece, but we were also ruing a miss by Scholes that would have put us 3-1 up prior to that. That's football, that's the difference and that's why we all love it and keep coming back for more.

No matter, it was a positive dressing-room and we felt we could go on and win. But those plans were slightly changed early in the second half when Beckham kicked out at Diego Simeone and was sent off. To me it's an incident that has been blown out of proportion. I played over 700 club games and 66 for England; things happen. The bigger the stage, the more it's highlighted. When you're in there playing though, they're everyday things. People get sent off, but because it was David it was a huge deal. When incidents happen you don't dwell on them. Your mind just switches on to the game. "We're down to ten men, this is what we're doing, let's get on with it. Let's shut up shop and try and grab a goal from a set-play."

As the game wore on I remember having to chase their number 10, Ortega, a lot. He was a tricky player and I was tiring. Then it seemed that Sol Campbell had won it for us with a late header, but as he was off celebrating the referee had disallowed it and the Argentineans were attacking my penalty box. I was never one to run off to celebrate and was running back to my half thinking "We've done it!" and suddenly I had defending to do.

Glenn made some changes deep into extra-time and we got to penalties. We had looked strong even with ten men, but now it was in the lap of the gods. I don't take penalties any more because I just don't think it's my department. Having said that I've taken three in my career and scored three so maybe I was harsh on myself. I was supposed to have the sixth against Germany in '96. I was getting ready, but Gareth went straight over to Terry and said "I'm having the next one." He was so confident. I thought "OK, good, go for it." I should have insisted looking back! At this point I just thought whatever will be will be and good luck chaps. I was just getting ready to console or to celebrate.

Seaman gave us hope by saving Hernan Crespo's penalty kick, but when Ince missed we were once more on level footing. Owen scored a very cool penalty for one so young, but we were trailing 4-3 with David Batty set to take the last. I don't think he had ever taken one and alas it showed as the keeper saved his effort and that was it, we were out. Batty was very pragmatic about it. I don't know if that was a façade.

There was a lot of distraught people about I can tell you. I admired Beckham for crying. I remember thinking I wish I could do that because it usually takes me about three years to come to terms with defeats and big football matches. I was the first one back in the dressing rooms and he was in tears then. I went over to him, and said "It's all your f***ing fault, you idiot. That was my last chance to do well in the World Cup and you ruined it!" He looked at me, eventually saw I was (semi) joking and it brought him out of his depression. "I've waited 20 years, but you've got plenty of chances!" I continued. That broke the depression slightly.

Not for Glenn though. He was gutted. We all react differently. I don't judge people for reacting how they do. Glenn was distraught, alone and gutted in the corner. We thought we had a hell of a chance. You win the lottery of a penalty shoot out and then who knows. It wasn't to be, though. Some are inconsolable, whilst some are a little bit more philosophical.

I would have loved to have gone on in the tournament and I was sad. I was having a nice time and it was a wonderful experience, but – and this is due to the battles I had fought on a personal front – I could put it in perspective. It wasn't everything. I didn't feel I had to go and get smashed out of my head like I did in 1996. It was all over, but I had other things in my life I could go back to and get on with. It was a huge disappointment but, one I could deal with as a sober man.

Back home we got a good reception and were all told how well we had done but, there is an element in me that doesn't like all of that. I am very proud to be English and I love what this country can stand for. I love the fact that Karl Marx chose to be buried in London and am proud of many of our other achievements, but we lost and to be applauded is typical of us. "Jolly well done chaps!" That's not right if you ask me. Americans would have been ignored and chastised even, but not here and I don't know how healthy that is in the long run.

It's hard for me to discuss it from a fan's point of view because I've never been one. The fans love seeing emotions and passion. This is why they love people like Stuart Pearce and they empathise with that. I love Stuart and I respect him for what he did as a player, but for me to love someone for their passion is ridiculous.

Adrian Chiles, who I became friendly with having done the *Match of the Day* stuff, has asked me to go on the West Bromwich Albion supporters coach for a game and I think I'd better because I want to find out what makes fans tick, because when you're playing you are a bit withdrawn from that. You're poles apart. You're a pro and it's work. It's a job that I love, don't get me wrong.

One man who didn't get much in the way of recognition on his return was David Beckham. He took a lot of stick. I gave him some advice. England came home from Euro '88 and some blamed me for our defeat to Holland. We arrived at Luton airport and I was chased to my car by disgruntled fans. I had won a Fiat Uno for being named Young Player of the Year and I ran to that and escaped. Things were low, but I made a bet with Jim Rosenthal that I would bounce back and Arsenal would win the title that season. We did and I think Jim still owes me £50. I was focused by the criticism and it made me better. George Graham said to me "Don't worry about England, they're crap, concentrate on us."

My point to David was that the best way to shut the critics up was to play well and prove your point. They'll throw a few things at you about your wife and about you, but the best way to respond is to win. United won the bloody treble didn't they that season, so it's all my fault!

That summer in France in 1998 was another chapter in my eventful career. It was lovely. That word may be a little too wet for a supposedly hard centre-half, but I did, I found it lovely. I was free. Sorry to use that word again, but I was. I was doing a job I loved doing, playing for my country. I'd just done the Double with Arsenal and OK the best thing would have been to win The World Cup, but you don't get everything you want, just what you need and I needed that experience.

JAPAN/SOUTH KOREA 2002

ENGLAND 1 v BRAZIL 2

World Cup Quarter-final
Friday 21 June 2002

Shizuoka Stadium, Shizuoka
Attendance 47,436

England wilt in the Japanese sun after taking the lead. Had they won their group they would have played Brazil at night in a semi-final

Teams

Sven-Göran Eriksson	**Managers**	Luis Felipe Scolari
David Seaman		Roberto Silva Marcos
Danny Mills		Cafu
Ashley Cole		Roberto Carlos
(Sub. Teddy Sheringham)		
Trevor Sinclair		José Roque Junior
(Sub. Kieron Dyer)		
Rio Ferdinand		Ferreira da Silva Lucio
Sol Campbell		José Kleberson
David Beckham		Gilberto Silva
Paul Scholes		José Gomes Edmilson
Emile Heskey		Rivaldo
Michael Owen		Ronaldinho
(Sub. Darius Vassell)		Ronaldo
		(Sub. Dias Batista Edilson)
Owen 23	**Scorer**	Rivaldo 45, Ronaldinho 49
	Sent Off	Ronaldinho 66

Referee: Felipe Ramos Rizo (Mexico)

AND SO TO Japan and South Korea. In 1950, when England belatedly entered the World Cup fray, it was under a cloud of conservative suspicion. Should the nation that had nurtured the rules and given the planet association football really embroil itself in this somewhat crude, global event? An event that was, to make matters worse, invented by the French. It was like the Lord of the Manor stepping from the comfort of his drawing room and joining the servants in their downstairs, late night booze-up.

England were to learn the hard way that summer in Brazil that they were far from the sport's gentry. They arrived as favourites, but were bamboozled by the United States, a nation that when it came to football could not even be classified as part-timers.

As the great Sir Tom Finney has indicated in the opening chapter of this book, it was a shock to all involved and one that would take years to recover from. Back then, though, despite being star-spangled by America, football was very much old school tie. We had been beaten by minnows, but no matter; that was a freak result and we remained the psychological doyens of the sport.

Hungary's famous win at Wembley in 1953 went a long way to denting the crowns worn by England's governing body, but had the men in blazers at the FA been told then that one day the countries of the world would gather in Japan to decide their champion, they would have murmured something about the war and politely asked you to leave the boardroom.

But that is exactly what happened, and oh what a joy it was. America (them again) had proved in 1994 that a nation outside of the game's *illuminati* could handle hosting the tournament. America had thrown glitter over the World Cup and painted it in razzmatazz, but still that month in Japan was so fresh, so new and so enthusiastic in terms of its hosts that it breathed life into FIFA's grand party like never before.

You will have noticed that this final chapter is not a chronicle of memories from one of the players present with the England team. The idea behind a book such as this is to have players recount their memories and reveal exactly what it was like to compete in the biggest games of their life, but when it came to 2002 this wasn't to be. No player from that squad was prepared to co-operate.

Myself and my fellow editor Louis Massarella have had the pleasure of meeting some of England's greatest ever heroes, who travelled the world representing the country. The great Sir Tom Finney, slowed only by the onset of old age (full-backs couldn't manage it) discussed that fateful trip to Brazil in 1950 with a grimace as if they had lost only yesterday.

Ivor Broadis, the ex-Manchester City, Newcastle and Sunderland inside-forward invited me into his home, gave me photos, cooked me a very tasty plate of egg and chips (washed down by a nice glass of red) and reminisced with glee about the summer of 1954 when he took on the world. Once more the country had fallen short, but to Ivor, 'Those were the best days of my life.'

Then there was Sir Bobby Robson, ever enthusiastic, giving Louis a lift to Newcastle station after their three hour interview. Roger Hunt, still revelling in the glories of '66, waxing lyrical. Peter Reid, chatting about the nightmare (literally) image of the impish Diego Maradona racing away from him and Tony Adams talking candidly about how the World Cup of 1998 had countered his personal battle with alcoholism.

These and the other gents involved all had different stories to tell; their stories. The inside, personal story of their World Cup. They all had different fortunes at their respective tournaments, but you sensed from them that they were days they would never forget and to share those memories was something they felt was for the benefit of their fans, England fans, football fans. It was far from a chore for them.

I don't want to jump on the 'aren't all modern footballers idle, overpaid brats' bandwagon. The vast majority of them aren't. The bottom line is though, over the six months it took us to put this book together, we could not get a member of the 2002 squad to chat about their summer in the Far East and that seems a real shame.

No need to name names, but one player's agent scoffed at the notion of us paying £1000 for forty-five minutes of their client's time ('Not for that f***ing money' he informed me), most simply said "No" or had contractual obligations with other publishers, while one finally said "Yes", but when push came to shove and deadlines were being extended time and time again, he decided to go missing and his mobile was switched off. None of them wanted to share their story with England fans up and down the land. None considered our fantastic charity, the Bobby Moore Fund for Cancer Research UK, a worthy enough cause to support. None wanted to be associated with the other greats within the pages of this book who had preceeded them in an England shirt in their attempt to win the greatest prize in football for their country. As I say, a real shame.

We hope this isn't indicative of the modern game and its much-hyped, possibly much-over-hyped protagonists.

It's a shame because those players who went to Japan were witness to a fascinating tournament in a fascinating country. They would have been able to tell us first hand just how fervent the local support was, especially for England and past players such as the late Brian Labone would readily confirm that the locals actually supporting the English was indeed a first.

As I say, I am not going to go bleary-eyed and lament the passing of our game in terms to accessibility to its stars. I'm sure one day a grey-haired Theo Walcott will invite a young writer into his living-room (OK, East Wing) and discuss the joys of South Africa 2010, but I think it is important that readers understand the hurdles writers today so often face.

Enough of that. The World Cup of 2002 and two nations, South Korea and Japan, who would embrace their responsibilities and in the former's case almost shock the world to its core by reaching the final. They failed, losing to the Germans in the semi-final, but memories of the Koreans in their millions draped in haemoglobin red T-shirts pulsating to their incredible team's fortunes, will live long in my memory.

For thankfully for the integrity of this book, I myself was there, in the Far East to witness this incredible jamboree at first hand. Highly paid superstar footballer I may not be - I'm told winning the Camden Sunday Football League doesn't quite qualify me to speak with total authority on the subject of World Cup football - but as a priviliged attendee of the 2002 World Cup, I can reveal what it was really like to be there.

So what of England? Sven-Göran Eriksson's side travelled to the land of the rising sun on the crest of a rising wave. Only months before, the Germans (the eventual runners-up remember) had been savaged 5-1 in Munich, while the inspirational David Beckham's last gasp free-kick against the Greeks had sent us to the World Cup salivating that this sexy team may just give us what we craved. It is - as this book tells us - a familiar tale. England were amongst the tournament favourites. And we all know what the end of that particular tale usually is.

The build up to the tournament was clouded by another recognisable element, one that has made all modern fans budding medical students. The Metatarsal. A modern dread. As I write, the healing of Master Rooney's metatarsal has consumed the nation, but back in 2002 it was that of skipper and talisman Beckham that had the front, back and middle pages bulging with concern and prognosis.

The fact that Gary Neville, Manchester United's sturdy right-back had been definitively sidelined by a broken metatarsal had been almost overlooked by the media scrum more interested in the fate of his team-mate and pal. In the end you could argue that Neville's absence caused considerable grief to the team, but no matter, the talk was of Beckham and would he or wouldn't he make it.

You know the drill by now. Oxygen tents, tabloid calls to prayer, finger crossing on a national level. England travelled to Dubai for a pre-World Cup training camp and the images in our papers were not of Messrs Owen, Ferdinand or Seaman going through their paces with a ball at their feet, but of the captain bouncing up and down on a trampoline.

He went up, he went down, he went up, and he went down. Like our hopes he bounced about trying to convince himself, the coaching staff, us and a tiny little bone that everything was going to be OK. It wasn't and for a while it seemed that the whole squad were inflicted with one ailment or another. In South Korea, they trained and played a friendly against their hosts, but it was the sight of Kieron Dyer flying home and Trevor Sinclair going back and forth like a tired air-hostess that had us all wondering about the fitness of the squad in general.

Beckham was desperate to play, of course. He had personal redemption to pursue. He had been ordered from the field four years previously and had to watch the country lose to that old foe, Argentina, on penalties on a small TV screen in the changing rooms. Now he was skipper, forgiven by the nation for his wrongdoings thanks to some wonderful displays and was, bad foot or no bad foot, vying to take on the world seemingly single-handed according to most of the red-tops. But England were in the proverbial Group of Death. Sweden and Nigeria were joined by who else? Argentina. The script had been written, but could the leading man deliver his lines?

'Are you fit?' came the simple question from a hopeful manager. Eriksson had watched Beckham up his training, but still there were doubts and this was the eve of the opening game against those stubborn opponents from Sweden, unbeaten by England for over 30 years.

'I'm fit,' said his captain.

'Good, let's go.' With that Beckham was in.

The game itself matched none of the soap opera that had preceded it. The question of whether Beckham would play or not had been answered, but the 1-1 draw left many questions. On this form were we good enough to go all the way? The jury was out. Sol Campbell had got that considerable and often troubled forehead to a Beckham corner to put us one up, but England had tired in the second half (a notable feature of the side as it turned out) and a mistake by Gary Neville's replacement, Danny Mills of Leeds United, had allowed Niclas Alexandersson to equalise.

The mood was sombre. In the press box the hacks suspected a summer of underachievement, on the terraces and on the sofas back home the fans pondered such anti-climax, and in the dressing room the players feared for their hopes. The latter had their manager to console them, a man usually so stoical, but now having to lift the troops. 'We've drawn,' he told the players. 'We didn't lose did we?' How practical. Managerial technique, Ikea style.

W hat history has taught us is that there is nothing like a game against Argentina to lift the spirits of a flagging nation. As Roger Hunt reminded us earlier, in 1966 we had qualified from the group stags in the most humdrum of circumstances. The football was flat, the nation flatter; but then came Argentina and a 1-0 win amid controversial scenes. 'Animals' Sir Alf called them, and a lifetime's of animosity has followed. Back in '66, suddenly the nation and the team were up for it.

In 2002 a game against the Argentineans meant even more scope for wild car-horn tooting and crazy face painting. It's a fixture that gets our blood boiling. Rattin refusing to leave the field of play, Maradona using his fist and his hips to destroy our dreams or Simeone goading Beckham into getting himself sent off, all evoke the best and worst of the game. Everyone loves a good villain and in Argentina us Englishman have a villain of Blofeld proportions.

The match was played in the incredible indoor arena in Sapporo. Oliver Holt, the chief Sports Writer of the *Daily Mirror* was present and recalls what an incredible experience that proved to be. 'There was something very odd about the atmosphere that night,' he says. 'We had all been to games under closed roofs at Cardiff or in the United States, but this seemed different. England fans packed the stadium and it felt like something special was about to happen. It felt like we were under the Big Top about to watch a circus.'

The ring leader that night, of course, would be David Beckham. It would have to be Beckham. Present on reputation? Maybe. Only half-fit? Definitely. But that night Beckham laid his demons to rest and gave England's World Cup campaign the shot in the arm it so desperately wanted.

England came out of the blocks like horny greyhounds. Michael Owen began to taunt the Argentinean defence, forcing them to relive the nightmare of St Etienne in 1998. The English defence stood firm to Gabriel Batistuta's menace, Seba Veron looked a shell of the player we knew he could be, and while superstars like that toiled, men such as Trevor Sinclair, Nicky Butt and Danny Mills took the occasion by storm.

Owen had already hit the post when he wriggled like an eel in their box and was upended by Pochettino. A Penalty? It was a clumsy tackle at worst, but to the delight of those present and those back home the referee Pierluigi Collina was pointing to the spot. There was only going to be one man taking it. Michael Owen offered his services, but got short shrift from Beckham, the fire of 1998 burning in his eyes.

Diego Simeone, his nemesis, made his presence felt in the box, even offering to shake Beckham's hand, but the England captain had more important things to deal with and was having none of it. The ball placed, the whistle blown, the nation hushed; he stepped up and launched the ball straight down the middle, caring little for penalty taking technique - but no matter, the net bulged and a nation went bloody wild! A proper mental.

'From a journalist's point of view it was simply the perfect story,' recalls Holt. 'For Beckham to step up that night and score what turned out to be the winner against the team who had contributed to his downfall in 1998 was incredible.' The winner it was. The Argentineans came at us hard in the second half and as ever England began to wilt, but there was something about that night. It was as if the roof above the pitch acted as some sort of pressure cooker and, unlike previous years, England's turnips were not going to overcook. 1-0 England and suddenly we had a World Cup on our hands.

I myself flew out to Japan just days after the Argentina win. I was, of course, full of hope after that epic victory, but that was tempered slightly by a mundane final group game against Nigeria that finished goalless. No matter, the performance didn't count for much, we were through, that was all that mattered surely and I for one had a ticket for the last sixteen match against Denmark in the north-eastern town of Niigata.

To arrive in Tokyo is to walk onto the set of an over-the-top sci-fi movie. The futuristic feel to everything strikes you between the eyes, but for me the most refreshing thing about Japan was the old fashioned love and enthusiasm for the sport and the tournament they were putting on for the world. Some nations that host these tournaments, us included, can give off an air of superiority. Our own 'Football's Coming Home,' slogan in 1996 drew on our heritage - which is great, but like other stalwart countries you sense an air of grandeur. The head boy who can do no wrong.

In Japan there was an infantile naivety and I mean that in a very good way. They smiled, they laughed, they cheered, they adopted the different colour of whoever was playing; in short, they got it right. My second day in the city saw Japan win their last group game to ensure they were through to the latter stages. Mayhem!

The rush hour traffic continued, but only amid joyous scenes as face-painted locals delighted in their team's victory. 'Nippon, Nippon, Nippon!' The fans were dancing in the streets, but, this being Japan, they would move back onto the pavement each time the futuristic traffic lights suggested they should.

To be part of it was so uplifting, especially when you consider the trouble that so often had reared its head in recent times. Oliver Holt underlines that sense of joy, rather than beer-stained aggression. 'The World Cup in Japan and Korea was such a breath of fresh air. I remember being over there and just thinking back to France in 1998, when I watched Marseille burn before England's opening game. I thought of the European Championships in 2000, when drunken England fans fought police water cannons in Charleroi. Those were nasty occasions, but here, in Japan we had such a lovely contrast. This, I thought, is what football is supposed to be about.'

While the Japanese rejoiced at their own team's fortunes, it was clear that their second team was most certainly England. Walking along the street in Tokyo, schoolgirls and boys would clamour around you asking for a picture and wondering if you could introduce them to David Beckham. There were stories of Beckham's hotel room being invaded - once he and England had moved on - by loved-up locals who tried to steal bed sheets and even touch the toilet seat used by the man himself. What a cheek!

England's next game was once more against Scandinavian opposition. Denmark were a well drilled team, compromised of plenty of Premiership players and a real threat to England. As I took my seat I was struck immediately by that sense of pro-England feeling among the fans. Beckham's Mohawk (his haircut of choice that summer) was mimicked everywhere, while local kids grinned inanely as they were marched about upon the shoulders of high-spirited Englishman who requested raucously that we all have a disco.

A lack of aggression filled the air. There was no police presence, although I am sure they were there in great numbers. Instead of water cannons and Alsatians you were greeted by a small, pretty Japanese girl with a smile, a bow and a goody bag containing a soft drink and a programme. Everyone was smiling and taking pictures with her, but I'd like to fantasise that if trouble had begun, she would have been ready with a high kick or two, whilst never losing that intoxicating smile.

Talking of smiles, England had us beaming with an incredible first half display and three goals from Rio Ferdinand, Michael Owen and Emile Heskey (remember him) that had the fans in raptures. 'Let's all have a disco, let's all have a disco.' It didn't matter that the second half was once more insipid compared to the first. The damage was done and a quarter-final against the favourites beckoned.

It was a long journey home back to Tokyo, but with the beer flowing talk was of how maybe this team could be the one. In hindsight it was a long shot, but I feel we got swept away by our hosts and their seemingly knowing belief that they - with their own side knocked out - had backed the winners.

'I for one began to think, maybe we could win,' says Holt. 'The morning of the game against Brazil I wrote a piece about how we could beat Brazil and in what areas we were better then them.' Holt wasn't alone. Suddenly Trevor

Sinclair was a world beater, Danny Mills a rock and Nicky Butt, well Nicky Butt according to Pelé was the best player out there.

The great man may have dropped too many viagras there, but what mattered was the incredible optimism that followed the fans as we made the trip to Shizuoka. The sun beat down on our typically pale English flesh, but surely could no longer add further warmth our hearts. We were here and we were going to do it. Weren't we?

The stadium, like many in Japan, rose from the horizon like a spaceship. A modern hulk for a modern World Cup. You sensed football had moved into the 21st Century and it was nothing short of a delight to be there.

Brazilian and English fans mingled with the Japanese. Embarrassingly out of tune and unrhythmic Englanders tried and failed to out-samba their Brazilian counterparts. Yeah, but we could out-conga the best of them. Holt was right. This was how it is supposed to be.

Once more England took to the field in a World Cup game vital to their chances in this greatest of global football jamborees with the nation expectant.

The game kicked off and England were strong starters. The heat was going to be a factor, but it was in fact the Brazilians, in their blue away kit that looked the more out of sorts. Midway through the half, Heskey played a speculative ball toward his Liverpool team-mate Michael Owen, whose presence alone put off Brazil's Lucio, who mis-controlled the pass and let the diminutive striker in on goal. Owen was carrying fitness concerns, but as he bore down on the penalty area in front of us, there was going to be only one outcome. GOAL!

I had grown up with tales from my dad, himself a football writer, about how he had been behind the goal when England played Brazil in Mexico during the 1970 World Cup. He had told me again and again about how in front of his very eyes Gordon Banks had made that save against Pelé. I loved hearing about it, of course, but for the next twenty minutes or so I truly believed that I now had my own tale, my own story to tell my kids. I was there when Owen scored against the mighty Brazil and sent us on our way to our second World Cup victory. I gloried in the moment, relieved it over and over again, seeing Owen clip the ball into Brazil's goal and the outpouring of joy which greeted the billowing net.

It wasn't to be.

I was actually on the mobile filling my Dad in and gloating at how I could match his moment when Beckham jumped and in a flash Ronaldinho fed Rivaldo and bing bang, 1-1. If you had blinked you would have missed it. The fans continued to enjoy every minute during half-time, but there was an unsaid feeling that our number was up.

Early in the second half those fears were realised when Ronaldinho lofted a free-kick from the right wing high and over the poor Seaman into the top corner. 'Jammy Bastard,' cried one fan. Maybe he was, maybe he wasn't, but today, having watched him scintillate in the Champions League, you have to give him the benefit of the doubt.

There was time for the little maestro to be sent off, but all that meant was even more huff and very little puff from the players and incredible frustration - that most World Cup of emotions for England fans down the ages - for us supporters. We had done all that we could. England's reserve tank was empty and while Eriksson could do nothing, but sit quietly on his bench, the life was literally sapped from his players by a team that gave the world a lesson in keeping possession.

If only we'd held on until half-time. If only England had beaten Nigeria and won the group, we would have met Brazil at a later stage in a night match rather than the sapping heat of the Japanese daytime. If only...

That night we continued to enjoy the hospitality of Tokyo, gleefully cheered by the locals, whose attentions had now begun to turn to Ronaldo whose goals in the semi-final and final would win the trophy for his rapturous nation. England had been beaten by the eventual winners once again.

'There is one image that remains with me from Japan,' recalls Holt. 'I was on the suburban train back to Tokyo after the match and despite the England team's exit, the fans were still singing, still laughing and were doing a conga down the train's corridors with locals and their kids joyously taking part. It put a smile on your face.'

It was however time to go home.

Leo Moynihan
May 2006